Donnya Piggott

Tech Innovator and LGBTQ Advocate in Barbados – Unfiltered

Tarek Ibrahim

ISBN: 9781779697035
Imprint: Telephasic Workshop
Copyright © 2024 Tarek Ibrahim.
All Rights Reserved.

Contents

Bibliography   15
The Influence of Family and Community   15
The Power of Education and Technology   26
The Birth of a Tech Innovator   37
A Journey of Self-Acceptance and Advocacy   49

Breaking the Shackles of Silence   59
Breaking the Shackles of Silence   59
Out of the Closet, Into the Limelight   61
Unmasking Homophobia and Discrimination   73
Speaking Up for LGBTQ Youth   84
Mental Health Advocacy and Support   96

Bibliography   99

Bibliography   103
Bridging the Gap: LGBTQ Rights and Religion   110

Bibliography   123

A Technological Revolution for Equality   125
A Technological Revolution for Equality   125
The Role of Technology in LGBTQ Advocacy   128
Digital Activism and Online Advocacy   139
Tech Startups as Catalysts for Change   151
Challenging Online Hate and Cyberbullying   163
Tech Education for All: Closing the Gender Gap   175

Bibliography   183

Breaking Boundaries and Going Global **189**
Breaking Boundaries and Going Global 189
From Barbados to the World Stage 191

Bibliography **195**
Facing Controversy and Resilience 205
The Future of LGBTQ Advocacy 218
Legacy and Inspiration 231

Index **243**

Embracing Identity and Discovery

In a world that often seeks to categorize and define individuals, the journey of embracing one's identity is both a personal and universal quest. For Donnya Piggott, this journey began in the vibrant surroundings of Bridgetown, Barbados, where the interplay of culture, tradition, and modernity shaped her understanding of self. This section explores the multifaceted aspects of identity and discovery, shedding light on the theoretical frameworks, societal challenges, and personal experiences that define this crucial stage of her life.

1.1.1 Growing Up in Bridgetown

Growing up in Bridgetown, Donnya was immersed in a rich tapestry of Caribbean culture, marked by its colorful festivals, music, and communal gatherings. However, beneath the surface of this vibrant community lay a complex web of expectations and norms that often stifled individual expression. The dichotomy between the celebratory aspects of Barbadian culture and the conservative attitudes towards sexuality posed significant challenges for Donnya as she sought to understand her own identity.

1.1.2 Early Signs of Curiosity and Activism

From a young age, Donnya exhibited signs of curiosity that set her apart from her peers. She was not only interested in the world around her but also in the injustices that plagued it. This early sense of activism can be understood through the lens of developmental psychology, particularly Erik Erikson's theory of psychosocial development, which posits that identity formation is a crucial stage during adolescence. Donnya's awareness of societal inequalities fueled her desire to advocate for change, leading her to engage with local issues and question the status quo.

1.1.3 Navigating the Intersection of Tech and LGBTQ Advocacy

As Donnya grew older, her passion for technology emerged alongside her commitment to LGBTQ advocacy. The intersection of these two domains became a defining feature of her identity. The theory of intersectionality, introduced by Kimberlé Crenshaw, provides a framework for understanding how overlapping social identities—such as gender, race, and sexual orientation—create unique modes of discrimination and privilege. For Donnya, navigating this intersection meant utilizing technology as a tool for empowerment and visibility within the LGBTQ community.

1.1.4 Discovering the Power of Self-Expression Through Art

Art became a powerful medium for Donnya to explore and express her identity. Through various forms of artistic expression—be it painting, poetry, or performance—she found a voice that transcended societal limitations. This aligns with the concept of expressive arts therapy, which posits that creative expression can facilitate personal growth and emotional healing. Donnya's journey through art not only helped her articulate her experiences but also inspired others to embrace their own identities.

1.1.5 Inspiring Others Through Personal Storytelling

The act of storytelling emerged as a vital component of Donnya's advocacy. By sharing her personal narrative, she created a space for connection and understanding within the LGBTQ community. Narrative therapy, developed by Michael White and David Epston, emphasizes the importance of personal stories in shaping identity and fostering resilience. Donnya's storytelling not only validated her experiences but also empowered others to share their journeys, thereby strengthening the collective voice of the LGBTQ community.

In conclusion, the journey of embracing identity and discovery is a complex interplay of personal experiences, societal influences, and the search for self-acceptance. For Donnya Piggott, this journey has been marked by curiosity, creativity, and a commitment to advocacy. As she continues to navigate the challenges and triumphs of her identity, she serves as a beacon of hope and inspiration for others on similar paths.

Embracing Identity and Discovery

The journey of embracing one's identity is often a multifaceted and deeply personal experience, particularly for those within the LGBTQ community. For Donnya Piggott, this journey began in the vibrant streets of Bridgetown, Barbados, where the rich culture and the complexities of a conservative society created a unique backdrop for self-discovery.

1.1.1 Growing up in Bridgetown

Growing up in Bridgetown, Donnya was surrounded by the warmth of Caribbean culture, which is both colorful and rich in tradition. However, this environment was also steeped in conservative values that often stifled individual expression, particularly for those who identified as LGBTQ. The juxtaposition of cultural pride and societal constraints created a fertile ground for early signs of curiosity and activism.

Donnya's childhood was marked by a keen awareness of societal norms and expectations. From a young age, she exhibited an innate curiosity about identity and self-expression. This curiosity was not merely a personal quest; it was the seed of activism that would later bloom into a passionate commitment to LGBTQ rights.

1.1.2 Early signs of curiosity and activism

As a child, Donnya often found herself questioning the rigid definitions of gender and sexuality that surrounded her. This questioning manifested in various forms, from her choice of clothing to the friends she chose to surround herself with. She began to understand that her identity was not confined to societal labels but was a fluid and evolving concept.

For instance, during her teenage years, Donnya participated in local art competitions where she expressed her views on identity through painting and poetry. These creative outlets became a means of exploring and articulating her feelings about the world around her. This early engagement with art not only provided a sanctuary for her thoughts but also served as a platform for activism.

1.1.3 Navigating the intersection of tech and LGBTQ advocacy

Donnya's journey took a pivotal turn when she discovered the world of technology. The intersection of tech and LGBTQ advocacy became a powerful arena for her activism. Technology offered new avenues for self-expression and community building, enabling her to connect with like-minded individuals both locally and globally.

In her exploration of technology, Donnya recognized the potential for digital platforms to amplify LGBTQ voices and foster inclusivity. This realization was grounded in theories of digital activism, which suggest that technology can serve as a catalyst for social change. For example, social media platforms have become vital tools for marginalized communities to share their narratives and advocate for their rights.

1.1.4 Discovering the power of self-expression through art

Art played a crucial role in Donnya's journey of self-discovery. Through painting, poetry, and performance, she found a voice that transcended the limitations imposed by societal expectations. This creative expression became a form of resistance against the homophobia and discrimination prevalent in her community.

Donnya's art often reflected her struggles and triumphs, serving as a mirror to her identity. She explored themes of love, acceptance, and resilience, which resonated with many within the LGBTQ community. The act of creating art not only empowered her but also inspired others to embrace their identities and share their stories.

1.1.5 Inspiring others through personal storytelling

As Donnya navigated her own journey, she began to understand the profound impact of personal storytelling. Sharing her experiences became a powerful tool for advocacy, allowing her to connect with others who faced similar challenges.

Through public speaking engagements, workshops, and online platforms, Donnya shared her narrative, emphasizing the importance of authenticity and self-acceptance. Her story became a beacon of hope for many LGBTQ individuals in Barbados and beyond, encouraging them to embrace their identities unapologetically.

In conclusion, the journey of embracing identity and discovery is complex and deeply personal. For Donnya Piggott, it was a path marked by curiosity, creativity, and a commitment to advocacy. By navigating the intersections of culture, technology, and personal experience, she not only found her voice but also inspired countless others to embark on their own journeys of self-discovery and empowerment.

ERROR. thisXsection() returned an empty string with textbook depth = 3.
ERROR. thisXsection() returned an empty string with textbook depth = 3.
ERROR. thisXsection() returned an empty string with textbook depth = 3.

Early signs of curiosity and activism

From a young age, Donnya Piggott exhibited a profound curiosity about the world around her, particularly regarding issues of identity and social justice. Growing up in Bridgetown, Barbados, she found herself questioning societal norms and the status quo, a trait that would later define her activism. This section explores the formative experiences that ignited her passion for advocacy and the early signs of her commitment to LGBTQ rights.

Donnya's curiosity was often sparked by her interactions with diverse groups of people. She was drawn to stories that challenged conventional narratives, whether they were shared by friends, family, or through literature. This engagement with various perspectives allowed her to cultivate a sense of empathy that would become the cornerstone of her activism.

One pivotal moment occurred during her early teenage years when she attended a community workshop focused on gender identity and expression. This workshop, facilitated by local LGBTQ activists, introduced her to concepts of gender fluidity and the spectrum of sexual orientation. The discussions were not just theoretical; they resonated deeply with her own experiences of feeling different and out of place.

Donnya's involvement in this workshop marked the beginning of her journey into activism. She began to understand the importance of representation and visibility for marginalized communities. As she learned about the struggles faced by LGBTQ individuals in Barbados, she felt a sense of urgency to contribute to the conversation. This realization propelled her into action, leading her to engage in local advocacy efforts, such as organizing awareness campaigns at her school.

However, her path was not without challenges. The conservative societal norms prevalent in Barbados often stifled open discussions about LGBTQ issues. Donnya faced resistance from peers and adults who were uncomfortable with the topics she was passionate about. Yet, this pushback only fueled her determination to advocate for change. She began to write articles for her school newspaper, addressing the misconceptions surrounding LGBTQ identities and advocating for acceptance and understanding.

In her writings, she employed a mix of personal anecdotes and research, illustrating the real-life implications of discrimination. For example, she referenced studies that highlighted the mental health disparities faced by LGBTQ youth, which she had encountered in her own community. One study indicated that LGBTQ youth were significantly more likely to experience depression and anxiety compared to their heterosexual peers. By incorporating this data, Donnya effectively communicated the urgency of addressing these issues, making a compelling case for inclusivity and support.

Donnya's early activism also included leveraging art as a form of expression and advocacy. She discovered that creating visual art allowed her to articulate her feelings and experiences in a way that words sometimes could not. Her artwork often depicted themes of identity, love, and resilience, resonating with others who shared similar struggles. This artistic outlet not only provided her with a means of self-expression but also served as a tool for raising awareness about LGBTQ issues in her community.

In addition to her artistic endeavors, Donnya sought out mentorship from established activists in Barbados. She attended meetings and events organized by local LGBTQ groups, where she learned about the history of LGBTQ rights in the Caribbean and the ongoing battles for equality. This exposure to seasoned activists provided her with invaluable insights into effective advocacy strategies and the importance of coalition-building.

Donnya's early signs of curiosity and activism laid the groundwork for her future endeavors. Through her experiences in workshops, writing, and art, she cultivated a deep understanding of the complexities surrounding LGBTQ identities and the systemic barriers faced by marginalized communities. This foundation not only shaped her identity but also ignited a lifelong commitment to fighting for equality and justice.

In summary, Donnya Piggott's early signs of curiosity and activism were characterized by her engagement with diverse perspectives, her determination to challenge societal norms, and her creative expression through art. These formative experiences served as a catalyst for her future work as a tech innovator and LGBTQ advocate, demonstrating that even the smallest sparks of curiosity can ignite powerful movements for change. Through her journey, she exemplifies the notion that activism can begin at any age, fueled by a desire to understand and uplift the voices of the marginalized.

Navigating the intersection of tech and LGBTQ advocacy

In the contemporary landscape, the intersection of technology and LGBTQ advocacy has emerged as a powerful arena for social change. This section explores how technological advancements are not only reshaping the ways in which LGBTQ issues are addressed but also how they enable activists to mobilize, organize, and amplify their voices in unprecedented ways.

The Role of Technology in Advocacy

Technology serves as a catalyst for LGBTQ advocacy by providing tools that facilitate communication, organization, and education. Social media platforms like Twitter, Instagram, and Facebook allow activists to reach a global audience, share their stories, and mobilize support quickly. For instance, the hashtag #LoveIsLove became a rallying cry for marriage equality, uniting voices across borders and cultures.

$$\text{Advocacy Reach} = \text{Number of Followers} \times \text{Engagement Rate} \qquad (1)$$

Where the engagement rate is defined as the ratio of interactions (likes, shares, comments) to total followers. This equation highlights the importance of not just having a large following but also engaging effectively with the audience to maximize impact.

Challenges Faced by LGBTQ Activists in the Digital Space

Despite the advantages technology offers, LGBTQ activists face significant challenges. One major issue is the prevalence of online harassment and cyberbullying, which disproportionately affects LGBTQ individuals. According to a report by the Pew Research Center, 70% of LGBTQ youth have experienced online harassment, which can deter them from engaging in digital activism.

$$\text{Harassment Rate} = \frac{\text{Number of Harassment Incidents}}{\text{Total Online Engagements}} \times 100 \qquad (2)$$

This equation illustrates the percentage of online engagements that result in harassment, underscoring the need for protective measures and supportive resources for those who choose to advocate online.

Empowering Marginalized Voices through Technology

One of the most significant ways technology intersects with LGBTQ advocacy is by empowering marginalized voices. Digital platforms provide a space for individuals from diverse backgrounds—especially those from underrepresented communities—to share their experiences and advocate for their rights. For example, initiatives like *The Trevor Project* utilize digital media to provide crisis intervention and suicide prevention services to LGBTQ youth, demonstrating the potential of technology to save lives.

Innovative Solutions for Visibility and Representation

Innovative tech solutions have emerged to enhance visibility and representation for LGBTQ individuals. Virtual reality (VR) experiences, for instance, allow users to step into the shoes of LGBTQ individuals, fostering empathy and understanding. Projects like *The Queer History Project* use immersive storytelling to educate users about LGBTQ history and the ongoing fight for rights.

$$\text{Empathy Score} = \frac{\text{User Engagement in VR}}{\text{Time Spent in VR}} \qquad (3)$$

This equation can be used to gauge how effectively VR experiences foster empathy among users, emphasizing the importance of engagement in achieving meaningful connections.

Bridging the Digital Divide

While technology offers numerous benefits, it is crucial to acknowledge the digital divide that exists within LGBTQ communities, particularly in developing countries. Access to technology and the internet can be limited due to economic disparities, leading to unequal opportunities for advocacy. Bridging this divide is essential for ensuring that all voices are heard.

Programs aimed at providing free or low-cost internet access and technology training to LGBTQ individuals in underserved areas are vital. For example, initiatives like *Tech for Good* focus on equipping LGBTQ activists with the skills needed to utilize technology effectively in their advocacy efforts.

The Future of Tech and LGBTQ Advocacy

As technology continues to evolve, its role in LGBTQ advocacy will likely expand. The rise of artificial intelligence (AI) and data analytics offers exciting possibilities for targeted advocacy campaigns. For instance, AI can analyze social media trends to identify emerging issues within the LGBTQ community, allowing activists to respond swiftly and effectively.

$$\text{Trend Prediction} = f(\text{Social Media Data}, \text{Historical Trends}) \qquad (4)$$

This function emphasizes the potential of combining current social media data with historical trends to predict future advocacy needs.

In conclusion, navigating the intersection of technology and LGBTQ advocacy presents both opportunities and challenges. By harnessing the power of technology, activists can amplify their voices, foster community, and drive meaningful change. However, it is essential to remain vigilant against the challenges posed by online harassment and the digital divide, ensuring that advocacy efforts are inclusive and equitable. As we look to the future, the integration of technology into LGBTQ advocacy will undoubtedly continue to shape the landscape of social justice, empowering individuals and communities to advocate for their rights and visibility in an increasingly digital world.

Discovering the power of self-expression through art

Art has always been a powerful medium for self-expression, particularly for marginalized communities. For Donnya Piggott, the act of creating art became a pivotal avenue for exploring and articulating her identity as a member of the LGBTQ community in Barbados. This section delves into how art served as both a personal refuge and a public platform for advocacy, highlighting the intersection of creativity and activism.

The Role of Art in Identity Formation

Art allows individuals to explore complex aspects of their identity in a way that is often more profound than verbal expression. Theories of identity formation, such as Erik Erikson's stages of psychosocial development, suggest that individuals grapple with identity crises throughout their lives. For LGBTQ individuals, this struggle can be intensified by societal pressures and expectations. Through art, Donnya was able to navigate these challenges, using various forms such as painting, poetry, and performance to articulate her experiences and emotions.

$$I = f(E, C, A) \qquad (5)$$

Where:

- I = Identity
- E = Expression through art
- C = Cultural context
- A = Activism

This equation posits that identity (I) is a function of artistic expression (E), the cultural context (C), and activism (A). Donnya's art was not just a reflection of her personal experiences but also a commentary on the cultural and societal dynamics surrounding LGBTQ issues in Barbados.

Art as a Tool for Advocacy

Donnya's artistic journey was not limited to personal exploration; it also became a vehicle for advocacy. The power of art in activism is well-documented, with scholars such as Judith Butler arguing that art can challenge dominant narratives and create spaces for marginalized voices. Donnya utilized her artistic talents to raise awareness about LGBTQ issues, often addressing themes of love, acceptance, and resilience in her work.

One notable example is her participation in local art exhibitions, where she showcased pieces that depicted the struggles and triumphs of LGBTQ individuals. These exhibitions served as safe spaces for dialogue, fostering understanding and empathy among attendees. By sharing her artwork, Donnya was able to humanize the LGBTQ experience, challenging stereotypes and misconceptions through visual storytelling.

The Intersection of Art and Technology

In today's digital age, technology has transformed the way art is created, shared, and experienced. Donnya embraced this shift, leveraging social media platforms to reach a wider audience and amplify her message. The integration of technology in art allows for innovative forms of expression, such as digital art, video installations, and interactive performances.

For instance, Donnya developed a digital art project that combined her visual artwork with augmented reality. This project invited viewers to engage with her art in an immersive way, allowing them to experience the narratives of LGBTQ individuals firsthand. By bridging the gap between art and technology, Donnya not only expanded her creative horizons but also created a unique platform for advocacy.

Challenges and Triumphs in Artistic Expression

Despite the empowering nature of art, Donnya faced significant challenges in her journey. The conservative societal norms in Barbados often stifled open discussions about LGBTQ issues, creating barriers for artists who wished to express their identities. Donnya's work sometimes faced backlash, but she remained undeterred, using these experiences as fuel for her creativity.

The tension between personal expression and societal acceptance is a common theme in LGBTQ art. Scholars like bell hooks emphasize the importance of art as a means of resistance against oppression. Donnya's resilience in the face of adversity not only strengthened her artistic voice but also inspired others in the LGBTQ community to embrace their identities through creative outlets.

Conclusion: The Transformative Power of Art

In conclusion, Donnya Piggott's discovery of the power of self-expression through art highlights the transformative potential of creativity in the LGBTQ advocacy landscape. Art provided her with a means to explore her identity, advocate for change, and connect with others. As she continues to push boundaries through her artistic endeavors, Donnya exemplifies how art can be a powerful tool for personal and collective empowerment, paving the way for future generations of LGBTQ activists to find their own voices.

Through the lens of art, Donnya's journey illustrates the profound impact that creativity can have on identity formation, social change, and community building. In a world where many still struggle to express their true selves, the importance of art as a medium for self-discovery and advocacy cannot be overstated.

Inspiring others through personal storytelling

Personal storytelling serves as a powerful tool for advocacy, especially within the LGBTQ community. It allows individuals to share their unique experiences, fostering connection, empathy, and understanding among diverse audiences. This section explores how Donnya Piggott harnesses the art of storytelling to inspire others, highlighting relevant theories, challenges, and practical examples that illustrate the transformative power of narratives.

Theoretical Framework

At the core of personal storytelling is the narrative paradigm theory proposed by Walter Fisher (1984), which posits that humans are natural storytellers and that narratives are fundamental to human communication. Fisher argues that stories can effectively convey truths that resonate on an emotional level, often more so than logical arguments. This is particularly relevant in the context of LGBTQ advocacy, where personal narratives can humanize complex social issues, making them more relatable and impactful.

Moreover, the concept of *intersectionality*, coined by Kimberlé Crenshaw (1989), emphasizes the interconnected nature of social categorizations such as race, class, and sexual orientation. By sharing personal stories that reflect these intersecting identities, advocates like Donnya can illuminate the unique challenges faced by individuals at the crossroads of multiple marginalized identities, thereby fostering a deeper understanding of the complexities within the LGBTQ community.

Challenges of Storytelling

While personal storytelling can be empowering, it also presents challenges. Many LGBTQ individuals grapple with the fear of vulnerability and potential backlash when sharing their stories. The stigma associated with being LGBTQ can lead to feelings of isolation and apprehension about revealing one's identity. Additionally, the risk of misrepresentation or appropriation of their narratives can deter individuals from speaking out.

Donnya Piggott acknowledges these challenges and emphasizes the importance of creating safe spaces for storytelling. She advocates for community storytelling workshops that encourage individuals to share their experiences in a supportive environment, reducing the fear of judgment and fostering a sense of belonging.

Examples of Impactful Storytelling

Donnya's personal journey exemplifies the power of storytelling in inspiring others. Through her public speaking engagements, she shares her experiences of growing up in Bridgetown, navigating the complexities of her identity, and her subsequent activism. One notable instance was her keynote speech at a local LGBTQ pride event, where she recounted her struggles with acceptance and the pivotal moment when she decided to embrace her true self. This candid narrative resonated with many attendees, prompting several individuals to approach her afterward, sharing their own stories of struggle and triumph.

Another example is her involvement in a documentary project that features LGBTQ individuals from Barbados. By showcasing diverse stories, the documentary aims to challenge stereotypes and promote understanding within the broader community. Donnya's commitment to amplifying marginalized voices through such projects underscores her belief in the collective power of storytelling to drive social change.

The Ripple Effect of Storytelling

The impact of personal storytelling extends beyond individual narratives; it creates a ripple effect that can inspire collective action. When individuals hear stories that mirror their own experiences, it fosters a sense of solidarity and encourages them to share their stories, thereby contributing to a larger narrative of resilience and empowerment within the LGBTQ community.

Donnya's storytelling initiatives have led to the establishment of mentorship programs that connect LGBTQ youth with activists who share similar backgrounds. These programs not only provide guidance but also emphasize the importance of storytelling as a means of empowerment. Participants are encouraged to articulate their experiences, helping them to develop confidence and a sense of agency.

Conclusion

In conclusion, inspiring others through personal storytelling is a vital component of LGBTQ advocacy. By sharing her own experiences, Donnya Piggott exemplifies how narratives can foster understanding, challenge stigma, and empower individuals to embrace their identities. Despite the challenges associated with storytelling, the potential for connection and collective action makes it an invaluable tool in the fight for LGBTQ rights. As more individuals share their stories, the tapestry of narratives continues to grow, creating a more inclusive and empathetic society.

Bibliography

[1] Fisher, W. R. (1984). *Narration as a Human Communication Paradigm: The Case of Public Moral Argument.* Communication Monographs, 51(1), 1-22.

[2] Crenshaw, K. (1989). *Demarginalizing the Intersection of Race and Sex: A Black Feminist Critique of Antidiscrimination Doctrine, Feminist Theory and Antiracist Politics.* University of Chicago Legal Forum, 1989(1), 139-167.

The Influence of Family and Community

Supportive parents and siblings

In the journey of self-discovery and advocacy, the role of family can be pivotal, often acting as a foundation of support or, conversely, a source of conflict. For Donnya Piggott, the unwavering support of her parents and siblings provided a safe harbor amid the turbulent waters of growing up in a conservative society. This section explores the profound impact of familial support on Donnya's identity formation and activism, drawing on psychological theories and real-world examples.

Theoretical Framework

The importance of familial support in the development of LGBTQ identities can be understood through several psychological theories. One key theory is the **Attachment Theory**, which posits that early relationships with caregivers shape an individual's emotional and social development. Secure attachment, characterized by responsive and nurturing parenting, fosters self-esteem and resilience, enabling individuals to navigate challenges more effectively. Conversely, insecure attachment can lead to difficulties in self-acceptance and increased vulnerability to mental health issues.

Another relevant framework is **Erikson's Psychosocial Development Theory**, particularly the stage of *Identity vs. Role Confusion*. During adolescence, individuals grapple with their identities, and supportive family dynamics can facilitate a positive resolution to this conflict. Donnya's experience exemplifies how a supportive family can provide the necessary affirmation for a young person to embrace their true self.

The Role of Parents

Donnya's parents played a crucial role in her development. From an early age, they encouraged open dialogue about identity and self-expression. In a society where LGBTQ identities are often stigmatized, having parents who affirm and support their child's sexual orientation can significantly mitigate feelings of isolation and fear. For instance, when Donnya first expressed her feelings of attraction towards the same sex, her parents responded with love and acceptance rather than rejection. This reaction not only reinforced her self-worth but also instilled a sense of belonging.

Research indicates that parental acceptance can lead to better mental health outcomes for LGBTQ youth. A study by Ryan et al. (2010) found that LGBTQ adolescents with accepting parents were 80% less likely to experience suicidal ideation compared to those with rejecting parents. This statistic underscores the importance of Donnya's family environment in her journey toward self-acceptance and activism.

Siblings as Allies

Donnya's siblings also played a significant role in her life. They acted as allies, providing companionship and understanding during her formative years. Sibling relationships can be particularly influential; they often serve as a source of support and can help buffer against external societal pressures. For Donnya, her siblings were not just family members but confidants who shared in her struggles and triumphs.

The concept of **Sibling Support** is vital in understanding the dynamics of family support in LGBTQ contexts. Research shows that supportive siblings can enhance resilience and promote positive identity development. For example, when Donnya faced bullying at school due to her sexual orientation, her siblings stood by her side, helping her navigate the challenges and reinforcing her sense of self-worth.

Challenges in a Conservative Society

Despite the supportive environment provided by her family, Donnya still encountered challenges inherent in growing up in a conservative society. Societal norms often clash with individual identity, leading to internal and external conflicts. Donnya's family, while supportive, also had to navigate their own discomfort with societal expectations. This duality illustrates the complexity of familial support in the face of external pressures.

For instance, during family gatherings, discussions around LGBTQ issues could become contentious, reflecting the broader societal attitudes towards sexual orientation. Donnya's parents often found themselves in a position where they had to defend their acceptance of her identity against relatives who held more traditional views. This dynamic highlights the ongoing struggle many LGBTQ individuals face, even within supportive families, as they advocate for their rights and identities.

Creating a Safe Space

To foster an environment of acceptance, Donnya's parents actively worked to create a safe space for open discussions about identity and sexuality. They encouraged family dialogues that allowed each member to express their thoughts and feelings without fear of judgment. This proactive approach not only strengthened familial bonds but also equipped Donnya with the tools necessary to advocate for herself and others in the LGBTQ community.

The establishment of safe spaces within families is crucial for the mental well-being of LGBTQ individuals. According to the **Family Acceptance Project**, families that engage in supportive behaviors can significantly reduce the risk of mental health issues and increase the likelihood of positive outcomes for LGBTQ youth.

Conclusion

In conclusion, the support of Donnya Piggott's parents and siblings played an instrumental role in shaping her identity and activism. Through the lens of psychological theories, we see how familial acceptance fosters resilience and empowers individuals to embrace their authentic selves. Donnya's experience underscores the vital importance of supportive family dynamics in the broader context of LGBTQ advocacy. As she continues her journey, the strength derived from her family's unwavering support serves as a beacon of hope, inspiring others to seek and provide similar affirmations in their own lives.

Encountering challenges in a conservative society

Growing up in Barbados, a nation steeped in rich cultural traditions and conservative values, Donnya Piggott faced a myriad of challenges as she began to embrace her identity as an LGBTQ individual. The societal norms in Barbados often painted a narrow view of acceptable behavior, particularly concerning sexual orientation and gender identity. This environment can be understood through the lens of social identity theory, which posits that individuals derive a sense of self from their group memberships. For many in conservative societies, this means conforming to heteronormative standards, leading to a significant internal conflict for those who do not fit the mold.

The conservative landscape of Barbados is characterized by deeply entrenched beliefs about gender roles and sexuality. According to the Pew Research Center, a significant portion of the population holds traditional views on marriage and family, often viewing LGBTQ identities as deviant. This societal backdrop created a hostile environment for Donnya, who faced both overt and subtle forms of discrimination. The challenges she encountered were not merely personal but reflected broader systemic issues that marginalized LGBTQ individuals.

One of the primary challenges was the pervasive stigma associated with being LGBTQ. Stigma, as defined by Goffman (1963), refers to the discrediting attribute that leads to individuals being devalued in society. In Barbados, the stigma surrounding homosexuality often manifested in derogatory language, social ostracism, and even violence. For instance, reports from local LGBTQ organizations indicated that many individuals faced harassment in schools, workplaces, and public spaces simply for expressing their identities. This created an atmosphere of fear and silence, where many felt compelled to hide their true selves to avoid backlash.

Additionally, the legal framework in Barbados posed significant challenges. The country's laws, which criminalize same-sex relationships under the Buggery Act, serve as a powerful deterrent against LGBTQ visibility and advocacy. This legal discrimination not only perpetuates stigma but also limits access to essential services, such as healthcare and mental health support. For Donnya, the fear of legal repercussions was a constant weight, influencing her decisions and actions as she navigated her identity and her activism.

In her journey, Donnya also encountered the challenge of familial acceptance. The importance of family support in the LGBTQ experience cannot be overstated, as highlighted by the Family Acceptance Project, which emphasizes the positive outcomes associated with supportive family environments. However, in a conservative society like Barbados, many LGBTQ individuals face rejection from their families, leading to increased rates of mental health issues, homelessness, and substance abuse. Donnya's experience was no different; she often felt torn between her love for her family and her need to be authentic. This internal struggle is common among LGBTQ youth in conservative societies, where the fear of rejection can stifle self-expression and lead to isolation.

Despite these challenges, Donnya found resilience through community support. The emergence of local LGBTQ support groups provided a safe haven for individuals to share their experiences and foster solidarity. These groups often organized events and initiatives aimed at raising awareness about LGBTQ issues and advocating for change. For Donnya, these spaces became crucial in her journey toward self-acceptance, allowing her to connect with others who shared similar struggles.

Moreover, the intersectionality of Donnya's identity—being both a woman and a member of the LGBTQ community—added another layer of complexity to her challenges. Crenshaw's (1989) theory of intersectionality highlights how overlapping identities can compound experiences of discrimination. In Barbados, Donnya often faced a dual burden: not only was she navigating the challenges of being LGBTQ, but she was also contending with the societal expectations placed upon women. This intersectional lens is vital in understanding the unique obstacles faced by LGBTQ individuals in conservative societies, as it emphasizes the need for nuanced approaches to advocacy and support.

In summary, the challenges Donnya Piggott encountered in the conservative society of Barbados were multifaceted and deeply rooted in cultural, legal, and social frameworks. From stigma and discrimination to the complexities of familial acceptance and intersectionality, each aspect played a significant role in shaping her identity and her activism. Yet, through resilience, community support, and a commitment to advocacy, Donnya began to carve out a path not only for herself but for others in the LGBTQ community who faced similar struggles. Her journey serves as a testament to the strength of the human spirit in the face of adversity and the power of community in fostering change.

Finding solace in local LGBTQ support groups

In the journey of self-discovery and acceptance, finding a community that understands and supports one's identity can be a transformative experience. For many individuals, including Donnya Piggott, local LGBTQ support groups serve as vital sanctuaries where they can express their true selves without fear of judgment or discrimination. These groups offer a safe space for individuals to share their experiences, connect with others facing similar challenges, and foster a sense of belonging.

The Importance of Community

The significance of community in the LGBTQ experience cannot be overstated. Research indicates that social support is a critical factor in the mental health and well-being of LGBTQ individuals. According to Meyer's Minority Stress Theory, individuals who identify as part of a marginalized group often experience unique stressors that can lead to adverse mental health outcomes. These stressors include discrimination, stigma, and internalized homophobia, which can be alleviated through supportive community networks.

$$\text{Mental Health} = \text{Social Support} - \text{Minority Stress} \tag{6}$$

This equation illustrates that the presence of social support can mitigate the negative effects of minority stress, highlighting the essential role of LGBTQ support groups in fostering mental health and resilience.

Local LGBTQ Support Groups: A Lifeline

In Barbados, where societal norms can be conservative and often hostile towards LGBTQ individuals, local support groups provide a lifeline. These groups not only offer emotional support but also serve as platforms for advocacy and empowerment. For instance, organizations such as the Barbados Gays and Lesbians Against Discrimination (BGLAD) create spaces for dialogue, education, and community building.

Donnya Piggott's involvement in these groups allowed her to witness firsthand the impact of collective action. By sharing stories of resilience and triumph, members inspire each other to challenge societal norms and advocate for their rights. This communal spirit fosters a sense of solidarity, encouraging individuals to embrace their identities and fight against discrimination.

Challenges Faced by Support Groups

Despite the positive influence of local LGBTQ support groups, they are not without challenges. Funding constraints, societal stigma, and a lack of visibility often hinder their ability to reach those in need. Many groups operate on limited budgets, relying on donations and volunteer efforts to provide services. This can restrict their capacity to organize events, offer resources, or engage in advocacy campaigns.

Moreover, the fear of exposure can deter individuals from seeking help. In a society where being LGBTQ is often met with hostility, many potential members may hesitate to join support groups, fearing repercussions from family, friends, or employers. This underscores the importance of creating safe, confidential environments where individuals can feel secure in their participation.

Examples of Impact

The impact of local LGBTQ support groups extends beyond individual experiences; they play a crucial role in shaping societal attitudes. For example, during Pride Month, many support groups organize events that celebrate LGBTQ identities while simultaneously raising awareness about the challenges faced by the community. These events not only promote visibility but also encourage allyship among the broader population.

Donnya Piggott's involvement in such initiatives exemplifies the power of community action. By participating in workshops, panel discussions, and outreach programs, she has helped to educate others about LGBTQ issues, fostering a more inclusive environment. The ripple effect of these efforts can lead to greater acceptance and understanding, ultimately contributing to the advancement of LGBTQ rights in Barbados.

Conclusion

Finding solace in local LGBTQ support groups is a crucial aspect of the journey towards self-acceptance and empowerment. These groups provide essential support, foster community, and serve as catalysts for change. While challenges persist, the resilience and determination of individuals like Donnya Piggott highlight the transformative power of solidarity within the LGBTQ community. As these support networks continue to grow and evolve, they will undoubtedly play a pivotal role in shaping a more inclusive future for all.

Creating a chosen family within the LGBTQ community

In a world where acceptance can often feel elusive, the concept of a chosen family emerges as a beacon of hope and solidarity for many within the LGBTQ community. This notion transcends traditional familial bonds, offering individuals a space where they can express their authentic selves without fear of judgment or rejection. A chosen family is not merely a support system; it is a lifeline, a sanctuary where love, understanding, and shared experiences flourish.

Theoretical Framework

The idea of chosen families is deeply rooted in social and psychological theories that emphasize the importance of social support networks. According to *Attachment Theory*, the bonds formed within chosen families can provide the same emotional security and stability as biological families. These relationships often fulfill fundamental human needs for belonging and acceptance, which are particularly crucial for LGBTQ individuals who may face estrangement from their biological families.

Furthermore, *Social Identity Theory* posits that individuals derive a sense of self from their group memberships. For LGBTQ individuals, being part of a chosen family can enhance their identity, providing a sense of pride and community that counters societal stigma. This collective identity fosters resilience, enabling individuals to navigate the challenges posed by discrimination and prejudice.

Challenges Faced by LGBTQ Individuals

Despite the profound benefits of chosen families, the journey toward establishing these connections is not without its challenges. Many LGBTQ individuals grapple with feelings of isolation, particularly in conservative societies where their identities may be marginalized. The stigma associated with their sexual orientation or gender identity can lead to social exclusion, making it difficult to find like-minded individuals who share similar experiences.

Moreover, the process of building a chosen family often involves navigating complex emotional landscapes. Individuals may experience grief over the loss of biological family support or struggle with the fear of rejection within new relationships. These challenges can be exacerbated by societal pressures that prioritize traditional family structures, leaving LGBTQ individuals feeling unsupported in their quest for belonging.

Creating a Chosen Family: Steps and Examples

Creating a chosen family involves intentionality and effort. Here are several steps that individuals can take to foster these meaningful connections:

1. **Seek Out Community Spaces:** LGBTQ community centers, support groups, and social events provide opportunities for individuals to connect with others who share similar experiences. Engaging in these spaces can help individuals find friends who understand their journey.

2. **Cultivate Authentic Relationships:** Building a chosen family requires vulnerability and openness. Sharing personal stories, struggles, and triumphs can deepen bonds and foster trust among individuals.

3. **Establish Traditions and Rituals:** Creating shared traditions, whether it be regular gatherings, celebrations of milestones, or even simple check-ins, can solidify the ties within a chosen family. These rituals reinforce a sense of belonging and commitment.

4. **Provide Mutual Support:** A chosen family thrives on reciprocity. Supporting one another through challenges, celebrating successes, and offering a listening ear fosters a nurturing environment where everyone feels valued.

5. **Advocate Together:** Engaging in activism as a chosen family can strengthen bonds. Working collectively towards common goals not only amplifies voices but also creates shared experiences that deepen connections.

A poignant example of chosen family dynamics can be found in the story of a young trans woman named Mia, who moved to Barbados seeking acceptance. Upon arriving, she struggled with isolation and discrimination. However, through local LGBTQ groups and online forums, she connected with others who had faced similar challenges. Together, they formed a chosen family, celebrating birthdays, supporting each other through transitions, and even advocating for local LGBTQ rights. This network became Mia's anchor, providing her with the strength to embrace her identity fully.

The Impact of Chosen Families on Mental Health

The formation of chosen families can have a profound impact on mental health outcomes for LGBTQ individuals. Research indicates that individuals with supportive social networks experience lower levels of anxiety and depression. The emotional support provided by chosen families can serve as a buffer against the negative effects of discrimination and social isolation.

Moreover, chosen families often create environments where individuals can explore their identities freely. This acceptance fosters self-love and confidence, which are crucial for mental well-being. The shared experiences within a chosen family can also lead to collective healing, as members navigate their journeys together, offering empathy and understanding.

Conclusion

In conclusion, the creation of chosen families within the LGBTQ community is a powerful testament to the resilience and strength of individuals seeking love and acceptance. These families provide not only emotional support but also a sense of identity and belonging that is often lacking in traditional familial structures. As society continues to evolve, the importance of chosen families will only grow, serving as a vital resource for empowerment and advocacy within the LGBTQ movement. By fostering these connections, individuals can navigate the complexities of their identities, challenge societal norms, and ultimately create a more inclusive world for all.

Empowering others through community outreach

Community outreach is a fundamental pillar in the fight for LGBTQ rights, particularly in conservative societies like Barbados. Donnya Piggott recognized early on that empowering individuals within the LGBTQ community was not only about advocating for rights but also about fostering a sense of belonging and support through collective action. This section delves into the strategies and impact of community outreach initiatives led by Donnya, highlighting relevant theories, challenges faced, and successful examples that illustrate the transformative power of community engagement.

Theoretical Framework

The empowerment theory posits that individuals gain power and agency through participation in community initiatives. This theory suggests that when individuals are involved in decision-making processes and have access to resources, they are more likely to take action to improve their circumstances. According to [?], empowerment involves a process of personal and collective growth that enables individuals to transform their social conditions.

In the context of LGBTQ advocacy, community outreach serves as a vehicle for empowerment by providing individuals with the tools, knowledge, and networks necessary to advocate for their rights. By creating safe spaces for dialogue and support, outreach initiatives help to dismantle the stigma and discrimination that often accompany LGBTQ identities.

Challenges in Community Outreach

Despite the potential benefits of community outreach, several challenges persist. One of the primary obstacles is the pervasive homophobia and discrimination within society, which can deter individuals from participating in outreach programs. As noted by [?], the fear of social ostracism can lead to a reluctance to engage in community activities, ultimately hindering the effectiveness of outreach efforts.

Additionally, limited resources and funding can restrict the scope of outreach initiatives. Many LGBTQ organizations operate on shoestring budgets, making it difficult to sustain programs that require ongoing support. This scarcity of resources can lead to burnout among activists and volunteers, as they strive to meet the needs of the community without adequate support.

Strategies for Effective Outreach

Donnya Piggott's approach to community outreach was multifaceted, incorporating various strategies to engage and empower LGBTQ individuals. One effective strategy was the establishment of local support groups, which provided a safe environment for individuals to share their experiences and connect with others facing similar challenges. These groups not only fostered a sense of community but also served as a platform for collective advocacy.

Moreover, Donnya emphasized the importance of collaboration with other organizations and stakeholders. By partnering with local businesses, educational institutions, and governmental agencies, outreach initiatives could leverage additional resources and expertise. For instance, a partnership with a local university allowed for the development of workshops focused on LGBTQ rights and advocacy, which educated both the LGBTQ community and the broader public.

Successful Examples of Community Outreach

One of the standout initiatives led by Donnya was the "Voices of Change" program, which aimed to amplify the stories of LGBTQ individuals in Barbados. This program encouraged participants to share their personal narratives through various mediums, including art, writing, and public speaking. By showcasing these stories, the initiative not only validated the experiences of LGBTQ individuals but also raised awareness about the issues they face within society.

The impact of the "Voices of Change" program was profound. Participants reported feeling more empowered and confident in their identities, while community members gained a deeper understanding of the LGBTQ experience. The program effectively illustrated the power of storytelling as a tool for advocacy, aligning with the narrative theory which posits that personal stories can influence public perception and policy change [?].

Conclusion

Empowering others through community outreach is a vital component of LGBTQ advocacy. Donnya Piggott's commitment to creating inclusive spaces and fostering collaboration has demonstrated the potential for outreach initiatives to effect meaningful change. By addressing the challenges faced by the LGBTQ community and implementing effective strategies, Donnya has not only empowered individuals but has also contributed to the broader movement for equality in Barbados. The lessons learned from these outreach efforts underscore the importance of community engagement in the ongoing fight for LGBTQ rights, inspiring future generations of activists to continue the work of empowerment and advocacy.

The Power of Education and Technology

A thirst for knowledge and learning

Donnya Piggott's journey into the realms of technology and LGBTQ advocacy began with an insatiable thirst for knowledge. This intrinsic motivation to learn was not just a personal trait but a vital component that shaped her identity and activism. Knowledge, in this context, can be viewed through several theoretical lenses, including constructivism, which posits that learning is an active, constructive process where individuals build new ideas based upon their current and past knowledge.

Constructivist theory suggests that knowledge is not merely transmitted from teacher to student; instead, it is constructed through experiences and interactions. For Donnya, this meant engaging with the world around her in Bridgetown, absorbing information from various sources—books, community leaders, and the vibrant LGBTQ community. This continuous engagement allowed her to develop a nuanced understanding of both technology and the sociopolitical landscape impacting LGBTQ rights.

One of the key problems that arose in her pursuit of knowledge was the accessibility of educational resources. In Barbados, as in many parts of the world, access to quality education can be significantly limited, particularly for marginalized communities. Donnya faced barriers such as inadequate funding for schools, a lack of representation in STEM fields, and societal stigma surrounding LGBTQ identities. These challenges, however, did not deter her; instead, they fueled her determination to seek knowledge through alternative means.

For example, Donnya often turned to online platforms, utilizing resources such as Coursera and edX to enroll in courses that expanded her understanding of technology and advocacy. This self-directed approach exemplifies the concept of lifelong learning, which emphasizes the importance of continuous education beyond formal schooling. The ability to adapt and learn from various sources became a cornerstone of her advocacy, allowing her to stay informed about the latest developments in technology and LGBTQ rights.

Moreover, Donnya recognized that knowledge is most powerful when shared. Inspired by her own learning journey, she began to mentor young LGBTQ individuals, fostering a community of learners who could support one another. This approach not only empowered others but also reinforced her understanding of the material, creating a cycle of knowledge dissemination that benefited the entire community.

In this context, the role of technology as a facilitator of learning cannot be overstated. The digital age has transformed how individuals access information, breaking down traditional barriers associated with education. Through social media and online forums, Donnya was able to connect with like-minded activists and tech innovators globally, expanding her perspective and enhancing her advocacy efforts.

In summary, Donnya Piggott's thirst for knowledge was not merely a personal endeavor; it was a transformative force that shaped her identity and activism. By embracing a constructivist approach to learning, overcoming barriers to education, and leveraging technology, she not only enriched her own life but also became a catalyst for change within the LGBTQ community. This foundational commitment to knowledge and learning continues to inspire her advocacy, as she works tirelessly to create a more inclusive and equitable world for all.

$$\text{Knowledge} = \text{Experience} + \text{Reflection} \tag{7}$$

This equation encapsulates the essence of Donnya's learning journey, emphasizing that knowledge is a product of both lived experiences and thoughtful reflection on those experiences.

Discovering the world of tech and its possibilities

In an age defined by rapid technological advancement, the intersection of technology and social advocacy has become a fertile ground for innovation and change. For Donnya Piggott, this discovery was not merely a fascination; it was a calling. Growing up in Barbados, she realized early on that technology was not just a tool for personal expression but a powerful vehicle for social justice and equality.

The digital age has transformed how we communicate, organize, and advocate for change. As Piggott delved into the world of technology, she quickly recognized its potential to amplify marginalized voices, particularly within the LGBTQ community. The possibilities seemed endless, ranging from creating digital platforms for visibility to utilizing data analytics to inform advocacy strategies.

One of the most significant theories underpinning the relationship between technology and social change is the **Diffusion of Innovations** theory, proposed by Everett Rogers. This theory posits that innovations are communicated through certain channels over time among the members of a social system. The process involves several stages: knowledge, persuasion, decision, implementation, and confirmation. For Piggott, understanding this theory was crucial as she sought to leverage technology to promote LGBTQ rights.

$$I = P \cdot C \cdot T \tag{8}$$

Where:

- I = Impact of the innovation
- P = Perceived benefits of the innovation
- C = Compatibility with existing values and needs
- T = Complexity of the innovation

In her exploration, Piggott encountered several challenges that LGBTQ individuals face in accessing technology. The digital divide—a term that describes the gap between those who have easy access to digital technology and those who do not—was particularly pronounced in marginalized communities. Many LGBTQ individuals, especially in conservative societies, faced barriers such as lack of resources, inadequate training, and societal stigma that hindered their ability to engage with technology.

To address these issues, Piggott became an advocate for inclusive tech education. She recognized that empowering LGBTQ youth with digital skills could open doors to opportunities that were previously inaccessible. By establishing workshops and mentorship programs, she aimed to bridge the gap and ensure that everyone, regardless of their background, could harness the power of technology.

A compelling example of this approach was her initiative to create a digital storytelling platform specifically for LGBTQ youth in Barbados. This platform not only allowed young individuals to share their stories but also provided them with technical training in web development and content creation. The project exemplified how technology could foster a sense of community and belonging while empowering individuals to express their identities authentically.

Moreover, Piggott understood the importance of data in driving advocacy efforts. By utilizing data analytics, she could identify trends, measure the impact of initiatives, and tailor her advocacy strategies to effectively address the unique needs of the LGBTQ community. For instance, through surveys and data collection, she discovered that mental health issues were prevalent among LGBTQ youth, prompting her to advocate for better mental health resources and support systems.

The integration of technology into advocacy also posed ethical considerations. Piggott was acutely aware of the potential for surveillance and data privacy issues, especially in environments where LGBTQ identities were criminalized or stigmatized. She emphasized the importance of ethical tech practices, advocating for transparency and consent in data collection and usage. This commitment to ethical considerations ensured that her initiatives not only aimed for impact but also respected the dignity and rights of individuals.

As Piggott navigated the tech landscape, she also recognized the transformative power of social media. Platforms like Twitter, Instagram, and Facebook became essential tools for mobilization and awareness. Through strategic campaigns, she was able to reach a global audience, raising awareness about LGBTQ issues in Barbados and beyond. The ability to create viral content and engage with supporters in real time was a game-changer for advocacy.

In conclusion, Donnya Piggott's journey into the world of technology was marked by discovery, empowerment, and a deep commitment to social justice. By recognizing the potential of tech to drive change, she not only transformed her own life but also inspired countless others to embrace their identities and advocate for equality. The possibilities within the tech realm are vast, and Piggott's story serves as a testament to the profound impact that technology can have when harnessed for the greater good.

Applying technology to advance LGBTQ rights

In the modern landscape of advocacy, technology has emerged as a powerful ally in the quest for LGBTQ rights. The intersection of technology and activism has created new avenues for raising awareness, mobilizing communities, and effecting change. This section explores how technology is applied to advance LGBTQ rights, the challenges faced, and the innovative solutions that have emerged.

Theoretical Framework

The application of technology in advancing LGBTQ rights can be understood through the lens of several theoretical frameworks. One such framework is the *Social Movement Theory*, which posits that social movements arise in response to perceived injustices and mobilize resources to bring about change. In this context, technology serves as a resource that can amplify voices, disseminate information, and foster community engagement.

Another relevant theory is the *Diffusion of Innovations Theory*, which explains how new ideas and technologies spread within a society. This theory highlights the importance of early adopters and opinion leaders in promoting technological tools that can be leveraged for advocacy. By utilizing technology, activists can reach broader audiences and create networks that transcend geographical boundaries.

Challenges in Technological Advocacy

While technology offers numerous advantages, it also presents challenges that must be addressed to effectively advance LGBTQ rights. One significant challenge is the digital divide, which refers to the gap between those who have access to technology and those who do not. Marginalized communities, including many LGBTQ individuals, may lack access to the internet or digital tools, hindering their ability to engage in advocacy efforts.

Additionally, online harassment and cyberbullying pose serious threats to LGBTQ activists. The anonymity of the internet can lead to increased instances of hate speech and discrimination, which can deter individuals from participating in online advocacy. As a result, it is crucial to develop strategies that not only promote LGBTQ rights but also ensure the safety and well-being of activists.

Innovative Applications of Technology

Despite these challenges, numerous innovative applications of technology have emerged to advance LGBTQ rights:

- **Social Media Campaigns:** Platforms like Twitter, Instagram, and Facebook have become vital tools for LGBTQ advocacy. Campaigns such as *#LoveIsLove* and *#TransRightsAreHumanRights* have successfully mobilized support and raised awareness about LGBTQ issues. These campaigns allow individuals to share their stories, connect with allies, and advocate for change in real-time.

- **Online Petitions and Crowdfunding:** Websites like Change.org and GoFundMe provide platforms for LGBTQ activists to launch petitions and fundraising campaigns. These tools enable activists to rally support for specific causes, such as legal reforms or community initiatives, and secure the necessary resources to effect change.

- **Virtual Support Communities:** Technology has facilitated the creation of virtual support groups and forums where LGBTQ individuals can connect, share experiences, and seek advice. Platforms like Reddit and Discord host communities that provide safe spaces for discussion and empowerment, fostering a sense of belonging among marginalized individuals.

- **Data Analytics for Advocacy:** The use of data analytics can enhance the effectiveness of LGBTQ advocacy efforts. By analyzing trends and patterns in public opinion, activists can tailor their campaigns to resonate with specific audiences. For instance, understanding the demographics of supporters can help in crafting messages that appeal to different groups, thereby maximizing impact.

- **Telehealth Services:** The rise of telehealth has revolutionized access to mental health services for LGBTQ individuals. Many organizations now offer online therapy and counseling tailored to the unique needs of the LGBTQ community. This accessibility is crucial in addressing mental health disparities and providing support to those who may face barriers to traditional healthcare services.

Case Studies

Several case studies illustrate the successful application of technology in advancing LGBTQ rights:

- **The Trevor Project:** This organization utilizes technology to provide crisis intervention and suicide prevention services for LGBTQ youth. Through their 24/7 helpline and digital resources, they offer immediate support and guidance, leveraging technology to reach those in need.
- **GLAAD:** GLAAD has effectively used social media to combat misinformation and promote LGBTQ visibility in media. Their campaigns encourage individuals to share positive representations of LGBTQ characters and stories, thereby influencing public perception and fostering acceptance.
- **Human Rights Campaign (HRC):** HRC has utilized data analytics to inform their advocacy strategies. By analyzing voter sentiment and demographic data, they have successfully targeted campaigns to mobilize support for LGBTQ rights legislation across the United States.

Conclusion

The application of technology in advancing LGBTQ rights is both a promising and complex endeavor. While challenges such as the digital divide and online harassment persist, the innovative use of technology has proven to be a transformative force in advocacy. By harnessing the power of social media, online communities, and data analytics, activists can amplify their voices, mobilize support, and create lasting change. As we continue to navigate the evolving landscape of technology, it is essential to remain vigilant in addressing the barriers that hinder access and participation, ensuring that all individuals can engage in the fight for LGBTQ rights.

Through collaboration, creativity, and commitment, technology will continue to play a pivotal role in shaping the future of LGBTQ advocacy, empowering individuals and communities to strive for equality and acceptance in all facets of life.

Bridging the digital divide for marginalized communities

In today's increasingly digital world, the concept of the digital divide has become a critical issue, particularly for marginalized communities. The digital divide refers to the gap between individuals who have access to modern information and communication technology and those who do not. This divide can be attributed to several factors, including socioeconomic status, geographic location, and education levels. Bridging this divide is essential for ensuring that all individuals, regardless of their background, can participate fully in society, access vital resources, and advocate for their rights effectively.

The digital divide can be understood through the lens of several theoretical frameworks. One prominent theory is the **Social Capital Theory**, which posits that individuals with access to networks and resources are more likely to succeed in various aspects of life. In the context of the digital divide, those without access to technology are often excluded from these valuable networks, thereby perpetuating cycles of poverty and disenfranchisement. According to Putnam (2000), social capital is crucial for fostering community engagement and civic participation. Thus, bridging the digital divide is not merely a technological issue but a social justice imperative.

$$\text{Digital Divide} = \text{Access} + \text{Skills} + \text{Usage} \qquad (9)$$

This equation illustrates that the digital divide encompasses not only access to technology but also the skills necessary to use it effectively and the frequency of its use. To address the digital divide, we must consider these three components holistically.

Challenges Faced by Marginalized Communities

Marginalized communities face numerous challenges that exacerbate the digital divide. One significant issue is the lack of infrastructure in rural and low-income areas. According to the Federal Communications Commission (FCC), approximately 19 million Americans lack access to high-speed internet, with rural areas being disproportionately affected. This lack of connectivity limits access to educational resources, job opportunities, and essential services.

Moreover, even when technology is available, there may be a lack of digital literacy skills among community members. A report by the Pew Research Center found that individuals from lower-income households are less likely to possess the skills necessary to navigate digital platforms effectively. This gap in skills can hinder their ability to engage in online advocacy, access health information, or pursue educational opportunities.

Examples of Bridging Initiatives

Several initiatives have emerged to bridge the digital divide for marginalized communities, demonstrating the potential for technology to empower individuals and foster advocacy. One noteworthy example is the work of **TechSoup**, a nonprofit organization that provides technology resources and support to nonprofits and libraries serving low-income communities. By offering discounted software and training, TechSoup helps organizations equip their communities with the tools needed to thrive in a digital world.

Another example is the **EveryoneOn** initiative, which aims to connect low-income families with affordable internet service and devices. Through partnerships with internet service providers and local organizations, EveryoneOn has successfully connected thousands of families, enabling them to access vital online resources for education, employment, and healthcare.

In addition, organizations like **Code.org** are working to promote digital literacy among youth, particularly in underserved communities. By providing free coding education and resources, Code.org empowers young people to develop essential skills that can lead to future career opportunities in the tech industry. Such initiatives not only help bridge the digital divide but also inspire the next generation of tech innovators and advocates.

The Role of Technology in Advocacy

Technology plays a crucial role in advocacy efforts aimed at bridging the digital divide. Social media platforms, for instance, have become powerful tools for raising awareness and mobilizing support for marginalized communities. Campaigns that utilize hashtags, such as #DigitalDivide, have successfully drawn attention to the issue, encouraging policymakers to take action.

Furthermore, online platforms can facilitate the sharing of resources and information among marginalized communities. For example, community-driven websites and forums allow individuals to share their experiences, access support, and collaborate on advocacy initiatives. This digital solidarity can amplify voices that have historically been silenced, fostering a sense of community and empowerment.

Conclusion

Bridging the digital divide for marginalized communities is a multifaceted challenge that requires a concerted effort from various stakeholders, including government agencies, nonprofits, and the private sector. By addressing issues of access, skills, and usage, we can create a more equitable digital landscape that empowers all individuals to advocate for their rights and participate fully in society. As we move forward, it is essential to recognize that technology is not just a tool for communication; it is a catalyst for social change and empowerment. By ensuring that marginalized communities have the resources and skills to navigate the digital world, we can pave the way for a more inclusive and equitable future.

Pioneering online education initiatives for LGBTQ youth

In the digital age, where information flows freely and connectivity knows no bounds, the potential for online education initiatives to empower LGBTQ youth is immense. These initiatives not only provide crucial resources but also create safe spaces for learning and self-expression. They serve as a beacon of hope for young individuals who may feel isolated due to their sexual orientation or gender identity.

Theoretical Framework

The foundation of these online education initiatives can be anchored in several key theories. One of the most relevant is *Social Learning Theory*, which posits that individuals learn from one another through observation, imitation, and modeling. For LGBTQ youth, seeing positive representations of themselves and their experiences can significantly impact their self-esteem and identity formation. Additionally, the *Constructivist Learning Theory* emphasizes the importance of social interaction and collaboration in learning. Online platforms can facilitate this by connecting youth with mentors, peers, and resources that foster a sense of community.

Challenges Faced by LGBTQ Youth

Despite the potential benefits, LGBTQ youth face numerous challenges that can hinder their educational experiences. These include:

- **Bullying and Discrimination:** Many LGBTQ youth encounter bullying in traditional educational settings, leading to decreased academic performance and mental health issues.

- **Lack of Resources:** In many regions, particularly in conservative societies, access to LGBTQ-inclusive educational materials is limited.

- **Mental Health Struggles:** LGBTQ youth are at a higher risk for mental health challenges, including anxiety and depression, which can affect their learning.

Addressing these issues through online education initiatives can create a more inclusive environment that recognizes and celebrates diversity.

Examples of Successful Online Education Initiatives

Several organizations have successfully pioneered online education initiatives tailored specifically for LGBTQ youth. These programs often combine educational content with community-building elements.

- **The Trevor Project:** This organization offers a plethora of resources, including online courses and webinars focused on mental health, advocacy, and self-acceptance. Their programs not only educate but also provide a platform for LGBTQ youth to connect with peers and mentors.
- **OUT for Safe Schools:** This initiative focuses on creating safe and inclusive school environments for LGBTQ students. Through online training modules, educators and administrators learn how to support LGBTQ youth effectively, fostering a culture of acceptance within schools.
- **GSA Network:** The Gay-Straight Alliance (GSA) Network offers online resources for students to establish and maintain GSAs in their schools. These alliances serve as crucial support systems, promoting advocacy and awareness while providing a safe space for LGBTQ youth.

The Role of Technology in Education

The integration of technology in education has transformed how information is disseminated and consumed. Online platforms allow for:

- **Accessibility:** LGBTQ youth can access educational resources from the comfort of their homes, reducing the fear of stigma or discrimination.
- **Interactivity:** Tools such as discussion forums, live chats, and webinars encourage active participation and engagement, making learning more dynamic.
- **Anonymity:** Online platforms provide a level of anonymity that can encourage youth to express themselves freely, share their experiences, and seek help without fear of judgment.

Future Directions

Looking ahead, the potential for online education initiatives for LGBTQ youth is vast. As technology continues to evolve, the following strategies can enhance these programs:

- **Gamification:** Incorporating game-like elements into educational content can make learning more engaging and enjoyable for youth.

- **Mobile Learning:** Developing mobile-friendly educational resources ensures that LGBTQ youth can access information on-the-go, meeting them where they are.

- **Collaboration with Tech Companies:** Partnering with tech companies can provide the necessary resources and expertise to create innovative educational tools tailored for LGBTQ youth.

Conclusion

Pioneering online education initiatives for LGBTQ youth is not just about providing information; it is about fostering a sense of belonging and empowerment. By leveraging technology and community support, these initiatives can break down barriers, inspire self-acceptance, and equip the next generation of LGBTQ advocates with the tools they need to thrive. As we move forward, it is essential to continue developing these programs, ensuring they remain inclusive, accessible, and responsive to the needs of LGBTQ youth worldwide.

The Birth of a Tech Innovator

Creating digital platforms for LGBTQ visibility

In an era where technology permeates every aspect of our lives, the creation of digital platforms has emerged as a vital tool for enhancing LGBTQ visibility. These platforms serve not only as spaces for community engagement but also as powerful means of advocacy, allowing marginalized voices to resonate in a society that often seeks to silence them.

The theory behind digital visibility can be rooted in the concept of *social presence theory*, which posits that the degree to which a person is perceived as "real" in a digital environment influences the quality of communication and interaction. In the context of LGBTQ advocacy, digital platforms such as social media, blogs, and dedicated websites create a sense of community and belonging, where individuals can express their identities freely and authentically.

Challenges in LGBTQ Visibility

Despite the potential of digital platforms, several challenges persist. One significant issue is the pervasive existence of online hate speech and cyberbullying. According to a report by the *Pew Research Center*, 70% of LGBTQ individuals have experienced some form of online harassment. This not only stifles expression but also discourages individuals from engaging with digital platforms that could otherwise serve as a source of support and information.

Moreover, there exists a digital divide that disproportionately affects marginalized communities, including LGBTQ individuals. Access to technology and the internet is not uniform; socioeconomic factors often dictate who can participate in the digital landscape. This disparity creates barriers to visibility and advocacy efforts, as those without access to technology are rendered invisible.

Examples of Successful Platforms

Despite these challenges, several initiatives have successfully harnessed the power of technology to amplify LGBTQ voices. One notable example is the social media platform *Instagram*, which has become a haven for LGBTQ individuals to share their stories and experiences. Hashtags such as #LGBTQ and #Pride have garnered millions of posts, creating a visual tapestry of diverse identities and experiences. This phenomenon not only fosters community but also raises awareness and promotes acceptance among wider audiences.

Another example is the creation of dedicated websites like *GLAAD* (Gay & Lesbian Alliance Against Defamation), which utilizes digital platforms to educate the public about LGBTQ issues and advocate for representation in media. GLAAD's campaigns leverage digital storytelling to challenge stereotypes and promote positive narratives about LGBTQ lives, demonstrating the potential of targeted digital advocacy.

Innovative Solutions for Visibility

To address the challenges of visibility, innovative solutions are being developed. For instance, the use of *augmented reality* (AR) and *virtual reality* (VR) technologies can create immersive experiences that educate users about LGBTQ history and issues. These technologies can help bridge the gap between understanding and empathy, allowing users to experience the struggles and triumphs of LGBTQ individuals firsthand.

Moreover, creating user-friendly digital platforms that prioritize accessibility is crucial. This includes ensuring that websites and applications are designed with inclusive features, such as screen reader compatibility and language options, to cater to a diverse audience. By employing principles of *universal design*, developers can create spaces that welcome all users, regardless of their background or abilities.

The Role of Community Engagement

Community engagement plays a critical role in the effectiveness of digital platforms. By actively involving LGBTQ individuals in the creation and management of these platforms, developers can ensure that the content is relevant and resonates with the target audience. Participatory design approaches, where community members contribute to the development process, can lead to more authentic and impactful platforms.

Furthermore, partnerships with LGBTQ organizations can enhance the reach and credibility of digital initiatives. Collaborations can lead to shared resources, knowledge, and networks, amplifying the visibility of LGBTQ issues on a larger scale. For instance, the partnership between *Facebook* and various LGBTQ organizations during Pride Month has resulted in campaigns that celebrate diversity and promote inclusion.

Conclusion

In conclusion, the creation of digital platforms for LGBTQ visibility is not merely a technological endeavor; it is a vital component of the broader struggle for equality and acceptance. By addressing the challenges of online harassment, access disparities, and the need for community engagement, advocates can harness the power of technology to create spaces that empower LGBTQ individuals and foster a culture of visibility. As we continue to innovate and adapt in the digital age, the potential for these platforms to drive social change remains boundless. Ultimately, the goal is to create a world where every LGBTQ individual can express their identity openly and without fear, paving the way for a more inclusive society.

Developing innovative solutions for marginalized communities

In the quest for social equity, the development of innovative solutions tailored for marginalized communities has emerged as a pivotal focus for advocates and technologists alike. This section delves into the strategies employed by Donnya Piggott, highlighting her commitment to leveraging technology as a means of empowerment and advocacy for those often overlooked.

Understanding Marginalization

Marginalized communities are often defined by their exclusion from mainstream social, economic, and political systems. This exclusion can manifest in various forms, including limited access to education, healthcare, and employment opportunities, as well as systemic discrimination based on sexual orientation, gender identity, race, or socioeconomic status. To effectively address these disparities, it is essential to first understand the unique challenges faced by these communities.

$$\text{Marginalization} = \text{Social Exclusion} + \text{Economic Disparity} + \text{Political Disempowerment} \tag{10}$$

This equation illustrates that marginalization is a multifaceted issue that requires comprehensive solutions that address each component.

Innovative Technological Solutions

Donnya Piggott has championed the use of technology as a transformative tool for marginalized communities. Her approach encompasses several key areas:

1. Digital Platforms for Visibility One of the primary barriers faced by marginalized communities is the lack of visibility in mainstream narratives. Piggott has developed digital platforms that amplify the voices of LGBTQ individuals in Barbados and beyond. These platforms serve as safe spaces for self-expression and community building, allowing users to share their stories and experiences.

For instance, the creation of an online storytelling platform enabled individuals to document their journeys, fostering a sense of belonging and solidarity. By showcasing diverse narratives, these platforms challenge stereotypes and promote understanding among wider audiences.

2. Access to Education and Resources Education is a critical component in breaking the cycle of marginalization. Piggott has initiated online education programs aimed at LGBTQ youth, providing them with access to resources that would otherwise be unavailable. These programs focus on essential skills such as coding, digital literacy, and entrepreneurship, empowering participants to navigate the tech landscape.

A notable example is the "Tech for Change" initiative, which offers workshops and mentorship opportunities for LGBTQ youth, equipping them with the tools needed to succeed in the digital economy. By bridging the educational gap, these initiatives not only enhance individual prospects but also strengthen the community as a whole.

3. **Health and Well-being Applications** Health disparities are prevalent in marginalized communities, particularly among LGBTQ individuals who often face discrimination within healthcare systems. Piggott has been instrumental in developing health and well-being applications that cater specifically to the needs of these communities.

These applications provide users with access to mental health resources, community support networks, and information about LGBTQ-friendly healthcare providers. For example, the "Wellness Connect" app allows users to find nearby support groups and mental health services while offering anonymous chat options for those hesitant to seek help in person.

4. **Economic Empowerment through Technology** Economic empowerment is crucial for marginalized communities seeking to achieve autonomy and stability. Piggott has collaborated with local entrepreneurs to create tech startups that focus on solving community-specific issues, such as access to affordable housing and job placement services.

By fostering an entrepreneurial spirit, these initiatives encourage innovation while creating job opportunities within the community. For example, a startup launched under Piggott's guidance developed a platform connecting local businesses with job seekers from marginalized backgrounds, thereby facilitating economic inclusion.

Challenges and Solutions

Despite the progress made, several challenges persist in the development of innovative solutions for marginalized communities.

1. **Digital Divide** The digital divide remains a significant barrier, as not all individuals have equal access to technology and the internet. Piggott addresses this issue by advocating for policies that promote affordable internet access and providing resources to underserved areas.

2. **Resistance to Change** Resistance from traditional institutions can hinder the implementation of innovative solutions. Piggott emphasizes the importance of building coalitions with stakeholders, including government entities, to foster a supportive environment for change.

Conclusion

Donnya Piggott's commitment to developing innovative solutions for marginalized communities exemplifies the intersection of technology and social advocacy. By harnessing the power of digital tools, she has created pathways for empowerment, visibility, and economic inclusion. As society continues to evolve, the need for such transformative solutions remains paramount in the pursuit of equality and justice for all.

In summary, the innovative solutions developed by Piggott not only address the immediate needs of marginalized communities but also lay the groundwork for sustainable change. By focusing on education, visibility, health, and economic empowerment, these initiatives serve as a model for future advocacy efforts, highlighting the critical role technology plays in shaping a more inclusive world.

Overcoming obstacles and making a name on the global stage

Donnya Piggott's journey to becoming a recognized name in the global LGBTQ advocacy and tech innovation landscape was not without its challenges. Growing up in Barbados, a nation with deeply rooted conservative values and a history of anti-LGBTQ sentiment, Donnya faced numerous obstacles that could have easily deterred her from pursuing her passions. However, it was through resilience, strategic thinking, and an unwavering commitment to her mission that she not only overcame these hurdles but also established herself as a formidable force on the international stage.

One of the primary obstacles Donnya encountered was the societal stigma attached to being openly LGBTQ in a conservative environment. The pervasive homophobia in Barbados manifested in various forms, from verbal harassment to systemic discrimination. According to the *International Lesbian, Gay, Bisexual, Trans and Intersex Association (ILGA)*, Caribbean nations, including Barbados, have some of the highest rates of reported hate crimes against LGBTQ individuals. This hostile environment often leads to a culture of silence, where individuals fear coming out and expressing their true selves.

Donnya recognized that silence was detrimental not only to her own journey but also to the broader LGBTQ community. Thus, she made a conscious decision to embrace her identity publicly. This decision, while empowering, was fraught with risks. She faced backlash from conservative factions within her community, including threats to her safety and well-being. Yet, she transformed these challenges into opportunities for dialogue, using her experiences to educate others about the importance of acceptance and understanding.

In her quest to make a name for herself globally, Donnya leveraged technology as a tool for advocacy. She understood that the digital realm offered a platform for marginalized voices to be heard, especially in regions where traditional media might shy away from LGBTQ issues. By utilizing social media platforms, she was able to amplify her message and connect with like-minded individuals across the globe. For instance, through campaigns on platforms like Twitter and Instagram, Donnya shared personal stories and insights that resonated with many, fostering a sense of community and support.

The power of digital activism cannot be overstated. Research by *Pew Research Center* indicates that social media has become a critical tool for advocacy, allowing individuals to mobilize support and raise awareness about pressing issues. Donnya's innovative use of these platforms exemplifies how technology can break down barriers and create global conversations around LGBTQ rights.

Moreover, Donnya faced the challenge of securing funding and resources for her initiatives. Many LGBTQ advocacy programs struggle with financial sustainability, particularly in regions where such work is often underfunded or overlooked. Donnya tackled this obstacle by forming strategic partnerships with international organizations that shared her vision. For example, she collaborated with the *Human Rights Campaign* and *OutRight Action International*, securing grants and resources that allowed her to expand her outreach efforts.

A significant aspect of Donnya's success was her ability to navigate the complexities of intersectionality. As a Black LGBTQ woman, she understood that her identity intersected with various social issues, including race, gender, and economic inequality. This awareness informed her advocacy work, allowing her to address the unique challenges faced by marginalized groups within the LGBTQ community. By fostering inclusivity in her initiatives, she created a more comprehensive approach to advocacy that resonated with a broader audience.

Furthermore, Donnya's commitment to education played a pivotal role in her journey. She recognized that empowering the next generation of activists was essential for the sustainability of the movement. By implementing workshops and mentorship programs, she cultivated a new wave of leaders who were equipped to continue the fight for equality. This investment in education not only strengthened the community but also established Donnya as a thought leader in both the tech and LGBTQ advocacy spaces.

In her pursuit of global recognition, Donnya faced the daunting task of representing the LGBTQ community on international platforms. She participated in conferences, panels, and discussions, where she eloquently articulated the challenges faced by LGBTQ individuals in the Caribbean. Her ability to share personal narratives while addressing systemic issues garnered respect and attention from global audiences. This visibility was crucial in shifting perceptions and fostering understanding of the unique struggles faced by LGBTQ individuals in conservative societies.

Donnya's resilience in the face of adversity is a testament to the power of determination and purpose. She embraced her identity, leveraged technology, formed strategic partnerships, and invested in education, all while navigating the complexities of intersectionality. Through her efforts, she not only overcame the obstacles in her path but also paved the way for others to follow.

Today, Donnya Piggott stands as a beacon of hope and inspiration, proving that with courage, creativity, and collaboration, it is possible to rise above challenges and make a significant impact on the global stage. Her story is a powerful reminder that the fight for equality is ongoing, and that every voice, no matter how marginalized, has the potential to create change.

Collaborating with tech giants on groundbreaking projects

In the rapidly evolving landscape of technology and advocacy, the collaboration between LGBTQ activists and major tech corporations has emerged as a powerful catalyst for change. Donnya Piggott, with her unique blend of passion for technology and commitment to LGBTQ rights, has been at the forefront of these groundbreaking initiatives. This section explores the dynamics of these collaborations, the challenges faced, and the transformative impact they have had on the LGBTQ community.

The Importance of Collaboration

Collaborating with tech giants allows LGBTQ advocates to leverage resources, expertise, and platforms that can amplify their voices and initiatives. These partnerships can take various forms, including:

- **Funding and Resources:** Tech companies often have substantial financial resources that can be directed towards LGBTQ advocacy projects. For instance, when Donnya partnered with a leading social media platform, they allocated funds to develop a digital campaign aimed at increasing awareness about LGBTQ issues in Barbados.

- **Technological Innovation:** Tech giants have the capability to create innovative solutions that address specific challenges faced by LGBTQ individuals. By collaborating with these companies, activists can harness

cutting-edge technology to develop apps and platforms that provide support, resources, and community connections.
- **Global Reach:** Collaborations with international tech companies can extend the reach of LGBTQ advocacy efforts beyond local boundaries. Donnya's partnership with a global tech firm enabled her to participate in international conferences, presenting LGBTQ issues to a wider audience and fostering global dialogue.

Challenges in Collaboration

Despite the potential benefits, collaborations with tech giants are not without challenges. Activists often face issues such as:

- **Corporate Interests vs. Advocacy Goals:** There can be a misalignment between the objectives of tech companies and the goals of LGBTQ advocacy. Donnya has often emphasized the importance of ensuring that corporate partnerships do not dilute the advocacy message or prioritize profit over people. This requires careful negotiation and clear communication of shared values.
- **Tokenism:** Activists must be vigilant against tokenism, where collaborations are superficial and do not lead to meaningful change. It is crucial for advocates to establish metrics for success and ensure that partnerships result in tangible benefits for the LGBTQ community.
- **Navigating Bureaucracy:** Working with large corporations can involve navigating complex bureaucratic structures, which may slow down the pace of project implementation. Donnya has shared experiences where project timelines were extended due to internal approvals and red tape within tech companies.

Successful Examples of Collaboration

Donnya's collaborations have yielded several successful projects that illustrate the potential of these partnerships:

1. **Digital Safety Initiatives:** In partnership with a major cybersecurity firm, Donnya helped launch a digital safety initiative aimed at educating LGBTQ individuals about online safety and privacy. This program included workshops,

online resources, and the development of a mobile app that provides real-time alerts about potential online threats.

2. Advocacy through Data: Collaborating with a data analytics company, Donnya spearheaded a project that utilized data to highlight the disparities faced by LGBTQ individuals in Barbados. By analyzing social media trends and public sentiment, the project provided valuable insights that informed advocacy strategies and policy recommendations.

3. Mentorship Programs: Donnya partnered with a tech giant to create a mentorship program for LGBTQ youth interested in pursuing careers in technology. This initiative not only provided guidance and support but also created networking opportunities, helping young individuals to build confidence and skills in a male-dominated field.

Theoretical Framework

The collaborations between LGBTQ activists and tech giants can be understood through the lens of **Social Exchange Theory**, which posits that relationships are formed based on the perceived benefits and costs of the interaction. In this context, both parties must see value in the partnership: tech companies gain positive public relations and fulfill corporate social responsibility goals, while LGBTQ advocates receive resources, visibility, and support for their causes.

Additionally, the **Diffusion of Innovations Theory** can be applied to understand how new ideas and technologies are adopted within the LGBTQ community. As tech giants introduce innovative solutions, the rate of adoption among LGBTQ individuals can vary based on factors such as awareness, perceived benefits, and compatibility with existing practices.

Conclusion

Collaborating with tech giants has proven to be a double-edged sword for LGBTQ activists like Donnya Piggott. While these partnerships can provide invaluable resources and visibility, they also require careful navigation of challenges to ensure that the true goals of advocacy are upheld. Through her innovative projects and strategic collaborations, Donnya has not only advanced LGBTQ rights in Barbados but has also set a precedent for how technology can be harnessed as a force for social change. The journey of collaboration is ongoing, and as the tech landscape continues to evolve, so too will the opportunities for meaningful partnerships that champion equality and justice for all.

Pushing the boundaries of tech innovation to create social impact

The intersection of technology and social impact is a fertile ground for innovation, particularly within the LGBTQ advocacy space. Donnya Piggott has consistently pushed the boundaries of tech innovation to create meaningful change, leveraging her expertise to address systemic issues faced by marginalized communities. This section explores the theoretical frameworks, challenges, and exemplary initiatives that illustrate how technology can be harnessed for social good.

Theoretical Frameworks

To understand the impact of technology on social issues, we can draw upon several theoretical frameworks:

- **Social Innovation Theory:** This theory posits that innovative solutions can address social needs and challenges. It emphasizes collaboration among various stakeholders, including nonprofits, government agencies, and private sectors, to create sustainable change.

- **Digital Divide Theory:** This framework addresses the gap between those who have access to digital technologies and those who do not. It highlights the importance of equitable access to technology as a means to empower marginalized groups.

- **Intersectionality:** Coined by Kimberlé Crenshaw, this theory emphasizes the interconnected nature of social categorizations such as race, class, and gender, which can create overlapping systems of discrimination. In the context of LGBTQ advocacy, intersectionality is crucial in understanding the diverse experiences of individuals within the community.

These frameworks guide the development of technology-driven initiatives aimed at advancing LGBTQ rights, ensuring that solutions are inclusive and responsive to the needs of the community.

Challenges in Tech Innovation for Social Impact

Despite the potential for technology to drive social change, several challenges persist:

- **Access and Affordability:** Many LGBTQ individuals, particularly in developing countries, face economic barriers that limit their access to technology. This digital divide exacerbates existing inequalities and hinders advocacy efforts.

- **Censorship and Surveillance:** In some regions, governments impose restrictions on internet access and monitor online activities. This creates a hostile environment for LGBTQ activists, who may fear repercussions for their online presence.

- **Lack of Representation:** The tech industry has historically been dominated by a homogenous group of individuals, leading to a lack of representation of LGBTQ voices in technology development. This can result in products and services that do not adequately address the needs of diverse communities.

Addressing these challenges requires innovative thinking and a commitment to inclusivity in technology development.

Examples of Tech Innovations for Social Impact

Donnya Piggott has been instrumental in pioneering several tech innovations that have had a profound social impact:

- **Digital Platforms for Visibility:** Piggott developed online platforms that amplify LGBTQ voices and stories. For instance, her initiative, *OutStories*, allows individuals to share their personal experiences, fostering a sense of community and visibility. This platform not only empowers users but also educates the broader public about LGBTQ issues.

- **Mobile Apps for Safety:** In response to rising incidents of violence against LGBTQ individuals, Piggott collaborated with developers to create a mobile app that provides users with real-time safety alerts and resources. The app connects users with local support services and allows them to report incidents anonymously, thereby enhancing personal safety.

- **Online Education Initiatives:** Recognizing the need for inclusive education, Piggott launched online courses aimed at LGBTQ youth. These courses cover topics such as self-advocacy, mental health, and digital literacy, equipping participants with the tools they need to navigate their identities in a digital world.

These examples illustrate how technology can be harnessed to create social impact, empowering LGBTQ individuals and fostering community engagement.

Conclusion

Pushing the boundaries of tech innovation to create social impact is not merely a goal; it is a necessity for advancing LGBTQ rights in an increasingly digital world. By leveraging theoretical frameworks, addressing challenges, and implementing innovative solutions, advocates like Donnya Piggott are paving the way for a more inclusive future. As technology continues to evolve, it is crucial to ensure that it serves as a tool for empowerment, bridging gaps and fostering connections within the LGBTQ community and beyond.

$$\text{Social Impact} = \text{Innovation} + \text{Access} + \text{Representation} \qquad (11)$$

This equation encapsulates the essence of Piggott's work: true social impact arises from a combination of innovative solutions, equitable access to technology, and the representation of diverse voices in the tech landscape. As we look to the future, it is essential to continue pushing these boundaries, ensuring that technology serves as a catalyst for social change and equality.

A Journey of Self-Acceptance and Advocacy

Embracing personal struggles and triumphs

Donnya Piggott's journey has been a tapestry woven with threads of personal struggles and triumphs, where each experience has contributed to her identity as a tech innovator and LGBTQ advocate. This section delves into the complexities of her life, illustrating how her challenges shaped her resilience and ultimately fueled her passion for advocacy.

At the heart of Donna's narrative is the struggle for self-acceptance. Growing up in Bridgetown, Barbados, in a conservative society, she faced the daunting task of reconciling her sexual orientation with societal expectations. The internal conflict between her true self and the persona she felt compelled to present often felt like a tug-of-war, leading to profound moments of self-doubt and isolation. This experience is not unique to Donnya; many LGBTQ individuals grapple with similar feelings, a phenomenon supported by the Minority Stress Theory, which posits that stigma, prejudice, and discrimination can lead to increased psychological stress among marginalized groups [1].

Donnya's early life was marked by moments of introspection and artistic expression, which served as her refuge. Art became a powerful medium through which she could articulate her feelings and experiences. For instance, she often found solace in painting, using colors and shapes to convey emotions that words could not encapsulate. This artistic outlet not only provided a therapeutic escape but also laid the groundwork for her future advocacy, illustrating how creativity can be a vital tool for self-discovery and empowerment.

The triumphs in Donnya's life are equally significant. Each milestone she achieved—whether it was coming out to her family or successfully leading a community initiative—was a testament to her resilience. Her decision to embrace her identity publicly was a pivotal moment, akin to breaking free from the shackles of silence. This act of courage resonated with many in her community, inspiring others to share their stories and embrace their authentic selves. The ripple effect of her bravery exemplifies the concept of collective empowerment, where individual triumphs contribute to the strength of the community as a whole [?].

Moreover, Donnya's journey highlights the importance of vulnerability in advocacy. By openly sharing her struggles with mental health, including anxiety and depression, she has humanized the often stigmatized topic of mental wellness within the LGBTQ community. This transparency has fostered a culture of openness, encouraging others to seek help and share their experiences. Research indicates that sharing personal narratives can significantly reduce stigma and promote understanding, thereby enhancing community support systems [?].

As she navigated the complexities of her identity, Donnya also faced external challenges, such as discrimination and societal backlash. These obstacles only strengthened her resolve to advocate for LGBTQ rights. For instance, after facing hostility during a public speaking engagement, she channeled that experience into her advocacy work, focusing on creating safe spaces for LGBTQ youth. This proactive approach not only addressed her personal struggles but also transformed them into a platform for collective action, illustrating the power of turning adversity into advocacy.

In summary, Donnya Piggott's journey of embracing personal struggles and triumphs is a profound testament to the resilience of the human spirit. Her experiences underscore the vital interplay between personal growth and community advocacy, demonstrating that individual journeys can inspire collective movements for change. As she continues to break barriers and challenge societal norms, Donnya serves as a beacon of hope for many, proving that through embracing our struggles, we can emerge stronger and more empowered.

Breaking barriers and challenging societal norms

Donnya Piggott's journey as an LGBTQ advocate is not just a personal narrative; it is a powerful testament to the resilience required to challenge and break through the societal norms that often constrain individual identity and expression. This section explores how Donnya navigated these barriers, employing both personal experience and broader advocacy strategies to effect change within her community and beyond.

Theoretical Framework: Social Norms and Identity

To understand the impact of societal norms on LGBTQ individuals, we can draw upon the theory of social norms, which posits that behaviors are influenced by the expectations and rules established by society. According to Cialdini et al. (1990), social norms can be divided into two categories: descriptive norms, which reflect what most people do, and injunctive norms, which reflect what most people approve or disapprove of. For LGBTQ individuals, these norms can create a restrictive environment that discourages authenticity and self-expression.

The pressure to conform to these norms can lead to a phenomenon known as internalized homophobia, where individuals may internalize society's negative attitudes towards their sexual orientation or gender identity. This internal conflict can manifest in various ways, including mental health challenges, decreased self-esteem, and reluctance to engage in advocacy.

Personal Experiences of Breaking Barriers

Donnya's own experiences exemplify the struggle against these societal expectations. Growing up in Bridgetown, she faced the dual challenge of reconciling her identity with the conservative values prevalent in her community. The stigma surrounding LGBTQ identities in Barbados often meant that those who dared to express their true selves faced ostracism, discrimination, and even violence.

One pivotal moment in Donnya's journey occurred during her teenage years when she attended a local LGBTQ support group for the first time. Here, she found a safe space where individuals shared their stories of struggle and resilience. This experience not only validated her feelings but also ignited her passion for advocacy. It was within this community that she began to understand the importance of challenging societal norms and the power of collective action.

Advocacy Strategies: Challenging Norms through Visibility

Donnya recognized that one of the most effective ways to challenge societal norms was through visibility. By sharing her story and the stories of others, she aimed to dismantle the misconceptions surrounding LGBTQ identities. This approach aligns with the concept of narrative therapy, which posits that personal storytelling can empower individuals to reclaim their identities and challenge oppressive narratives.

For instance, Donnya launched a digital campaign called *My Truth, My Voice*, which encouraged LGBTQ individuals to share their experiences online. The campaign quickly gained traction, with participants from various backgrounds contributing their stories. By amplifying these voices, Donnya not only fostered a sense of community but also challenged the prevailing narratives that often marginalized LGBTQ identities.

Creating Dialogue: Engaging with Conservative Perspectives

While visibility is crucial, Donnya also understood the importance of engaging with those who hold conservative views. This approach is rooted in the theory of dialogue, which emphasizes the value of open communication in bridging divides. By initiating conversations with community leaders, religious figures, and policymakers, Donnya aimed to challenge stereotypes and promote understanding.

One notable initiative was a series of community forums where LGBTQ individuals and conservative leaders were invited to share their perspectives. These forums often sparked heated debates, but they also created opportunities for empathy and connection. For example, during one forum, a local pastor expressed his concerns about LGBTQ rights, citing traditional beliefs. Donnya responded with compassion, sharing her own experiences and the importance of love and acceptance in all communities. This dialogue not only humanized the LGBTQ experience but also encouraged some attendees to reconsider their views.

The Role of Education in Challenging Norms

Education plays a pivotal role in challenging societal norms. Donnya recognized that many misconceptions about LGBTQ individuals stem from a lack of understanding. To address this, she collaborated with local schools to implement inclusive education programs that addressed LGBTQ issues and promoted diversity.

These programs included workshops that educated students about sexual orientation, gender identity, and the importance of acceptance. By fostering an environment of understanding and respect, Donnya aimed to reduce the stigma surrounding LGBTQ identities and empower young people to embrace their authentic selves.

Conclusion: The Ongoing Journey of Advocacy

Breaking barriers and challenging societal norms is an ongoing journey, one that requires courage, resilience, and a commitment to advocacy. Donnya Piggott's work serves as a reminder that while societal norms can be deeply entrenched, they are not immutable. Through visibility, dialogue, and education, individuals can challenge these norms and create a more inclusive society.

As Donnya continues her advocacy, she inspires others to join the fight for equality, reminding us all that it is possible to break free from societal constraints and live authentically. Her journey illustrates that the path to change is often fraught with challenges, but with determination and collective action, barriers can be dismantled, paving the way for a more equitable future for all.

Becoming a voice for the voiceless in the LGBTQ community

In the vibrant tapestry of LGBTQ activism, few threads shine as brightly as the voices of those who have chosen to stand up for the marginalized and voiceless. For Donnya Piggott, becoming a voice for the voiceless was not merely a role; it was a calling rooted in personal experience and a profound understanding of the systemic barriers faced by many within the LGBTQ community.

At the heart of this advocacy lies the recognition of intersectionality, a theory developed by Kimberlé Crenshaw, which posits that individuals experience overlapping social identities—such as race, gender, sexual orientation, and class—that can compound discrimination and oppression. For many LGBTQ individuals, particularly those from marginalized backgrounds, this intersectionality creates a unique set of challenges that often go unheard. Donnya's commitment to amplifying these voices reflects an understanding that advocacy must be inclusive and representative of all experiences within the community.

$$\text{Intersectionality} = \sum_{i=1}^{n} \text{Identity}_i \times \text{Discrimination}_i \qquad (12)$$

This equation illustrates how various identities contribute to the overall experience of discrimination, emphasizing the need for a multifaceted approach to advocacy. Donnya recognized that to truly advocate for the voiceless, one must listen to their stories, understand their struggles, and elevate their narratives in spaces where they are often silenced.

In her journey, Donnya encountered numerous challenges while advocating for LGBTQ rights in Barbados, a society where traditional values often clash with the quest for equality. The stigma surrounding homosexuality and the lack of legal protections for LGBTQ individuals created an environment ripe for discrimination. For instance, reports of violence against LGBTQ persons, particularly transgender individuals, were alarmingly prevalent. Donnya understood that simply being an advocate was not enough; she needed to be a conduit for the stories of those who felt they had no platform.

One of the pivotal moments in her advocacy came when she organized a storytelling event that showcased the lived experiences of LGBTQ individuals in Barbados. This event was not just about sharing stories; it was about creating a safe space where individuals could express their truths without fear of judgment or reprisal. The success of this event demonstrated the power of personal narratives in fostering understanding and empathy within the broader community.

Moreover, Donnya utilized digital platforms to amplify these voices. By harnessing social media, she created campaigns that highlighted the struggles faced by LGBTQ individuals, particularly those who were most vulnerable. For example, a campaign titled #VoicesUnheard featured short videos of individuals sharing their experiences with discrimination and violence. The campaign quickly gained traction, drawing attention from local and international media, thereby providing a larger platform for these voices.

In addition to storytelling, Donnya emphasized the importance of mentorship within the LGBTQ community. She established programs that paired young LGBTQ individuals with experienced activists, fostering a sense of belonging and empowerment. By providing guidance and support, these mentorship programs helped to cultivate the next generation of advocates who could continue the fight for equality.

Donnya's advocacy also extended to policy change, where she became a vocal critic of laws that perpetuated discrimination against LGBTQ individuals. By collaborating with local and international organizations, she worked to draft proposals aimed at reforming legislation that criminalized homosexuality. This effort was not without its challenges; she faced backlash from conservative factions within society who viewed her actions as a threat to traditional values. However, Donnya remained resolute, understanding that the fight for equality often requires courage in the face of adversity.

The impact of Donnya's work is evident in the growing visibility and acceptance of LGBTQ issues in Barbados. Her efforts have inspired many to speak out against injustice, creating a ripple effect that encourages others to share their stories and advocate for their rights. As a result, the LGBTQ community in

Barbados is gradually becoming more empowered to challenge societal norms and demand change.

In conclusion, becoming a voice for the voiceless in the LGBTQ community is a profound responsibility that requires dedication, empathy, and resilience. Through her advocacy, Donnya Piggott exemplifies the power of storytelling, mentorship, and policy reform in elevating marginalized voices. Her journey serves as a reminder that while the path to equality may be fraught with challenges, the collective strength of the LGBTQ community can pave the way for a more inclusive and just society. By continuing to amplify the voices of the voiceless, advocates like Donnya not only honor their struggles but also ignite hope for a brighter future.

Transforming personal experiences into collective empowerment

In the journey of LGBTQ advocacy, the transformation of personal experiences into collective empowerment serves as a powerful catalyst for change. This process involves the sharing of individual narratives that resonate with broader societal issues, ultimately fostering a sense of community and solidarity among marginalized groups. The act of storytelling not only validates personal experiences but also highlights systemic injustices that need to be addressed.

The Importance of Personal Narratives

Personal narratives are crucial in LGBTQ activism as they humanize the struggles faced by individuals within the community. According to [?], personal stories can challenge stereotypes and foster empathy among those who may not have direct experience with LGBTQ issues. This aligns with the theory of narrative identity, which posits that individuals construct their identities through the stories they tell about themselves [?]. By sharing their experiences, activists like Donnya Piggott create a tapestry of narratives that collectively illustrate the challenges and triumphs of LGBTQ individuals.

Creating Safe Spaces for Storytelling

To effectively transform personal experiences into collective empowerment, it is essential to create safe spaces where individuals feel comfortable sharing their stories. Piggott has been instrumental in establishing forums, workshops, and online platforms that encourage open dialogue among LGBTQ individuals. These safe spaces allow for the exploration of identity, the sharing of experiences, and the building of community. According to [?], such environments not only promote healing but also empower individuals to take ownership of their narratives.

Collective Action and Advocacy

Once personal stories are shared, they can serve as a foundation for collective action. By highlighting common experiences, individuals can unite to advocate for systemic change. For example, Piggott's initiative to compile personal testimonies of LGBTQ individuals in Barbados led to the creation of a comprehensive report that was presented to policymakers. This report not only illustrated the lived realities of LGBTQ individuals but also provided concrete recommendations for legislative reform. As noted by [?], collective action is often fueled by shared grievances, making personal narratives a vital component of advocacy.

Empowerment through Visibility

The visibility of personal experiences can also empower others within the community. When individuals see their stories reflected in the narratives of others, it fosters a sense of belonging and validation. Piggott's use of social media platforms to amplify LGBTQ voices exemplifies this phenomenon. By sharing her journey and those of others, she has created a virtual community that offers support, encouragement, and inspiration. The concept of visibility politics, as discussed by [?], emphasizes the importance of representation in achieving social change. The more visible LGBTQ individuals become, the more likely they are to challenge existing norms and advocate for their rights.

Challenges in Transforming Experiences

While the transformation of personal experiences into collective empowerment is a powerful tool for activism, it is not without challenges. One significant barrier is the fear of backlash or discrimination that individuals may face when sharing their stories. Piggott has often spoken about the need to navigate the complexities of vulnerability and safety. As highlighted by [?], the act of coming out or sharing one's experiences can lead to potential risks, including social ostracism and violence. Therefore, it is essential to approach storytelling with sensitivity and an understanding of the potential consequences.

Conclusion

In conclusion, transforming personal experiences into collective empowerment is a fundamental aspect of LGBTQ advocacy. Through the sharing of narratives, individuals can foster community, challenge systemic injustices, and inspire collective action. Donnya Piggott's work exemplifies how personal stories can be harnessed to create a more inclusive and equitable society. By prioritizing safe spaces for storytelling and amplifying the voices of marginalized individuals, activists can continue to drive meaningful change in the pursuit of LGBTQ rights. The journey from personal narrative to collective empowerment is not only transformative for individuals but also essential for the advancement of the entire LGBTQ movement.

Amplifying LGBTQ causes through public speaking and media engagements

In a world where voices often go unheard, public speaking and media engagements serve as powerful platforms for LGBTQ advocates like Donnya Piggott to amplify their causes. The act of sharing personal narratives and experiences not only fosters understanding but also creates a ripple effect that can lead to social change. This section delves into the significance of these platforms, the challenges faced, and the strategies employed by Piggott to elevate LGBTQ issues on a global stage.

Public speaking allows advocates to connect with diverse audiences, breaking down barriers of ignorance and prejudice. According to the *Social Identity Theory*, individuals are more likely to empathize with those they perceive as similar to themselves. By sharing her journey as a LGBTQ individual, Piggott creates a relatable narrative that encourages listeners to reflect on their own biases and assumptions. The emotional resonance of storytelling can be transformative, as it humanizes the statistics and facts often associated with LGBTQ issues.

Moreover, media engagements—whether through interviews, podcasts, or social media—offer a broader reach. In an age dominated by digital communication, the ability to disseminate messages widely is crucial. For instance, when Piggott participated in a panel discussion at an international tech conference, her insights on the intersection of technology and LGBTQ rights not only informed attendees but also reached thousands through live streaming and recorded content. This multiplicative effect is vital for raising awareness and mobilizing support.

However, public speaking and media engagements are not without their challenges. Advocates often face backlash from conservative factions, and the pressure to represent the entire LGBTQ community can be overwhelming. Piggott has encountered instances where her messages were misinterpreted or distorted, leading to public controversy. In such moments, it is essential to employ strategies that reinforce the core message while addressing misconceptions. For example, Piggott has utilized follow-up interviews and social media posts to clarify her stance and provide context to her statements.

Furthermore, the effectiveness of public speaking can be enhanced through the incorporation of data and research. By grounding her narratives in empirical evidence, Piggott strengthens her arguments and showcases the urgent need for change. For instance, when discussing mental health issues within the LGBTQ community, she often cites studies that highlight the disproportionate rates of depression and anxiety faced by LGBTQ youth compared to their heterosexual peers. This data-driven approach not only informs but also empowers audiences to advocate for policy changes and support initiatives that address these disparities.

In addition, collaboration with other activists and organizations amplifies the impact of public speaking and media engagements. By forming coalitions, advocates can pool resources, share platforms, and create a united front. Piggott's partnership with international LGBTQ rights organizations has led to joint campaigns that leverage the strengths of each group, thereby reaching a wider audience and fostering a sense of solidarity. The collective voice of multiple advocates can be more persuasive than that of a single individual, further enhancing the visibility of LGBTQ causes.

Moreover, the role of social media cannot be overstated in the context of public speaking. Platforms like Twitter, Instagram, and TikTok have transformed how messages are communicated and received. Piggott has adeptly used these platforms to share snippets of her speeches, engage in live Q&A sessions, and participate in trending discussions. By capitalizing on the virality of social media, she has been able to mobilize support quickly and effectively, demonstrating the power of digital advocacy in the modern age.

In conclusion, amplifying LGBTQ causes through public speaking and media engagements is a multifaceted endeavor that requires skill, resilience, and strategic thinking. Donnya Piggott exemplifies how personal storytelling, data-driven narratives, and collaborative efforts can create significant social impact. As advocates continue to navigate the complexities of public discourse, the lessons learned from Piggott's journey can serve as a guiding light for future generations of LGBTQ activists seeking to make their voices heard in an ever-evolving landscape.

Breaking the Shackles of Silence

Breaking the Shackles of Silence

Breaking the Shackles of Silence

In this chapter, we delve into the transformative journey of Donnya Piggott as she navigates the complex landscape of identity, advocacy, and the often-uncharted territory of coming out. The phrase "breaking the shackles of silence" encapsulates the profound act of embracing one's truth and the subsequent ripple effects it has on personal relationships, social acceptance, and the broader LGBTQ community.

Embracing Personal Truth and Coming Out

Coming out is not merely a personal choice; it is a courageous act that reverberates through the lives of those around us. For Donnya, this journey began in the vibrant streets of Bridgetown, where the juxtaposition of her identity and the conservative societal norms created a battleground of emotions. The process of coming out can be understood through the lens of *Erving Goffman's theory of stigma*, which posits that individuals with a stigmatized identity often experience internal conflict and societal rejection. This theory provides a framework for understanding the psychological implications of living in a society that may not fully accept one's identity.

Donnya's coming out was not a singular event but rather a gradual unfolding of her truth. Each revelation to friends and family was met with a range of reactions, from unconditional support to confusion and resistance. This mirrors the findings of *The Williams Institute*, which highlights that LGBTQ individuals often face varying degrees of acceptance based on their social circles and community dynamics.

The Impact on Personal Relationships and Social Acceptance

The act of coming out can significantly alter personal relationships. Donnya experienced both the joy of acceptance and the pain of rejection. For instance, her close-knit family initially struggled with her identity, reflecting the broader societal reluctance to embrace LGBTQ individuals. This experience is not uncommon; research indicates that nearly 40% of LGBTQ youth report being rejected by their families upon coming out, leading to increased risks of mental health challenges.

As Donnya navigated these turbulent waters, she found solace in supportive friendships, which became a lifeline during her most challenging moments. The concept of a *chosen family* emerged as a crucial support system, allowing her to cultivate relationships that affirmed her identity and provided a sense of belonging. This is particularly important in LGBTQ communities, where chosen families often replace biological ones that may not offer acceptance.

Paving the Way for Others to Live Authentically

Donnya's journey of self-acceptance became a beacon of hope for others in her community. By sharing her story publicly, she created a platform for dialogue and empowerment, encouraging others to embrace their truth. This aligns with the principles of *social learning theory*, which posits that individuals learn from one another through observation and imitation. Donnya's visibility inspired others to break their silence, fostering a culture of authenticity and acceptance.

Moreover, her advocacy work emphasized the importance of representation in mainstream media. By championing LGBTQ visibility, Donnya aimed to dismantle stereotypes and challenge societal norms. This effort is supported by *George Gerbner's cultivation theory*, which suggests that media exposure can shape perceptions and attitudes toward marginalized groups. Thus, Donnya's presence in the media landscape became a vital tool for normalizing LGBTQ identities.

Navigating the Complexities of Intersectional Identities

Donnya's advocacy also highlighted the complexities of intersectional identities, where race, gender, and sexual orientation intersect to create unique experiences of discrimination and privilege. The work of *Kimberlé Crenshaw* on intersectionality underscores the necessity of understanding how overlapping social identities can compound experiences of oppression. Donnya, as a Black queer woman, faced distinct challenges that required her to navigate multiple layers of identity in her activism.

This intersectional approach informed her advocacy strategies, as she sought to uplift voices that were often marginalized within the LGBTQ movement. By collaborating with other activists and organizations, Donnya aimed to create a more inclusive narrative that recognized the diverse experiences within the community.

Championing LGBTQ Visibility in Mainstream Media

The chapter culminates in Donnya's commitment to championing LGBTQ visibility in mainstream media. She recognized that representation matters, not just for those within the community but for society at large. By advocating for more inclusive storytelling and diverse characters in media, Donnya aimed to challenge the prevailing stereotypes that often perpetuate discrimination.

In conclusion, Chapter 2 of Donnya Piggott's biography illustrates the profound impact of breaking the silence surrounding one's identity. Through her personal journey, she not only embraced her truth but also paved the way for others to do the same. By navigating the complexities of relationships, intersectionality, and media representation, Donnya emerged as a powerful advocate for LGBTQ rights, inspiring countless individuals to live authentically and fearlessly.

Out of the Closet, Into the Limelight

Embracing personal truth and coming out

Coming out is a deeply personal journey that involves embracing one's identity and sharing it with the world. For many in the LGBTQ community, this process is not just a single event, but a series of revelations that unfold over time. It can be both liberating and daunting, as it challenges individuals to confront societal norms and expectations. This section explores the complexities of coming out, its emotional impact, and the theoretical frameworks that underpin this significant life event.

Theoretical Frameworks

The process of coming out can be understood through various psychological and sociological theories. One prominent framework is the **Minority Stress Theory**, which posits that LGBTQ individuals experience unique stressors due to their marginalized status. These stressors can include societal stigma, discrimination, and internalized homophobia, which can significantly affect mental health and overall well-being. The theory emphasizes that coming out can serve as a coping mechanism, allowing individuals to reduce the burden of secrecy and embrace their identity.

Another relevant framework is the **Identity Development Theory**, particularly the model proposed by Cass (1979). Cass identified six stages of sexual identity formation:

1. Identity Confusion
2. Identity Comparison
3. Identity Tolerance
4. Identity Acceptance
5. Identity Pride
6. Identity Synthesis

These stages illustrate the evolution of an individual's understanding and acceptance of their sexual orientation, culminating in the decision to come out. Each stage presents its own challenges and triumphs, reflecting the complexity of navigating one's identity in a society that may not always be accepting.

The Emotional Landscape

The emotional landscape of coming out is multifaceted. For many, it is a mix of excitement and fear. The exhilaration of living authentically can be overshadowed by concerns about rejection, loss, and discrimination. Research indicates that individuals who come out often report feelings of relief and empowerment, but the process can also trigger anxiety and stress related to potential negative reactions from family, friends, and colleagues.

For instance, a study by [1] found that LGBTQ individuals who had supportive environments during their coming out reported higher levels of self-esteem and lower levels of depression compared to those who faced rejection. This highlights the importance of a supportive network in facilitating a positive coming-out experience.

Cultural Considerations

Cultural context plays a significant role in shaping the coming-out experience. In conservative societies, where traditional values may stigmatize LGBTQ identities, the stakes can be particularly high. For example, in Barbados, where cultural norms often emphasize heteronormativity, coming out can lead to social ostracism or even violence. This reality forces many individuals to weigh the risks of coming out against the desire for authenticity.

In contrast, more progressive environments may provide a supportive backdrop for coming out. In these contexts, individuals may find role models and community resources that encourage openness and acceptance. The difference in societal attitudes can significantly influence the timing and manner of an individual's coming out.

Personal Narratives

Personal stories of coming out can serve as powerful testaments to the journey of self-acceptance. For example, Donnya Piggott's own experience of coming out was marked by a blend of fear and hope. Growing up in Bridgetown, she often felt the weight of societal expectations pressing down on her. However, through the support of friends and LGBTQ groups, she found the courage to embrace her truth.

Donnya recalls the moment she decided to come out to her family. "I took a deep breath, my heart racing like it was auditioning for the Olympics," she humorously reflects. "But when I finally said the words, it felt like I was shedding a heavy coat I had worn for years." This moment of vulnerability not only marked a turning point in her life but also inspired others in her community to seek their own truths.

Navigating Relationships

Coming out inevitably affects personal relationships. The reactions of family and friends can vary widely, ranging from unconditional love to shock and rejection. Navigating these responses requires sensitivity and resilience. For instance, Donnya faced mixed reactions from her loved ones. While some embraced her authenticity, others struggled to accept her identity. This dichotomy is common, as individuals often grapple with their own beliefs and biases when confronted with a loved one's truth.

The process of coming out can also lead to the formation of chosen families—supportive networks of friends and allies who provide emotional sustenance and understanding. These relationships can be particularly vital for individuals who face rejection from biological families. The concept of chosen family is a cornerstone of LGBTQ culture, emphasizing the importance of community and solidarity.

Conclusion

In summary, embracing personal truth and coming out is a profound journey that involves navigating emotional, cultural, and relational complexities. Theoretical frameworks such as Minority Stress Theory and Identity Development Theory provide valuable insights into the challenges faced by LGBTQ individuals during this process. Personal narratives, like that of Donnya Piggott, illustrate the transformative power of coming out, highlighting both the struggles and triumphs that accompany this significant life event. Ultimately, coming out is not just about revealing one's identity; it is about embracing authenticity and fostering connections that empower both the individual and the broader community.

The impact on personal relationships and social acceptance

Coming out is often heralded as a moment of liberation, a time when individuals can finally breathe freely in their own skin. However, it is also a complex journey that can significantly impact personal relationships and social acceptance. For Donnya Piggott, this journey was no different, as she navigated the intricate web of connections that defined her life in Barbados.

The Ripple Effect on Relationships

When Donnya came out, the immediate effect was a seismic shift in her relationships with family and friends. The fear of rejection loomed large, as many LGBTQ individuals experience a profound anxiety regarding how their loved ones will react. Research has shown that approximately 40% of LGBTQ individuals report strained relationships with family members post-coming out [1]. For Donnya, the initial response from her family was mixed; while her parents offered support, some extended family members struggled to accept her identity, creating a rift that would take time to heal.

The impact on friendships was equally profound. Some friends rallied around her, offering unconditional support, while others distanced themselves, unable to reconcile their beliefs with Donnya's truth. This phenomenon is not uncommon; studies indicate that social acceptance can fluctuate dramatically within peer groups, often leading to a re-evaluation of friendships [?]. Donnya found solace in those who embraced her authenticity, forming deeper bonds with individuals who shared similar experiences.

Navigating Social Acceptance

Social acceptance is a multifaceted concept, encompassing not only personal relationships but also the broader societal context. In a conservative society like Barbados, where traditional values often prevail, Donnya faced significant challenges. The social landscape can be hostile, with prevailing attitudes toward LGBTQ individuals often steeped in stigma and discrimination. The impact of these societal norms on personal relationships cannot be overstated; individuals often find themselves grappling with the fear of ostracism or backlash from their communities.

Donnya's experience highlights the importance of safe spaces—environments where individuals can express their identities without fear of judgment. These spaces, often found within LGBTQ support groups, provide a refuge for individuals navigating the complexities of acceptance. Through her involvement in local advocacy, Donnya was able to foster a sense of community, creating opportunities for connection among individuals who faced similar struggles.

The Role of Intersectionality

The intersection of various identities—race, gender, socio-economic status—further complicates the dynamics of personal relationships and social acceptance. Donnya, being a Black queer woman, faced unique challenges that required her to navigate multiple layers of identity. According to Crenshaw's theory of intersectionality, individuals who embody multiple marginalized identities often experience compounded discrimination [?].

In Donnya's case, this meant that her coming out was not just about her sexual orientation but also about confronting societal expectations tied to her race and gender. The intersectional nature of her identity shaped her relationships, as she sought allies who understood the complexities of her experience. This journey of self-discovery allowed her to advocate not only for LGBTQ rights but also for broader social justice issues, creating a ripple effect that encouraged others to embrace their multifaceted identities.

The Power of Visibility

Visibility plays a crucial role in shaping social acceptance. When Donnya stepped into the limelight as an LGBTQ advocate, she became a beacon for others in her community. The act of being visible can challenge stereotypes and foster empathy, paving the way for greater acceptance. Research indicates that increased visibility of

LGBTQ individuals in media and society correlates with a decrease in homophobic attitudes [?].

Donnya's public advocacy work, including her participation in pride events and media interviews, served to humanize the LGBTQ experience in Barbados. By sharing her story, she not only validated her own identity but also provided a voice for those who felt voiceless. This act of visibility can have profound implications, as it encourages others to come out and assert their identities, ultimately fostering a more inclusive society.

Conclusion

The impact of coming out on personal relationships and social acceptance is a nuanced journey that varies from individual to individual. For Donnya Piggott, this journey was marked by both challenges and triumphs. While she faced the fear of rejection and the complexities of navigating societal norms, she also discovered the power of community, visibility, and intersectionality. Through her advocacy, Donnya not only transformed her own relationships but also contributed to a broader movement toward acceptance and equality in Barbados. As she continues to inspire others, her story serves as a testament to the resilience of the LGBTQ community and the ongoing fight for love and acceptance.

Paving the way for others to live authentically

Living authentically is a journey that many individuals in the LGBTQ community aspire to, yet it often comes with a myriad of challenges and societal pressures. For Donnya Piggott, this journey was not only personal but also a catalyst for broader societal change. By embracing her own truth, she created a pathway for others to follow, demonstrating the profound impact of authenticity on both individual lives and the collective LGBTQ community.

The Importance of Authenticity

Authenticity refers to the quality of being genuine or true to oneself. In the context of LGBTQ identities, it encompasses the courage to embrace one's sexual orientation or gender identity openly, without succumbing to societal expectations or prejudices. Research indicates that living authentically can lead to improved mental health outcomes, increased self-esteem, and a stronger sense of community belonging. According to a study by [?], LGBTQ individuals who feel accepted and supported in their identities experience significantly lower levels of depression and anxiety.

Challenges to Authenticity

Despite the benefits of authenticity, many individuals face substantial barriers when attempting to live openly. In conservative societies, such as Barbados, the stigma surrounding LGBTQ identities can lead to discrimination, ostracization, and even violence. This societal pressure often forces individuals back into the metaphorical closet, stifling their true selves. A 2018 report by [?] highlighted that over 70% of LGBTQ individuals in the Caribbean have experienced some form of discrimination due to their sexual orientation.

Donnya's experience exemplifies these challenges. Growing up in a society where traditional values often overshadowed personal truths, she encountered significant resistance not only from the external community but also within her own family. However, she recognized that her journey was not just about her own liberation; it was about creating a space where others could feel safe to express their identities.

Creating Safe Spaces

One of the pivotal strategies employed by Donnya was the establishment of safe spaces for LGBTQ individuals. These environments foster acceptance, understanding, and support, allowing individuals to explore their identities without fear of judgment. By collaborating with local organizations, Donnya helped create community centers and support groups where LGBTQ youth could gather, share their experiences, and empower one another.

For instance, the establishment of the "Pride Hub" in Bridgetown became a beacon of hope for many. This initiative provided resources, mentorship, and a sense of belonging to those grappling with their identities. As documented in qualitative interviews conducted by [?], participants reported feeling a renewed sense of hope and determination after engaging with the Pride Hub, highlighting the transformative power of community support.

Advocating for Visibility

Donnya understood that visibility is a crucial element in paving the way for others to live authentically. By sharing her own story through various media platforms, she challenged the prevailing stereotypes and misconceptions surrounding LGBTQ identities. Her public speaking engagements and social media presence served as powerful tools for advocacy, amplifying the voices of those often marginalized.

The impact of visibility cannot be overstated. A 2020 study by [?] found that increased representation of LGBTQ individuals in media significantly correlates with greater societal acceptance and reduced stigma. By being unapologetically herself, Donnya inspired countless others to embrace their identities, fostering a culture of authenticity that rippled through the community.

Empowering Future Generations

Empowerment is a key component in the quest for authenticity. Donnya's advocacy extended beyond her immediate community; she sought to equip future generations with the tools necessary to navigate their identities confidently. Through workshops and mentorship programs, she instilled resilience and self-acceptance in LGBTQ youth, encouraging them to embrace their uniqueness.

For example, the "Authenticity Workshop" series, which Donnya spearheaded, focused on self-discovery, self-acceptance, and the importance of living one's truth. Feedback from participants revealed a significant shift in mindset, with many expressing newfound confidence in their identities. As one participant noted, "Donnya showed me that being myself is not just okay; it's powerful."

Conclusion

In conclusion, paving the way for others to live authentically is a multifaceted endeavor that requires courage, resilience, and a commitment to community. Donnya Piggott's journey is a testament to the transformative power of authenticity, illustrating how one individual's bravery can inspire a collective movement towards acceptance and understanding. By creating safe spaces, advocating for visibility, and empowering future generations, she has laid a foundation for others to embrace their true selves without fear or hesitation. As the LGBTQ community continues to navigate the complexities of identity and acceptance, the path paved by pioneers like Donnya will undoubtedly guide many toward a brighter, more authentic future.

Navigating the complexities of intersectional identities

In the realm of LGBTQ advocacy, understanding intersectionality is crucial. Coined by legal scholar Kimberlé Crenshaw in 1989, intersectionality refers to the ways in which various forms of social stratification, such as race, gender, sexual orientation, and class, intersect to create unique dynamics of discrimination and privilege. This framework allows us to comprehend how individuals experience overlapping systems of oppression. For instance, a Black lesbian may face challenges that are distinct from those encountered by a white gay man, highlighting the necessity of a nuanced approach to advocacy.

The complexities of intersectional identities can be illustrated through the following theoretical framework:

$$P = \sum_{i=1}^{n} \left(\frac{D_i}{V_i} \right) \qquad (13)$$

Where P represents the overall privilege or disadvantage an individual experiences, D_i is the degree of discrimination faced due to identity i, and V_i is the visibility or recognition of that identity in society. For example, if an individual identifies as both LGBTQ and a person of color, they may experience compounded discrimination that is not adequately addressed by focusing on either identity in isolation.

Navigating these complexities requires a multifaceted approach to advocacy. One major problem arises when LGBTQ advocacy groups prioritize certain identities over others, often sidelining the voices of those who embody multiple marginalized identities. For example, a study by the Human Rights Campaign revealed that LGBTQ youth of color are disproportionately affected by bullying and mental health issues, yet their experiences are frequently overlooked in mainstream LGBTQ discourse.

An illustrative case is that of Marsha P. Johnson, a Black transgender activist who played a pivotal role in the Stonewall uprising. Johnson's contributions have often been overshadowed by the narratives of white, cisgender activists. By recognizing and amplifying the contributions of intersectional figures like Johnson, advocacy can become more inclusive and representative of the diverse experiences within the LGBTQ community.

Moreover, the concept of "double jeopardy" is pertinent here. Individuals with intersecting marginalized identities may experience discrimination that is more severe than those with a single marginalized identity. This phenomenon can be mathematically represented as:

$$R = D + (D \times I) \qquad (14)$$

Where R is the resultant discrimination faced, D is the base level of discrimination, and I is the index of intersectionality that quantifies the multiplicative effect of holding multiple marginalized identities. For instance, a transgender woman of color may face both transphobia and racism, leading to a compounded effect that significantly impacts her quality of life.

To effectively navigate these complexities, it is essential for LGBTQ advocates to employ an intersectional lens in their strategies. This involves:

1. **Inclusive Representation**: Ensuring that the voices of individuals from diverse backgrounds are included in leadership roles within LGBTQ organizations. This can be achieved by actively recruiting and supporting leaders from various intersectional identities.
2. **Tailored Programs**: Developing advocacy programs that specifically address the unique challenges faced by individuals with intersectional identities. For example, creating mental health resources that cater to the needs of LGBTQ youth of color, incorporating culturally competent practices.
3. **Collaborative Efforts**: Building coalitions with other social justice movements, such as racial justice and women's rights organizations, to address the overlapping issues of discrimination. This collaboration can amplify the impact of advocacy efforts and foster a more holistic approach to social justice.
4. **Education and Awareness**: Conducting training sessions and workshops that educate advocates on the importance of intersectionality. This can help dismantle biases within the LGBTQ community and promote understanding of the diverse experiences of its members.

In conclusion, navigating the complexities of intersectional identities is not merely an academic exercise but a vital aspect of effective LGBTQ advocacy. By embracing intersectionality, advocates can better understand the unique challenges faced by individuals at the crossroads of multiple marginalized identities, ultimately leading to a more inclusive and equitable movement. As we continue to fight for LGBTQ rights, let us remember that our strength lies in our diversity and our ability to uplift every voice within our community.

Championing LGBTQ visibility in mainstream media

In an era where representation matters more than ever, championing LGBTQ visibility in mainstream media has become a pivotal aspect of advocacy. The media acts as a mirror reflecting societal values, beliefs, and norms. When LGBTQ individuals are portrayed positively and authentically, it can significantly influence public perception and acceptance. Conversely, negative or stereotypical portrayals can perpetuate stigma and discrimination. This section delves into the importance of visibility, the challenges faced, and the strategies employed to enhance representation.

The Importance of Visibility

Visibility in media serves several crucial functions:

- **Normalization:** By showcasing LGBTQ characters and stories, media can normalize diverse identities and experiences. This normalization fosters acceptance and reduces prejudice, as audiences become familiar with LGBTQ narratives that reflect their own lives or those of their peers.

- **Empowerment:** Representation empowers LGBTQ individuals by affirming their identities. Seeing oneself reflected in media can bolster self-esteem and provide a sense of belonging. It sends a message that LGBTQ lives are valid and worthy of recognition.

- **Education:** Media serves as a powerful educational tool. Through storytelling, it can inform audiences about LGBTQ issues, history, and culture, promoting understanding and empathy. This education is vital in combating ignorance and fostering inclusivity.

Challenges to Visibility

Despite the importance of visibility, numerous challenges hinder the representation of LGBTQ individuals in mainstream media:

- **Stereotyping:** Often, LGBTQ characters are relegated to stereotypes, such as the flamboyant gay best friend or the tragic queer character. These narrow portrayals fail to capture the diversity of LGBTQ experiences and can reinforce harmful clichés.

- **Censorship:** In many regions, particularly those with conservative cultural norms, LGBTQ content faces censorship or backlash. This can limit the stories told and the authenticity of the representation, as creators may feel pressured to conform to societal expectations.

- **Lack of Authentic Voices:** A significant issue in media representation is the lack of LGBTQ individuals in decision-making roles. When LGBTQ creators are excluded from the narrative process, the resulting portrayals may lack authenticity and depth.

Strategies for Enhancing Visibility

To champion LGBTQ visibility, several strategies can be employed:

- **Inclusive Storytelling:** Media creators should prioritize inclusive storytelling that reflects the complexities of LGBTQ lives. This includes developing multi-dimensional characters who embody a range of experiences and identities, moving beyond stereotypes.

- **Collaboration with LGBTQ Creators:** Engaging LGBTQ writers, directors, and producers can lead to more authentic representations. Their lived experiences can inform narratives that resonate with audiences and accurately depict LGBTQ realities.

- **Advocacy for Policy Change:** Advocating for policies that promote diversity in media can help increase LGBTQ representation. This includes pushing for funding for LGBTQ projects and supporting initiatives that hold media organizations accountable for their portrayals.

Examples of Successful Representation

Several examples illustrate the positive impact of championing LGBTQ visibility in mainstream media:

- **Television Series:** Shows like *Pose* and *Schitt's Creek* have garnered acclaim for their authentic representation of LGBTQ characters and stories. *Pose*, in particular, highlights the lives of transgender individuals and the ballroom culture, showcasing the richness of LGBTQ experiences often overlooked.

- **Film:** The film *Moonlight* received widespread praise for its nuanced portrayal of a Black gay man navigating his identity amidst societal challenges. By centering the story on a marginalized identity, it opened discussions around intersectionality and representation.

- **Social Media Campaigns:** Campaigns like #RepresentationMatters have gained traction on platforms like Twitter and Instagram, highlighting the importance of visibility in media. These movements empower individuals to share their stories and advocate for better representation.

Conclusion

Championing LGBTQ visibility in mainstream media is not just about representation; it is about creating a world where all individuals can see themselves reflected in the stories that shape our culture. By addressing the challenges and implementing strategic approaches, advocates like Donnya Piggott are paving the way for a more inclusive media landscape. This visibility not only fosters acceptance but also empowers the LGBTQ community to embrace their identities fully. As we continue to push for diverse representations, we must remember that every story matters, and every voice deserves to be heard.

Unmasking Homophobia and Discrimination

Addressing social stigma through advocacy

Social stigma surrounding LGBTQ identities remains a pervasive challenge, particularly in regions like Barbados, where conservative cultural norms often dictate societal attitudes. Advocacy plays a crucial role in dismantling these stigmas, fostering a more inclusive environment for LGBTQ individuals. This section explores the theoretical frameworks, challenges, and practical examples of advocacy efforts aimed at addressing social stigma.

Theoretical Frameworks

To understand the dynamics of social stigma, we can draw on Erving Goffman's seminal work in *Stigma: Notes on the Management of Spoiled Identity* (1963). Goffman categorizes stigma into three types: physical deformities, character blemishes, and tribal identities. LGBTQ identities often fall under the category of character blemishes, where societal perceptions frame these identities as deviant or abnormal.

The *Social Identity Theory* (Tajfel & Turner, 1979) further elucidates how individuals derive a sense of self from their group memberships. When LGBTQ individuals are marginalized, their social identity is negatively impacted, leading to internalized stigma and diminished self-worth. Advocacy efforts must therefore focus on reshaping societal narratives and promoting positive representations of LGBTQ identities.

Challenges in Addressing Stigma

Despite the progress made in LGBTQ advocacy, several challenges persist:

- **Cultural Resistance:** In conservative societies, traditional beliefs often perpetuate stigma. Advocacy initiatives must navigate these cultural landscapes delicately to avoid backlash.
- **Misinformation:** Misunderstandings about LGBTQ identities can lead to fear and prejudice. Advocacy must prioritize education and awareness to combat misinformation.

♦ **Institutional Barriers:** Legal and institutional frameworks may reinforce stigma, limiting the effectiveness of advocacy efforts. This includes discriminatory laws that marginalize LGBTQ individuals.

Practical Examples of Advocacy Efforts

1. **Public Awareness Campaigns:** Initiatives such as the *It Gets Better Project* have successfully addressed stigma by sharing uplifting stories of LGBTQ individuals overcoming adversity. These narratives foster empathy and understanding, challenging negative stereotypes.

2. **Educational Workshops:** Organizations like *PFLAG* (Parents, Families, and Friends of Lesbians and Gays) conduct workshops aimed at educating families and communities about LGBTQ issues. By promoting dialogue, these workshops help dismantle misconceptions and foster acceptance.

3. **Media Representation:** Advocacy groups have worked to increase positive representation of LGBTQ individuals in media. Shows like *Pose* and *Queer Eye* not only entertain but also educate audiences about the complexities of LGBTQ lives, challenging harmful stereotypes.

4. **Collaborative Initiatives:** Partnerships between LGBTQ organizations and mainstream entities (such as corporations or educational institutions) can amplify advocacy efforts. For instance, corporate allyship during Pride Month can signal broader societal acceptance and encourage others to join the movement.

Conclusion

Addressing social stigma through advocacy is an ongoing battle that requires a multifaceted approach. By combining theoretical insights with practical strategies, advocates can effectively challenge societal norms and promote acceptance of LGBTQ identities. As Donnya Piggott exemplifies through her work, advocacy is not just about raising awareness; it is about creating a world where LGBTQ individuals can thrive without fear of stigma or discrimination.

$$\text{Stigma Reduction} = \text{Awareness} + \text{Education} + \text{Representation} \qquad (15)$$

In this equation, we see that reducing stigma requires a holistic approach that encompasses awareness campaigns, educational efforts, and positive representation in media. By employing these strategies, advocates can pave the way for a more inclusive society, transforming perceptions and ultimately improving the lives of LGBTQ individuals in Barbados and beyond.

Battling systemic discrimination in Barbados

Systemic discrimination against the LGBTQ community in Barbados is deeply rooted in historical, cultural, and legal frameworks that perpetuate inequality and marginalization. This section delves into the various dimensions of systemic discrimination faced by LGBTQ individuals in Barbados, examining the socio-legal environment, cultural attitudes, and the ongoing struggle for rights and recognition.

Historical Context

The roots of systemic discrimination in Barbados can be traced back to colonial laws that criminalized homosexuality and reinforced heteronormative standards. The remnants of these laws continue to influence contemporary attitudes and policies. The historical context is crucial for understanding the current landscape of LGBTQ rights in the Caribbean. For instance, Section 9 of the Barbados Sexual Offences Act criminalizes "buggery," which is defined as anal intercourse, and Section 12 criminalizes "serious indecency." These laws not only stigmatize LGBTQ individuals but also embolden discrimination and violence against them.

Cultural Attitudes and Social Norms

Cultural attitudes in Barbados often reflect a conservative and religiously influenced society where heteronormativity is the norm. The pervasive stigma surrounding LGBTQ identities leads to social ostracism and discrimination in various spheres of life, including employment, healthcare, and education. According to a survey conducted by the Caribbean Policy Development Centre, approximately 70% of respondents expressed negative attitudes towards LGBTQ individuals, indicating the prevalence of homophobia in everyday interactions.

Social norms dictate that individuals conform to traditional gender roles, and any deviation is met with hostility. This cultural backdrop creates an environment where LGBTQ individuals fear coming out, often leading to mental health issues, isolation, and a lack of community support.

Legal Framework and Human Rights Violations

Despite the global movement towards LGBTQ rights, Barbados has lagged in legal reforms. The lack of comprehensive anti-discrimination laws leaves LGBTQ individuals vulnerable to various forms of discrimination. For example, a study by the International Lesbian, Gay, Bisexual, Trans and Intersex Association (ILGA) highlighted that LGBTQ individuals in Barbados face discrimination in employment, with many reporting being fired or denied jobs based solely on their sexual orientation.

Moreover, the absence of legal protections against hate crimes exacerbates the risks faced by LGBTQ individuals. Reports of violence, harassment, and discrimination are prevalent, yet victims often hesitate to report incidents to law enforcement due to fear of further victimization or lack of support from authorities.

Activism and Resistance

In response to systemic discrimination, LGBTQ activists in Barbados have mobilized to advocate for their rights. Organizations such as the Barbados Gazeebo and the Coalition of Caribbean LGBTQ Organizations have emerged as critical voices in the fight against discrimination. These organizations engage in public awareness campaigns, legal advocacy, and community outreach to challenge the status quo and promote acceptance.

One notable example of activism is the annual Pride celebration, which serves as a platform for visibility and solidarity. Despite facing pushback from conservative factions, these events foster a sense of community and empower individuals to embrace their identities. Activists also work to build alliances with international organizations to amplify their voices and bring global attention to local issues.

Challenges Ahead

Battling systemic discrimination in Barbados remains a daunting task. The interplay of cultural, legal, and social factors creates significant barriers to progress. Activists face opposition not only from conservative segments of society but also from within the LGBTQ community, where internalized homophobia can hinder collective action. Additionally, the COVID-19 pandemic has exacerbated existing inequalities, with many LGBTQ individuals facing increased vulnerability due to economic instability and lack of access to support services.

Conclusion

In conclusion, systemic discrimination against LGBTQ individuals in Barbados is a multifaceted issue that requires a concerted effort from activists, allies, and policymakers. Addressing the historical, cultural, and legal dimensions of discrimination is essential for fostering an inclusive society. By continuing to advocate for legal reforms, raising awareness, and building community support, Barbados can move towards a future where LGBTQ individuals are recognized, respected, and empowered to live authentically.

$$\text{Discrimination Index} = \frac{\text{Number of Discriminatory Incidents}}{\text{Total Population}} \times 100 \quad (16)$$

This equation represents a simplified model to quantify discrimination within a population, highlighting the need for comprehensive data collection and analysis to inform advocacy efforts. By understanding the scope of discrimination, activists can better strategize their initiatives and drive change.

The role of legislation in protecting LGBTQ rights

Legislation plays a crucial role in the advancement and protection of LGBTQ rights, serving as both a shield against discrimination and a sword for achieving equality. In many countries, including Barbados, the legal framework directly influences the societal treatment of LGBTQ individuals. This section explores the significance of legislation, the problems that arise from inadequate legal protections, and examples of successful legal reforms that have positively impacted LGBTQ communities.

The Importance of Legal Protections

Legal protections for LGBTQ individuals are essential for several reasons:

- **Establishing Equality:** Laws that explicitly protect LGBTQ individuals from discrimination in areas such as employment, housing, and healthcare establish a formal recognition of their rights. This recognition is crucial for fostering an inclusive society where everyone can thrive without fear of persecution.

- **Providing Recourse:** Legislation provides a mechanism for individuals to seek justice in cases of discrimination or violence. Anti-discrimination laws empower victims to hold perpetrators accountable, thereby deterring future offenses.

- **Promoting Visibility:** Laws that protect LGBTQ rights contribute to greater visibility and acceptance within society. When legal protections are in place, it signals to the public that LGBTQ individuals are valued members of the community deserving of equal rights.

Challenges in Legislative Frameworks

Despite the importance of legislation, many LGBTQ individuals face significant challenges due to inadequate legal protections. Some of these challenges include:

- **Criminalization:** In several countries, same-sex relationships are criminalized, leading to arrests, violence, and social stigma. In Barbados, the existence of laws that criminalize same-sex relations creates a hostile environment for LGBTQ individuals, effectively silencing their voices and limiting their rights.

- **Lack of Comprehensive Protections:** Even in countries where some protections exist, gaps often remain. For instance, while anti-discrimination laws may protect against employment discrimination, they may not extend to housing or healthcare, leaving LGBTQ individuals vulnerable in these critical areas.

- **Resistance to Change:** Efforts to reform legislation are often met with resistance from conservative factions within society. This resistance can stem from cultural beliefs, religious doctrines, or political agendas that prioritize traditional values over human rights.

Successful Legislative Reforms

Despite these challenges, there have been notable examples of successful legislative reforms that have advanced LGBTQ rights globally. These examples illustrate the potential for change when advocacy efforts are combined with strategic legislative action:

- **Marriage Equality:** One of the most significant victories for LGBTQ rights has been the legalization of same-sex marriage in various countries. For instance, the United States Supreme Court's decision in *Obergefell v. Hodges* (2015) affirmed the constitutional right to marry for same-sex couples, setting a precedent that has inspired similar movements worldwide.

- **Anti-Discrimination Laws:** Countries like Canada have implemented comprehensive anti-discrimination laws that protect LGBTQ individuals in multiple areas, including employment, housing, and public services. These laws have been instrumental in reducing discrimination and fostering a more inclusive society.

- **Legal Recognition of Gender Identity:** Many jurisdictions have enacted laws that allow individuals to legally change their gender on identification documents without invasive procedures. This recognition is crucial for affirming the identities of transgender and non-binary individuals, thereby promoting their dignity and autonomy.

The Role of Advocacy in Legislative Change

Advocacy plays a pivotal role in driving legislative change. LGBTQ activists and organizations work tirelessly to raise awareness, mobilize communities, and lobby lawmakers for reforms. Some key strategies employed in advocacy include:

- **Grassroots Mobilization:** Engaging the community at the grassroots level is essential for building support for legislative change. Activists organize rallies, educational campaigns, and community forums to raise awareness about LGBTQ issues and the need for legal protections.

- **Coalition Building:** Forming coalitions with other marginalized groups can amplify the impact of advocacy efforts. By uniting with allies, LGBTQ organizations can leverage collective power to challenge discriminatory laws and promote inclusive policies.

- **Engaging Policymakers:** Direct engagement with policymakers is critical for influencing legislative agendas. Advocates often meet with lawmakers, provide testimonies, and share personal stories to humanize the issues at stake and encourage legislative action.

Conclusion

In conclusion, legislation is a fundamental pillar in the fight for LGBTQ rights. While significant challenges remain, successful reforms and advocacy efforts demonstrate the potential for progress. By continuing to push for comprehensive legal protections, LGBTQ activists can pave the way for a future where everyone, regardless of their sexual orientation or gender identity, can live freely and authentically. The journey toward equality is ongoing, and the role of legislation will remain central to this vital cause.

Collaborating with international organizations in the fight against homophobia

In the ongoing battle against homophobia, collaboration with international organizations has emerged as a pivotal strategy for LGBTQ advocacy. These partnerships amplify local voices, provide essential resources, and foster a global network of support that transcends geographical and cultural barriers. This section explores the theoretical foundations, key challenges, and successful examples of such collaborations.

Theoretical Framework

The collaboration between local LGBTQ advocates and international organizations can be understood through several theoretical lenses, including social movement theory, globalization theory, and the theory of transnational advocacy networks.

Social Movement Theory posits that social movements are collective efforts aimed at challenging existing power structures. By partnering with international organizations, local activists can leverage additional resources, visibility, and legitimacy, thereby enhancing their capacity to effect change.

Globalization Theory emphasizes the interconnectedness of societies in the modern world. As issues of human rights become global concerns, international organizations play a crucial role in shaping policies and norms that support LGBTQ rights. This interconnectedness allows local activists to draw attention to their struggles on a global stage, garnering support from a diverse array of stakeholders.

Transnational Advocacy Networks consist of activists, organizations, and individuals who collaborate across borders to promote social change. These networks facilitate the exchange of information, strategies, and resources, creating a robust framework for fighting homophobia.

Challenges in Collaboration

Despite the potential benefits of collaboration, several challenges can hinder effective partnerships between local LGBTQ advocates and international organizations:

- **Cultural Sensitivity:** International organizations may not always fully understand the local cultural context, leading to initiatives that are perceived as imposing foreign values or agendas. This can create resistance among local communities and activists.

- **Resource Allocation:** Disparities in resource allocation can lead to tensions, with local activists feeling sidelined or underrepresented in decision-making processes. Ensuring equitable participation is crucial for successful collaboration.

- **Political Backlash:** Collaborating with international organizations can attract negative attention from conservative factions within a country, leading to increased hostility towards local activists.

Successful Examples of Collaboration

Several successful collaborations between local LGBTQ activists and international organizations illustrate the potential of these partnerships:

1. **The Global Fund for Human Rights** has been instrumental in supporting LGBTQ rights initiatives worldwide. By providing funding and resources to local activists, the organization has enabled grassroots movements to flourish. For instance, their support in the Caribbean region has helped facilitate workshops and training sessions that empower local advocates to combat homophobia effectively.

2. **OutRight Action International** is another prominent organization that collaborates with local LGBTQ groups to promote human rights. Their initiatives in countries like Barbados have included advocacy training and capacity-building programs, allowing local activists to develop skills necessary for effective advocacy.

3. **The United Nations Free & Equal Campaign** aims to promote equal rights and fair treatment for LGBTQ individuals globally. By partnering with local organizations, the campaign has successfully raised awareness of LGBTQ issues and mobilized support for policy changes in several countries, demonstrating the power of international collaboration in combating homophobia.

Conclusion

Collaboration with international organizations is a vital component in the fight against homophobia. By leveraging the strengths of these partnerships, local

LGBTQ advocates can amplify their voices, access resources, and foster a supportive global network. However, to maximize the effectiveness of these collaborations, it is essential to address the challenges of cultural sensitivity, resource allocation, and political backlash. Through careful navigation of these complexities, the collective efforts of local and international actors can lead to significant advancements in LGBTQ rights and the dismantling of homophobic structures worldwide.

Empowering LGBTQ individuals to stand up against discrimination

Empowering LGBTQ individuals to stand up against discrimination is a multifaceted approach that requires a combination of education, community support, and advocacy strategies. This empowerment not only enhances individual confidence but also fosters a collective strength within the LGBTQ community, enabling members to confront and challenge discriminatory practices effectively.

Understanding Discrimination

Discrimination against LGBTQ individuals often manifests in various forms, including but not limited to, social stigma, verbal harassment, employment discrimination, and systemic inequalities. According to the *American Psychological Association*, discrimination can be defined as *"the unjust or prejudicial treatment of different categories of people, especially on the grounds of race, age, or sex."* In the context of LGBTQ individuals, discrimination can lead to significant psychological distress, impacting mental health and overall well-being.

$$D = \frac{H}{C} \qquad (17)$$

Where D represents the level of discrimination experienced, H is the frequency of harmful incidents, and C is the capacity of the individual or community to cope with such incidents. As the frequency of harmful incidents increases, the capacity to cope diminishes, leading to a higher level of perceived discrimination.

Education as a Tool for Empowerment

Education plays a pivotal role in empowering LGBTQ individuals. By providing comprehensive education on LGBTQ rights, individuals can better understand their rights and the tools available to combat discrimination. Programs that focus on educating both LGBTQ individuals and the broader community about inclusivity and diversity can foster a more supportive environment.

For example, workshops that educate participants on the legal protections available to LGBTQ individuals can significantly increase awareness and encourage individuals to advocate for their rights. This is particularly important in regions where legal protections are still lacking or poorly enforced.

Community Support and Solidarity

Creating safe spaces within the community is essential for empowering LGBTQ individuals. Support groups, community centers, and online forums provide platforms where individuals can share their experiences and strategies for coping with discrimination.

$$S = \frac{C}{R} \qquad (18)$$

Where S represents the strength of community support, C is the collective resources available within the community, and R is the level of resistance against discrimination. A strong community support system can lead to a higher resilience against discrimination, fostering a sense of belonging and solidarity among members.

Advocacy Strategies

Advocacy is a critical component of empowerment. LGBTQ individuals must be equipped with the tools and resources necessary to advocate for themselves and their community. This includes training in effective communication, negotiation skills, and understanding the legislative process.

Examples of successful advocacy include the campaigns led by organizations such as *Human Rights Campaign* and *GLAAD*, which have mobilized LGBTQ individuals to speak out against discriminatory laws and practices. These organizations provide resources, training, and platforms for individuals to share their stories, thereby amplifying their voices.

Real-World Examples

One notable example of empowerment through advocacy is the *It Gets Better Project*, which encourages LGBTQ individuals to share their stories of resilience and hope. This initiative has not only provided a platform for individuals to stand up against discrimination but has also fostered a sense of community and support among LGBTQ youth.

Additionally, the work of activists like Donnya Piggott, who has utilized technology and social media to advocate for LGBTQ rights, demonstrates the power of modern tools in mobilizing individuals against discrimination. By leveraging digital platforms, Piggott has created spaces for dialogue, education, and activism, empowering individuals to take a stand.

Conclusion

Empowering LGBTQ individuals to stand up against discrimination is a vital process that requires an integrated approach encompassing education, community support, and active advocacy. By fostering a sense of agency and providing the necessary tools, LGBTQ individuals can challenge discrimination effectively, promote inclusivity, and pave the way for a more equitable society. The collective strength of empowered individuals can lead to significant societal change, ultimately contributing to the advancement of LGBTQ rights globally.

Speaking Up for LGBTQ Youth

Supporting mental health and well-being

Mental health is a crucial aspect of overall well-being, particularly within the LGBTQ community, where individuals often face unique challenges and stressors. Research has shown that LGBTQ individuals are at a higher risk for mental health issues, including depression, anxiety, and suicidal ideation, due to factors such as discrimination, social stigma, and rejection. According to the *National Alliance on Mental Illness (NAMI)*, LGBTQ youth are more than twice as likely to experience a mental health condition compared to their heterosexual peers.

One of the primary theories relevant to understanding mental health in the LGBTQ community is the **Minority Stress Theory**. This theory posits that individuals from marginalized groups experience chronic stress due to their societal stigma, prejudice, and discrimination. This stress can lead to negative mental health outcomes. The equation for stress can be represented as:

$$S = E + D + R$$

where S represents the overall stress experienced, E is the external stigma from society, D is the internalized discrimination, and R is the relational stress from family and friends.

To combat these challenges, it is essential to create supportive environments that promote mental health and well-being for LGBTQ individuals. This can be achieved through various strategies:

- **Creating Safe Spaces:** Establishing safe spaces where LGBTQ individuals can express themselves without fear of judgment is vital. These spaces can be physical locations, such as community centers, or virtual environments, like online forums and support groups. For example, organizations like *The Trevor Project* provide crisis intervention and suicide prevention services specifically for LGBTQ youth, creating a safe and supportive environment for those in need.

- **Promoting Mental Health Education:** Education about mental health issues and resources available to LGBTQ individuals can empower them to seek help. Workshops and seminars that focus on mental health awareness can be organized in schools and community centers. For instance, the *Human Rights Campaign* has developed educational materials aimed at increasing awareness of mental health issues among LGBTQ youth.

- **Advocating for Inclusive Mental Health Services:** It is crucial to advocate for mental health services that are inclusive and culturally competent. Mental health professionals should be trained to understand the unique experiences of LGBTQ individuals. Access to therapists who specialize in LGBTQ issues can significantly improve the quality of care. A study by *The American Psychological Association* found that LGBTQ individuals who received care from LGBTQ-affirmative therapists reported higher satisfaction and better mental health outcomes.

- **Fostering Peer Support:** Peer support programs can play a significant role in promoting mental health among LGBTQ individuals. These programs provide opportunities for individuals to connect with others who have similar experiences, fostering a sense of belonging and understanding. For example, peer-led support groups can help LGBTQ youth navigate their mental health challenges while providing a platform for sharing experiences and coping strategies.

- **Implementing School-Based Mental Health Programs:** Schools can be a significant source of stress for LGBTQ youth. Implementing school-based mental health programs that include LGBTQ-inclusive curricula and support services can create a more supportive environment. Programs like

GLSEN (Gay, Lesbian & Straight Education Network) work to create safe and affirming schools for LGBTQ students by providing resources and training for educators.

In conclusion, supporting the mental health and well-being of LGBTQ individuals requires a multifaceted approach that includes creating safe spaces, promoting education, advocating for inclusive services, fostering peer support, and implementing school-based programs. By addressing these factors, we can help mitigate the mental health disparities faced by the LGBTQ community and promote a healthier, more inclusive society. As we continue to champion mental health advocacy, it is essential to recognize the resilience of LGBTQ individuals and the importance of community support in their journeys toward well-being.

Creating safe spaces for LGBTQ youth

Creating safe spaces for LGBTQ youth is a critical component of fostering an inclusive environment where young individuals can express their identities without fear of discrimination or violence. Safe spaces serve as supportive environments that promote acceptance, understanding, and empowerment, allowing LGBTQ youth to flourish both personally and socially.

The Importance of Safe Spaces

Research indicates that LGBTQ youth are at a higher risk for mental health issues, including anxiety, depression, and suicidal ideation, often stemming from societal stigma and discrimination. According to the *2019 National School Climate Survey* by the Gay, Lesbian, and Straight Education Network (GLSEN), 59.1% of LGBTQ students felt unsafe at school because of their sexual orientation, and 40.6% felt unsafe because of their gender expression. These statistics underscore the urgent need for safe spaces where LGBTQ youth can find solace and support.

Defining Safe Spaces

Safe spaces can take various forms, including:

- **Physical Spaces:** Designated areas within schools, community centers, or organizations where LGBTQ youth can gather, socialize, and engage in activities without fear of harassment.

- **Online Spaces:** Virtual platforms such as forums, social media groups, and chat rooms that provide LGBTQ youth with a sense of community and belonging, especially for those who may feel isolated in their physical environments.

- **Support Groups:** Organized meetings that allow LGBTQ youth to share their experiences, challenges, and triumphs in a safe and confidential setting, often facilitated by trained professionals or peers.

Challenges in Creating Safe Spaces

Despite the necessity of safe spaces, several challenges persist in their establishment and maintenance:

- **Societal Resistance:** In many communities, there is still significant stigma surrounding LGBTQ identities, leading to pushback against the creation of safe spaces. This resistance can manifest through protests, negative media coverage, or even legislative actions aimed at limiting LGBTQ rights.

- **Funding and Resources:** Developing and sustaining safe spaces often requires financial support and resources, which can be scarce, particularly in underfunded schools or communities. Many organizations struggle to secure grants or donations to maintain these crucial programs.

- **Awareness and Training:** For safe spaces to be effective, facilitators and staff must be adequately trained to understand LGBTQ issues and foster an inclusive environment. Lack of training can lead to unintentional harm or exclusion, negating the purpose of the safe space.

Examples of Successful Safe Spaces

Numerous organizations and initiatives have successfully created safe spaces for LGBTQ youth, serving as models for others to emulate:

- **The Trevor Project:** This organization provides crisis intervention and suicide prevention services for LGBTQ youth. Through its online platform, it offers a safe space for young individuals to seek help and connect with peers who understand their struggles.

- **Gender and Sexuality Alliances (GSAs):** Many schools have established GSAs, which are student-led organizations that promote inclusivity and support for LGBTQ students. These alliances create safe spaces within the school environment, allowing students to advocate for their rights and educate their peers.

- **Local Community Centers:** Various community centers across the globe have dedicated programs for LGBTQ youth, offering workshops, social events, and counseling services in a safe and welcoming environment. These centers often collaborate with schools to provide resources and support to students.

The Role of Educators and Allies

Educators and allies play a pivotal role in the creation and sustainability of safe spaces for LGBTQ youth. By advocating for inclusive policies, promoting awareness, and actively participating in initiatives, they can help dismantle barriers and foster an environment where all students feel valued and respected.

$$\text{Safe Space Impact} = \text{Support} + \text{Visibility} + \text{Empowerment} \tag{19}$$

This equation illustrates that the impact of safe spaces is a product of the support provided to LGBTQ youth, the visibility of their identities, and the empowerment they experience through community engagement and advocacy.

Conclusion

Creating safe spaces for LGBTQ youth is not merely a matter of providing a physical location; it involves cultivating an atmosphere of acceptance, understanding, and empowerment. By addressing the challenges and leveraging successful models, society can work towards ensuring that every LGBTQ youth has access to a safe space where they can thrive, express their identities, and build a brighter future. The journey towards inclusivity begins with the commitment to create environments where all young individuals can feel safe and valued, paving the way for a more equitable society.

Empowering the next generation of activists

Empowering the next generation of activists is crucial for the sustainability and growth of the LGBTQ movement. As society evolves, so do the challenges and opportunities faced by LGBTQ individuals. This section explores the importance of mentorship, education, and community engagement in fostering a new wave of advocates who are equipped to tackle these challenges head-on.

The Importance of Mentorship

Mentorship plays a pivotal role in empowering young activists. By providing guidance, support, and a sense of belonging, mentors can help youth navigate the complexities of activism. Research indicates that mentorship can significantly impact the personal and professional development of young people, enhancing their confidence and leadership skills. For instance, a study by [?] found that mentees are more likely to pursue leadership roles and engage in community service than those without mentors.

Creating Safe Spaces

Creating safe spaces for LGBTQ youth is essential for fostering their activism. Safe spaces allow individuals to express themselves without fear of judgment or discrimination. Programs such as LGBTQ youth centers provide resources, support groups, and activities that promote self-acceptance and community building. These environments encourage young people to share their experiences and develop their voices, which is crucial for effective advocacy.

Education and Awareness

Education is a powerful tool for empowerment. Implementing inclusive curricula in schools can help raise awareness about LGBTQ issues and foster understanding among peers. By integrating LGBTQ history, literature, and rights into educational programs, students can learn about the struggles and contributions of LGBTQ activists. This not only validates the experiences of LGBTQ youth but also educates their peers, creating a more inclusive environment.

For example, the *Safe Schools Coalition* has been instrumental in advocating for inclusive education policies across various school districts. Their efforts have led to the implementation of training programs for educators on LGBTQ issues, which, in turn, creates a more supportive atmosphere for students.

Leadership Opportunities

Providing leadership opportunities for young activists is vital for their development. Programs that encourage youth to take on leadership roles in community projects, advocacy campaigns, and organizational initiatives help cultivate their skills and confidence. For instance, the *Youth Leadership Program* by the *Human Rights Campaign* empowers LGBTQ youth by equipping them with the tools needed to advocate for change in their communities. Participants engage in workshops, mentorship, and hands-on projects that enhance their leadership capabilities.

Utilizing Technology for Engagement

In the digital age, technology serves as a powerful platform for activism. Social media, blogs, and online campaigns provide young activists with the tools to amplify their voices and connect with like-minded individuals. Encouraging youth to harness these platforms can lead to innovative advocacy strategies. For example, the *#YouthForEquality* campaign on social media mobilized thousands of young people to advocate for LGBTQ rights, demonstrating the potential of digital activism.

Building a Network of Support

Empowering the next generation also involves building a strong network of support among activists. By fostering connections between youth and established activists, young individuals can benefit from shared experiences and resources. Initiatives such as intergenerational workshops and conferences can facilitate dialogue and collaboration between different generations of activists, ensuring that knowledge and strategies are passed down.

Conclusion

In conclusion, empowering the next generation of LGBTQ activists is a multifaceted endeavor that requires mentorship, safe spaces, education, leadership opportunities, and the utilization of technology. By investing in these areas, we can cultivate a robust and dynamic movement that not only addresses current challenges but also paves the way for future generations to thrive. The commitment to nurturing young activists is essential for the ongoing fight for LGBTQ rights and equality. As Donnya Piggott exemplifies, the legacy of activism is built on the shoulders of those who come after us, and it is our responsibility to ensure they are equipped to lead the charge.

Implementing Inclusive Education Policies for LGBTQ Students

Inclusive education policies play a critical role in ensuring that LGBTQ students feel safe, respected, and supported in their educational environments. The implementation of these policies is not merely an act of compliance with legal standards, but rather a commitment to fostering an equitable and nurturing atmosphere for all students, regardless of their sexual orientation or gender identity.

Theoretical Framework

The foundation for inclusive education policies can be rooted in several theoretical frameworks, including Social Justice Theory and Intersectionality. Social Justice Theory emphasizes the need to address inequalities and promote fairness within educational systems. It advocates for the recognition of diverse identities and the elimination of discrimination based on sexual orientation and gender identity. Intersectionality, on the other hand, examines how various social identities (such as race, class, and gender) intersect to create unique experiences of oppression or privilege. This theory is particularly relevant for LGBTQ students who may also belong to other marginalized groups.

The following equation illustrates the concept of intersectionality, where the total experience of discrimination (D) is a function of multiple identities ($I_1, I_2, \ldots, I_n$):

$$D = f(I_1, I_2, \ldots, I_n)$$

This equation emphasizes that the experience of discrimination cannot be understood by examining identities in isolation but rather as a complex interplay of multiple factors.

Identifying Problems in Current Education Systems

Despite the theoretical support for inclusive policies, many educational institutions still face significant challenges in implementing them effectively. Some common problems include:

- **Lack of Awareness and Training:** Many educators may not have received adequate training on LGBTQ issues, leading to unintentional biases and a lack of understanding of the unique challenges faced by LGBTQ students.

- **Bullying and Harassment:** LGBTQ students often experience bullying and harassment, which can lead to negative academic outcomes and mental health issues. According to a study by the Gay, Lesbian and Straight Education Network (GLSEN), 70.1% of LGBTQ students reported being bullied at school.

- **Absence of Supportive Policies:** Many schools lack formal policies that specifically address LGBTQ inclusivity, leaving students vulnerable to discrimination and exclusion.
- **Resistance to Change:** There may be resistance from school administrators, parents, or community members who hold conservative views regarding LGBTQ rights.

Strategies for Implementation

To effectively implement inclusive education policies for LGBTQ students, educational institutions can adopt several strategies:

1. **Develop Comprehensive Policies:** Schools should create and enforce policies that explicitly protect LGBTQ students from discrimination and harassment. These policies should include clear definitions of bullying and harassment, reporting procedures, and consequences for violators.

2. **Provide Training for Educators:** Professional development programs should include training on LGBTQ issues, cultural competency, and inclusive teaching practices. Educators should be equipped with the knowledge and skills necessary to create a supportive classroom environment.

3. **Create Safe Spaces:** Schools should establish safe spaces, such as Gay-Straight Alliances (GSAs), where LGBTQ students can find support and community. These spaces can serve as a refuge for students to express themselves freely.

4. **Incorporate LGBTQ Curriculum:** Integrating LGBTQ topics into the curriculum can help normalize diverse identities and experiences. This can include literature by LGBTQ authors, discussions about historical figures, and lessons on LGBTQ rights movements.

5. **Engage Families and Communities:** Schools should involve families and community members in discussions about LGBTQ inclusivity. This can help to build understanding and support for inclusive policies.

Examples of Successful Implementation

Several schools and districts have successfully implemented inclusive education policies, serving as models for others:

- **California's Safe Schools Program:** California has implemented statewide policies that require schools to create safe environments for LGBTQ students. This includes anti-bullying policies and the incorporation of LGBTQ history into the curriculum.

- **New York City Department of Education:** NYC has launched initiatives to support LGBTQ students, including training for educators, the creation of LGBTQ-inclusive curricula, and the establishment of GSAs in schools.

- **The Trevor Project:** This national organization provides resources and support for LGBTQ youth, including educational materials for schools to promote inclusivity and mental health resources.

Conclusion

Implementing inclusive education policies for LGBTQ students is essential for promoting equity and fostering a safe and supportive learning environment. By addressing the theoretical foundations, recognizing current challenges, and employing effective strategies, educational institutions can create a culture of acceptance that empowers LGBTQ students to thrive academically and personally. Ultimately, these efforts contribute not only to the well-being of LGBTQ students but also to the enrichment of the entire school community, fostering a spirit of diversity and inclusion that benefits everyone.

Fostering mentorship programs and leadership opportunities

In the realm of LGBTQ advocacy, fostering mentorship programs and leadership opportunities is crucial for empowering the next generation of activists. Mentorship provides a vital support system that can guide young individuals through the complexities of their identities and the challenges they face in society. By establishing structured mentorship initiatives, we can create pathways for personal and professional growth, ensuring that LGBTQ youth have access to the tools and resources they need to thrive.

The Importance of Mentorship

Mentorship plays a significant role in personal development, particularly for marginalized groups. Research indicates that mentorship can lead to increased self-esteem, improved academic performance, and enhanced career prospects. According to a study by the *National Mentoring Partnership*, mentored youth are

55% more likely to enroll in college and 78% more likely to volunteer regularly in their communities. These statistics highlight the transformative power of mentorship, particularly in the LGBTQ community, where individuals may face unique challenges that require tailored support.

Challenges Faced by LGBTQ Youth

LGBTQ youth often encounter a myriad of challenges, including societal stigma, discrimination, and mental health issues. The *Trevor Project* reports that LGBTQ youth are more than twice as likely to experience bullying and harassment compared to their heterosexual peers. This environment can lead to feelings of isolation and hopelessness, making mentorship even more vital. By connecting LGBTQ youth with mentors who understand their struggles, we can provide them with a sense of belonging and the encouragement needed to pursue their goals.

Implementing Effective Mentorship Programs

To create successful mentorship programs, several key elements must be considered:

- **Training and Support:** Mentors should receive training on LGBTQ issues, cultural competency, and effective communication skills. This ensures they are equipped to provide meaningful guidance and support.

- **Matching Process:** A thoughtful matching process between mentors and mentees is essential. Factors such as shared interests, backgrounds, and experiences should be taken into account to foster a strong connection.

- **Goal Setting:** Mentorship programs should encourage mentees to set personal and professional goals. Regular check-ins can help track progress and provide accountability.

- **Community Building:** Creating opportunities for mentors and mentees to connect with one another fosters a sense of community. Group activities, workshops, and networking events can enhance the mentorship experience.

Examples of Successful Mentorship Initiatives

Several organizations have successfully implemented mentorship programs for LGBTQ youth:

- The *Trevor Project* offers a mentorship program that connects LGBTQ youth with trained mentors who provide guidance on various life challenges, including coming out and navigating relationships.

- **OUT for Undergrad** hosts programs that connect LGBTQ undergraduates with mentors in various professional fields, helping them to develop their careers while fostering a supportive network.

- The *LGBTQ+ Youth Mentorship Program* in Canada pairs youth with mentors who have similar life experiences, providing a safe space for discussion and growth.

These programs demonstrate the effectiveness of mentorship in fostering leadership skills and resilience among LGBTQ youth. By sharing experiences and knowledge, mentors empower their mentees to become advocates for themselves and their communities.

Leadership Opportunities for LGBTQ Youth

In addition to mentorship, providing leadership opportunities is essential for cultivating the next generation of LGBTQ advocates. Leadership programs can equip youth with the skills needed to navigate advocacy work and inspire change. These programs often include:

- **Workshops and Training:** Leadership workshops that focus on public speaking, advocacy strategies, and community organizing can empower youth to take on leadership roles within their communities.

- **Internships and Volunteer Opportunities:** Partnering with local organizations to offer internships and volunteer opportunities allows youth to gain hands-on experience in advocacy work, further enhancing their skills and confidence.

- **Youth Councils:** Establishing youth councils within LGBTQ organizations can give young people a voice in decision-making processes, allowing them to influence policies and programs that affect their lives.

Conclusion

Fostering mentorship programs and leadership opportunities for LGBTQ youth is essential for building a more inclusive and equitable society. By providing the necessary support and resources, we can empower young individuals to embrace their identities, advocate for their rights, and become leaders in their communities. As we continue to champion LGBTQ rights, it is imperative that we invest in the next generation, ensuring that they have the tools to break barriers and create lasting change.

$$\text{Empowerment} = \text{Mentorship} + \text{Leadership Opportunities} \qquad (20)$$

In conclusion, the synergy between mentorship and leadership development forms a powerful equation for empowerment, allowing LGBTQ youth to rise above challenges and make significant contributions to the advocacy movement.

Mental Health Advocacy and Support

Personal experiences with mental health challenges

Mental health is a nuanced and often stigmatized topic, particularly within the LGBTQ community, where individuals frequently face compounded stressors related to their identity. As Donnya Piggott navigated her journey as a queer individual in Barbados, she encountered various mental health challenges that shaped her understanding of self and her advocacy work. This section delves into her personal experiences, highlighting the intersection of mental health and LGBTQ identity, and the broader implications for the community.

Growing up in a conservative society, Donnya faced societal pressures and expectations that often contradicted her authentic self. The internal conflict between her identity and societal norms led to feelings of isolation, anxiety, and depression. According to the Minority Stress Theory, LGBTQ individuals often experience chronic stress arising from stigma, discrimination, and social rejection, which can lead to adverse mental health outcomes. This theory posits that the unique stressors faced by marginalized groups can significantly impact their mental well-being.

Donnya's early experiences with mental health challenges manifested through intense feelings of anxiety, particularly in social situations where her identity was questioned or invalidated. For instance, during her teenage years, she vividly recalls attending community events where heteronormative expectations were prevalent. The pressure to conform to these expectations often triggered panic attacks, leaving her feeling trapped and unworthy. Such experiences align with research indicating that LGBTQ youth are at a higher risk for anxiety disorders compared to their heterosexual peers.

Furthermore, the lack of accessible mental health resources in Barbados exacerbated Donnya's struggles. The stigma surrounding mental health issues often deterred individuals from seeking help. This societal barrier is reflected in the work of Meyer (2003), who noted that stigma not only prevents individuals from accessing necessary care but also contributes to the internalization of negative societal attitudes. In Donnya's case, the fear of being judged for seeking help compounded her feelings of loneliness and despair.

Donnya also experienced the pervasive impact of depression, which often left her feeling disconnected from her peers and community. The feelings of hopelessness and worthlessness were exacerbated by the conservative cultural backdrop, where LGBTQ identities were often demonized. This aligns with findings from the American Psychological Association, which report that LGBTQ individuals are more likely to experience depressive symptoms due to societal rejection and discrimination.

In her journey toward healing, Donnya began to explore various coping mechanisms. She found solace in creative expression, particularly through art and writing. Engaging in creative outlets allowed her to process her emotions and articulate her experiences. This aligns with the therapeutic benefits of art as a form of expression, which can facilitate emotional release and promote mental well-being (Malchiodi, 2005). By sharing her story through art, Donnya not only found personal healing but also inspired others to embrace their narratives, fostering a sense of community and solidarity among those facing similar challenges.

Moreover, Donnya's experiences underscored the importance of peer support and community connection in addressing mental health challenges. She actively sought out local LGBTQ support groups, where she found a safe space to share her struggles and connect with others who understood her journey. Research indicates that social support is a critical protective factor for mental health among LGBTQ individuals, helping to mitigate the effects of minority stress (Budge et al., 2013). These connections provided Donnya with a sense of belonging and validation, reinforcing her resilience in the face of adversity.

Donnya's advocacy work also emerged from her personal experiences with mental health challenges. Recognizing the urgent need for mental health resources tailored to the LGBTQ community, she began to champion initiatives aimed at promoting mental health awareness and accessibility. Her advocacy efforts included collaborating with mental health professionals to develop programs specifically designed for LGBTQ youth, addressing the unique challenges they face.

In conclusion, Donnya Piggott's personal experiences with mental health challenges reflect the broader struggles faced by LGBTQ individuals in navigating their identities within a society that often marginalizes them. By embracing her journey and advocating for mental health awareness, Donnya not only transformed her own narrative but also became a beacon of hope for others in the LGBTQ community. Her story serves as a reminder of the importance of mental health advocacy and the need for inclusive support systems that empower individuals to live authentically and thrive.

Bibliography

[1] Meyer, I. H. (2003). Prejudice, social stress, and mental health in gay men. *American Psychologist*, 58(5), 161-173.

[2] Malchiodi, C. A. (2005). *Expressive therapies: History, theory, and practice.* New York: Guilford Press.

[3] Budge, S. L., Adelson, J. L., & Howard, K. A. (2013). Anxiety and depression in transgender individuals: The roles of social support and social identity. *Journal of Consulting and Clinical Psychology*, 81(3), 545-557.

Shedding light on the mental health struggles of LGBTQ individuals

The mental health challenges faced by LGBTQ individuals are multifaceted and deeply rooted in societal stigma, discrimination, and the unique stressors associated with non-heteronormative identities. Understanding these struggles is crucial for developing effective support systems and interventions.

Theoretical Frameworks

To comprehend the mental health struggles of LGBTQ individuals, we can utilize several theoretical frameworks. One prominent theory is the Minority Stress Theory, which posits that LGBTQ individuals experience chronic stress due to their marginalized status. According to Meyer (2003), this stress arises from external sources, such as discrimination and violence, as well as internal sources, including internalized homophobia and fear of rejection. The equation representing Minority Stress can be expressed as:

$$MS = E + I + S \qquad (21)$$

where MS is Minority Stress, E represents external stressors (e.g., discrimination), I denotes internal stressors (e.g., internalized stigma), and S stands for social stigma.

Prevalence of Mental Health Issues

Research indicates that LGBTQ individuals are at a higher risk for various mental health issues compared to their heterosexual counterparts. According to the National Alliance on Mental Illness (NAMI), LGBTQ youth are significantly more likely to experience depression, anxiety, and suicidal ideation. For example, a survey conducted by the Trevor Project found that 40% of LGBTQ youth seriously considered attempting suicide in the past year, compared to 14% of heterosexual youth.

Factors Contributing to Mental Health Struggles

Several factors contribute to the mental health struggles of LGBTQ individuals:

- **Discrimination and Stigma:** LGBTQ individuals often face discrimination in various aspects of life, including employment, healthcare, and education. This discrimination can lead to feelings of isolation and hopelessness.

- **Family Rejection:** Many LGBTQ individuals experience rejection from their families, which can result in profound emotional distress. Studies show that LGBTQ youth who are rejected by their families are more than eight times as likely to attempt suicide compared to those who are accepted.

- **Internalized Homophobia:** Internalized negative beliefs about one's sexual orientation can lead to low self-esteem and self-hatred, exacerbating mental health issues. This internal struggle often manifests in anxiety and depression.

- **Social Isolation:** The lack of supportive social networks can further exacerbate mental health struggles. LGBTQ individuals may feel isolated, particularly in conservative communities where their identities are not accepted.

Examples of Mental Health Struggles

To illustrate the mental health struggles faced by LGBTQ individuals, consider the following examples:

- **Case Study of Jamie:** Jamie, a 17-year-old transgender girl, faced bullying at school and rejection from her peers. As a result, she developed severe anxiety and depression, leading her to isolate herself from friends and family. Jamie's story highlights the critical need for supportive environments in schools.

- **Case Study of Alex:** Alex, a gay man in his twenties, struggled with internalized homophobia due to his conservative upbringing. He often felt unworthy of love and acceptance, leading to substance abuse as a coping mechanism. Alex's experience underscores the importance of addressing internalized stigma in mental health interventions.

Implications for Mental Health Advocacy

Given the unique challenges faced by LGBTQ individuals, it is imperative to advocate for inclusive mental health services. This includes:

- **Training for Mental Health Professionals:** Mental health providers must be trained to understand the specific needs of LGBTQ clients, including cultural competence and sensitivity to the issues they face.

- **Creating Safe Spaces:** Establishing safe spaces for LGBTQ individuals to share their experiences and seek support can significantly improve mental health outcomes. This can be achieved through community centers, support groups, and online forums.

- **Policy Advocacy:** Advocating for policies that protect LGBTQ rights and promote mental health resources is crucial. This includes pushing for anti-discrimination laws and funding for mental health services tailored to LGBTQ individuals.

In conclusion, shedding light on the mental health struggles of LGBTQ individuals is essential for fostering understanding and support. By addressing the unique stressors they face and advocating for inclusive mental health services, we can help improve the well-being of LGBTQ individuals and create a more equitable society.

Bibliography

[1] Meyer, I. H. (2003). Prejudice, Social Stress, and Mental Health in Gay Men. *American Psychologist*, 58(5), 161-173.

[2] The Trevor Project. (2021). National Survey on LGBTQ Youth Mental Health 2021. Retrieved from https://www.thetrevorproject.org

[3] National Alliance on Mental Illness. (2021). LGBTQ Mental Health. Retrieved from https://www.nami.org

Advocating for inclusive mental health services

In recent years, the importance of mental health awareness has gained significant traction, particularly within marginalized communities, including the LGBTQ population. Inclusive mental health services are essential in addressing the unique challenges faced by LGBTQ individuals, who often experience heightened levels of discrimination, stigma, and social isolation. This section delves into the advocacy for inclusive mental health services, exploring theoretical frameworks, existing problems, and practical examples of successful initiatives.

Theoretical Frameworks

The advocacy for inclusive mental health services is grounded in several psychological and sociological theories. One such framework is the **Minority Stress Theory**, which posits that individuals from stigmatized groups experience chronic stress due to their social environment. This stress arises from experiences of discrimination, expectations of rejection, and internalized homophobia, leading to adverse mental health outcomes such as anxiety and depression [1].

Mathematically, the relationship between minority stress and mental health can be conceptualized as follows:

$$M = S + R + I \tag{22}$$

Where: - M = Mental health outcomes (e.g., anxiety, depression) - S = Social stigma - R = Rejection sensitivity - I = Internalized stigma

This equation illustrates that increased levels of social stigma, rejection sensitivity, and internalized stigma contribute to poorer mental health outcomes in LGBTQ individuals.

Problems in Current Mental Health Services

Despite the growing recognition of mental health issues in the LGBTQ community, numerous barriers persist that hinder access to inclusive services. Some of the most pressing problems include:

- **Lack of Cultural Competency:** Many mental health professionals lack training in LGBTQ-specific issues, which can lead to misunderstandings and inadequate care. Research has shown that only a fraction of mental health providers receive training in LGBTQ cultural competency, resulting in a reluctance among LGBTQ individuals to seek help [3].

- **Stigmatization of LGBTQ Identities:** The persistent stigma surrounding LGBTQ identities can lead to negative experiences within healthcare settings. This stigma can manifest as discriminatory language, lack of empathy, or outright refusal to provide care, further alienating those in need of support [?].

- **Economic Barriers:** Many LGBTQ individuals face economic disadvantages, which can limit their access to mental health services. The intersection of socioeconomic status and sexual orientation often exacerbates mental health disparities, making it crucial to address financial barriers [?].

Examples of Successful Initiatives

To combat these challenges, several organizations and initiatives have emerged to advocate for inclusive mental health services for LGBTQ individuals. Notable examples include:

- **The Trevor Project:** This organization provides crisis intervention and suicide prevention services to LGBTQ youth. Their trained counselors are equipped to handle the unique challenges faced by LGBTQ individuals, offering a safe space for those in distress. The Trevor Project also conducts outreach and educational programs to raise awareness about mental health issues in the LGBTQ community [?].

- **LGBTQ+ Affirmative Therapy:** Many therapists are now adopting LGBTQ+ affirmative therapy approaches, which recognize and validate the identities of LGBTQ clients. This therapeutic model emphasizes the importance of understanding clients' experiences within the context of societal stigma and discrimination. By fostering an inclusive environment, therapists can help clients navigate their mental health challenges more effectively [3].

- **Community-Based Mental Health Programs:** Various community organizations have developed mental health programs specifically tailored for LGBTQ individuals. For instance, the *LGBTQ Youth Resource Center* in San Francisco offers workshops, peer support groups, and counseling services designed to meet the needs of LGBTQ youth. These programs not only provide mental health support but also foster a sense of community and belonging [?].

Conclusion

Advocating for inclusive mental health services is a critical component of promoting overall well-being within the LGBTQ community. By addressing the unique challenges faced by LGBTQ individuals and implementing culturally competent practices, mental health professionals can create a more supportive environment. Continued advocacy efforts are essential to dismantle the barriers that hinder access to care and to ensure that all individuals, regardless of their sexual orientation or gender identity, receive the mental health support they deserve.

Collaborating with mental health professionals to address LGBTQ-specific concerns

The intersection of mental health and LGBTQ advocacy is crucial in creating a supportive environment for individuals navigating their identities in a society that may not always be accepting. Mental health professionals play a pivotal role in addressing the unique challenges faced by LGBTQ individuals, and collaboration between activists and mental health experts can lead to significant advancements in care and support.

Understanding LGBTQ-Specific Mental Health Issues

LGBTQ individuals often experience higher rates of mental health issues compared to their heterosexual counterparts. Research indicates that factors such as societal stigma, discrimination, and internalized homophobia contribute to these disparities. The **Minority Stress Theory** provides a framework for understanding how these external pressures lead to negative mental health outcomes. According to this theory, LGBTQ individuals face unique stressors that can result in chronic stress, anxiety, and depression.

$$\text{Mental Health Disparities} = \text{Societal Stigma} + \text{Discrimination} + \text{Internalized Homoph} \tag{23}$$

This equation highlights the cumulative effect of these stressors on mental health, emphasizing the need for targeted interventions.

Collaborative Approaches to Mental Health Care

Collaboration between LGBTQ activists and mental health professionals can take various forms, including:

- **Training and Education:** Mental health professionals can benefit from training that addresses LGBTQ-specific issues, helping them to understand the unique challenges their clients may face. Workshops and seminars led by LGBTQ advocates can provide valuable insights into the lived experiences of LGBTQ individuals.

- **Resource Development:** Together, activists and mental health experts can develop resources that cater to the needs of LGBTQ individuals. This includes creating informational pamphlets, online resources, and support networks that specifically address LGBTQ mental health concerns.

- **Creating Safe Spaces:** Establishing safe spaces within mental health settings is essential. This can be achieved by fostering an environment where LGBTQ individuals feel comfortable discussing their identities and experiences without fear of judgment or discrimination.

- **Advocacy for Inclusive Policies:** Mental health professionals can advocate for policies that promote inclusivity within healthcare systems. This includes pushing for insurance coverage for LGBTQ-specific therapies and services, as well as ensuring that mental health facilities are welcoming to all individuals, regardless of their sexual orientation or gender identity.

Examples of Successful Collaborations

Several successful collaborations between LGBTQ advocates and mental health professionals have emerged as models for effective intervention:

- **The Trevor Project:** This organization provides crisis intervention and suicide prevention services to LGBTQ youth. By collaborating with mental health professionals, they offer a 24/7 helpline staffed by trained counselors who understand the unique challenges faced by LGBTQ youth.

- **The LGBT National Help Center:** This organization offers free and confidential support through its helplines and online resources. By partnering with mental health professionals, they ensure that the support provided is informed by the latest research and best practices in LGBTQ mental health.

- **Local Community Initiatives:** Many local LGBTQ organizations collaborate with mental health clinics to provide workshops and support groups tailored to the needs of their community. These initiatives often lead to increased awareness and understanding of LGBTQ issues among mental health providers.

Challenges and Future Directions

Despite the progress made in collaboration, several challenges remain:

- **Lack of Awareness:** Many mental health professionals may still lack awareness of the specific needs of LGBTQ individuals, leading to inadequate care. Continued education and training are essential to bridge this gap.

- **Cultural Competence:** Mental health providers must develop cultural competence to effectively work with LGBTQ clients. This involves understanding the nuances of LGBTQ identities and the impact of societal factors on mental health.

- **Funding and Resources:** Securing funding for LGBTQ-specific mental health initiatives can be challenging. Collaborative efforts must seek to address these financial barriers to ensure sustainability.

Looking ahead, the collaboration between LGBTQ activists and mental health professionals should focus on:

- Expanding access to mental health services for LGBTQ individuals, particularly in underserved communities.

- Advocating for research that explores the mental health needs of diverse LGBTQ populations, including those of different races, ethnicities, and gender identities.

- Developing innovative digital mental health solutions, such as teletherapy, which can provide accessible support to LGBTQ individuals, especially in regions where in-person services are limited.

In conclusion, the collaboration between LGBTQ activists and mental health professionals is essential in addressing the unique mental health concerns of LGBTQ individuals. By working together, they can create a more inclusive and supportive environment that empowers individuals to thrive in their identities. Through education, resource development, and advocacy, this partnership can lead to significant improvements in mental health outcomes for the LGBTQ community.

Establishing LGBTQ-inclusive therapy programs and support groups

The establishment of LGBTQ-inclusive therapy programs and support groups is a critical step towards addressing the unique mental health challenges faced by LGBTQ individuals. These programs not only provide a safe space for individuals to express their feelings and experiences but also foster a sense of community and belonging.

Understanding the Need

Research has shown that LGBTQ individuals are at a higher risk for mental health issues, including anxiety, depression, and suicidal ideation, compared to their heterosexual counterparts. The *American Psychological Association* (APA) highlights that societal stigma, discrimination, and the internalization of negative societal attitudes can significantly impact the mental health of LGBTQ individuals. Consequently, the need for tailored therapeutic interventions and support systems is paramount.

Theoretical Framework

To effectively establish these programs, it is essential to ground them in relevant psychological theories. One such theory is the *Minority Stress Theory*, which posits that marginalized groups experience chronic stress due to societal stigma, discrimination, and prejudice. This stress can lead to adverse mental health outcomes. By recognizing the impact of minority stress, therapists can develop targeted interventions that address the specific needs of LGBTQ clients.

Core Components of LGBTQ-Inclusive Therapy Programs

1. **Culturally Competent Therapists:** Therapists should undergo training in LGBTQ issues to ensure they are sensitive to the unique experiences of their clients. This includes understanding the complexities of gender identity, sexual orientation, and the impact of societal norms.

2. **Safe Spaces:** Therapy programs must create an environment that feels safe and welcoming for LGBTQ individuals. This can be achieved through inclusive language, representation in materials, and visibly affirming practices.

3. **Peer Support Groups:** Establishing peer-led support groups can provide LGBTQ individuals with a platform to share their experiences, challenges, and triumphs. These groups can foster connection and reduce feelings of isolation.

4. **Holistic Approaches:** Integrating holistic practices such as mindfulness, art therapy, and body positivity can enhance the therapeutic experience. These approaches can help clients navigate their emotions and develop healthier coping mechanisms.

Examples of Successful Programs

Several organizations have pioneered LGBTQ-inclusive therapy programs that serve as models for others. For instance, the *Trevor Project* offers crisis intervention and suicide prevention services tailored specifically for LGBTQ youth. Their trained counselors provide support through various channels, including a 24/7 hotline, chat, and text services.

Another example is the *LGBTQ Center* in various cities across the United States, which provides mental health services, support groups, and community outreach programs. These centers have become vital resources for LGBTQ individuals seeking mental health support and community connection.

Challenges in Implementation

Despite the importance of establishing LGBTQ-inclusive therapy programs, several challenges remain. Funding is often a significant barrier, as many organizations struggle to secure the necessary resources to implement and sustain these initiatives. Additionally, there may be resistance from traditional mental health institutions that do not prioritize or understand the specific needs of LGBTQ clients.

Conclusion

Establishing LGBTQ-inclusive therapy programs and support groups is essential for addressing the mental health disparities faced by LGBTQ individuals. By creating safe, supportive, and affirming environments, these programs can empower individuals to explore their identities, process their experiences, and foster resilience. As society continues to evolve, it is crucial that mental health services adapt to meet the needs of all individuals, regardless of their sexual orientation or gender identity.

$$\text{Mental Health} = (\text{Individual Factors}) + (\text{Societal Factors}) + (\text{Support Systems}) \tag{24}$$

This equation highlights the interplay between individual experiences, societal influences, and the availability of support systems in determining mental health outcomes. By investing in LGBTQ-inclusive therapy programs, we can significantly improve the mental health landscape for LGBTQ individuals, ultimately leading to a more equitable society.

Bridging the Gap: LGBTQ Rights and Religion

Navigating the complexities of faith and sexual orientation

The intersection of faith and sexual orientation is a multifaceted and often contentious domain that many LGBTQ individuals navigate. This complexity is underscored by the diverse interpretations of religious texts and the varying degrees of acceptance within different faith communities. For many, their sexual identity can create a profound conflict with their religious beliefs, leading to a struggle for acceptance both from within and outside their communities.

One of the primary issues faced by LGBTQ individuals within religious contexts is the doctrine of many faiths that traditionally views homosexuality as sinful or immoral. For instance, in Christianity, passages from the Bible, such as Leviticus 18:22, which states, "You shall not lie with a male as with a woman; it is an abomination," are frequently cited to justify exclusion and discrimination against LGBTQ individuals. Similarly, in Islam, certain interpretations of the Quran have led to the belief that same-sex relationships are forbidden. These interpretations can lead to internalized homophobia among LGBTQ individuals, manifesting as guilt, shame, and anxiety regarding their sexual orientation.

However, there is a growing movement within various religious communities that seeks to reconcile faith and sexual orientation. Progressive religious groups and LGBTQ-affirming congregations are emerging, advocating for an inclusive interpretation of sacred texts. For example, the United Church of Christ in the United States has been at the forefront of LGBTQ inclusion, actively supporting same-sex marriage and the ordination of LGBTQ clergy. These communities provide safe spaces for individuals to explore their faith without compromising their sexual identity.

The problem of navigating faith and sexual orientation is further complicated by cultural and societal norms. In many cultures, adherence to religious beliefs is tightly woven into the fabric of identity and community. For instance, in Barbados, where Donnya Piggott grew up, religious beliefs are often intertwined with national identity, making it particularly challenging for LGBTQ individuals to assert their identities without facing ostracization. The fear of rejection from family and community can lead to a painful silence, where individuals feel compelled to hide their true selves to maintain familial and societal bonds.

The theory of intersectionality, as posited by Kimberlé Crenshaw, provides a framework for understanding how overlapping identities—including race, gender, class, and sexual orientation—create unique experiences of discrimination and privilege. LGBTQ individuals of faith often navigate multiple layers of identity, where their sexual orientation intersects with their religious beliefs, leading to distinct challenges. For example, a Black LGBTQ individual may face not only homophobia but also racism within both religious and LGBTQ spaces, complicating their quest for acceptance.

To illustrate this complexity, consider the story of a young woman named Sarah, who grew up in a conservative Christian household in Barbados. From an early age, Sarah felt an attraction to women, but she was taught that such feelings were sinful. Struggling with her identity, she sought solace in her faith, hoping to find acceptance. However, as she began to explore her sexual orientation, she felt increasingly alienated from her church community. The turning point came when she discovered an LGBTQ-affirming church that embraced her wholeheartedly. This experience not only allowed her to reconcile her faith with her identity but also empowered her to advocate for others facing similar struggles.

The journey of navigating faith and sexual orientation is not without its challenges, but it is also marked by resilience and hope. Many LGBTQ individuals find strength in their faith, using it as a source of empowerment and community. Activists like Donnya Piggott are instrumental in fostering dialogue between LGBTQ individuals and religious communities, promoting understanding and acceptance. By engaging in interfaith initiatives, they work to dismantle prejudices and build bridges, emphasizing that love and acceptance are at the core of most religious teachings.

In conclusion, navigating the complexities of faith and sexual orientation requires courage, resilience, and a commitment to authenticity. As societal attitudes continue to evolve, there is hope for greater acceptance within religious communities. By fostering inclusive dialogues and creating safe spaces, LGBTQ individuals can embrace both their faith and their identity, paving the way for a more inclusive future for all.

$$\text{Acceptance} = f(\text{Understanding, Dialogue, Community}) \qquad (25)$$

Promoting dialogue and understanding within religious communities

In a world where faith and sexual orientation often collide, fostering dialogue and understanding within religious communities is paramount to creating an inclusive environment for LGBTQ individuals. The intersection of faith and identity can be a complex terrain, fraught with challenges. However, it also presents a unique opportunity for growth, empathy, and acceptance. This section explores the methods and theories that can facilitate constructive conversations between LGBTQ advocates and religious groups, ultimately paving the way for greater understanding and acceptance.

Theoretical Framework

To promote dialogue within religious communities, it is essential to understand the theoretical frameworks that underpin such discussions. One prominent theory is the **Social Identity Theory**, which posits that individuals derive a sense of self from their group memberships. This can lead to in-group favoritism and out-group discrimination. In the context of LGBTQ individuals within religious communities, it is crucial to recognize how these identities interact and influence perceptions of each other. By fostering an understanding of shared humanity, advocates can work to bridge the gap between LGBTQ identities and religious beliefs.

Another relevant theory is **Contact Theory**, which suggests that under certain conditions, interpersonal contact is one of the most effective ways to reduce prejudice between groups. This theory emphasizes the importance of creating safe spaces for LGBTQ individuals and religious leaders to engage in open dialogue. By facilitating interactions that promote understanding, empathy can flourish, allowing both groups to learn from one another.

Challenges to Dialogue

Despite the potential for productive conversations, several challenges hinder dialogue between LGBTQ advocates and religious communities. One significant barrier is the prevalence of **homophobia** and **transphobia** within certain religious doctrines. Many religious texts have been interpreted in ways that condemn LGBTQ identities, leading to a culture of exclusion and stigmatization. This can create a hostile environment for LGBTQ individuals, making it difficult for them to engage with their faith communities.

Additionally, the fear of backlash can deter LGBTQ individuals from initiating conversations within their religious communities. Many may worry about losing their support systems, facing rejection, or being ostracized. This fear can perpetuate silence and misunderstanding, further entrenching divisions between LGBTQ individuals and religious groups.

Strategies for Promoting Dialogue

To overcome these challenges, several strategies can be employed to promote dialogue and understanding within religious communities:

- **Facilitated Discussions:** Organizing facilitated discussions that include both LGBTQ advocates and religious leaders can create a safe space for dialogue. These discussions should focus on shared values, such as love, compassion, and acceptance, which are central to many faith traditions. By emphasizing common ground, participants can begin to dismantle preconceived notions and foster empathy.

- **Educational Workshops:** Hosting workshops that educate religious communities about LGBTQ issues can be an effective way to promote understanding. These workshops can cover topics such as the spectrum of sexual orientation and gender identity, the impact of discrimination, and the importance of inclusion. By equipping religious leaders with knowledge, they can better support LGBTQ individuals within their congregations.

- **Storytelling Initiatives:** Encouraging LGBTQ individuals to share their personal stories within religious settings can humanize their experiences and foster empathy among congregants. Storytelling initiatives can take various forms, such as panel discussions, written narratives, or video testimonials. By hearing firsthand accounts, religious communities can begin to challenge stereotypes and misconceptions.

- **Interfaith Dialogues:** Engaging in interfaith dialogues can provide a broader perspective on LGBTQ inclusion. By bringing together diverse religious communities, advocates can share best practices and learn from one another's experiences. These dialogues can also highlight the commonalities across faith traditions that promote love and acceptance, fostering a sense of unity.

- **Creating Allies:** Identifying and empowering allies within religious communities can be a powerful strategy for promoting dialogue. Allies can advocate for LGBTQ inclusion and serve as bridges between LGBTQ individuals and religious leaders. Training programs that equip allies with the tools to engage in meaningful conversations can help create a more inclusive environment.

Examples of Successful Initiatives

Several successful initiatives demonstrate the potential for promoting dialogue and understanding within religious communities:

1. **The Reformation Project:** This organization works to educate and empower LGBTQ Christians and their allies to advocate for inclusion within their churches. Through conferences, workshops, and educational resources, they facilitate conversations that challenge harmful interpretations of scripture and promote acceptance.

2. **PFLAG:** Parents, Families, and Friends of Lesbians and Gays (PFLAG) is an organization that encourages dialogue between LGBTQ individuals and their families, including those with religious backgrounds. PFLAG's support groups provide a platform for sharing experiences and fostering understanding among family members, which can extend to religious communities.

3. **The Interfaith Alliance:** This organization promotes dialogue among diverse faith communities, advocating for LGBTQ rights and inclusion. By

engaging in interfaith discussions, they highlight the importance of love and acceptance across religious traditions, challenging discriminatory practices.

Conclusion

Promoting dialogue and understanding within religious communities is essential for fostering acceptance and inclusion of LGBTQ individuals. By employing theoretical frameworks such as Social Identity Theory and Contact Theory, advocates can navigate the complexities of these conversations. While challenges remain, implementing strategies such as facilitated discussions, educational workshops, storytelling initiatives, interfaith dialogues, and allyship can create meaningful change. Successful examples from organizations like The Reformation Project, PFLAG, and The Interfaith Alliance demonstrate that dialogue is not only possible but can lead to transformative outcomes. Ultimately, by promoting understanding within religious communities, we can work towards a future where LGBTQ individuals are embraced and celebrated within their faith traditions.

Building bridges between LGBTQ individuals and their religious backgrounds

In a world where faith and identity often intersect, the journey of LGBTQ individuals within religious contexts can be fraught with challenges. Many LGBTQ individuals find themselves navigating a complex landscape where their sexual orientation or gender identity is at odds with the doctrines and beliefs of their religious communities. This section explores the importance of building bridges between LGBTQ individuals and their religious backgrounds, focusing on fostering understanding, acceptance, and dialogue.

Theoretical Framework

The intersectionality theory, developed by Kimberlé Crenshaw, provides a crucial framework for understanding how multiple identities—such as sexual orientation, gender identity, and religious affiliation—interact to shape individual experiences. Intersectionality posits that people experience overlapping systems of discrimination or disadvantage. For LGBTQ individuals, the combination of their sexual or gender identity with their religious beliefs can lead to unique challenges, including exclusion, discrimination, and internal conflict.

Challenges Faced by LGBTQ Individuals in Religious Contexts

The first challenge LGBTQ individuals often face is the stigma associated with their identities within many religious communities. This stigma can manifest in various forms, including:

- **Rejection and Exclusion:** Many LGBTQ individuals report being ostracized by their religious communities upon coming out. This rejection can lead to a profound sense of isolation and loss of community, which are vital for spiritual and emotional support.

- **Internalized Homophobia:** The negative messages received from religious teachings can lead to internalized homophobia, where LGBTQ individuals struggle to accept their identities due to the perceived conflict with their faith.

- **Misinterpretation of Religious Texts:** Many religious texts are interpreted in ways that condemn LGBTQ identities. This misinterpretation can create barriers to acceptance and understanding, both within religious communities and among LGBTQ individuals themselves.

Building Bridges: Strategies for Connection

To foster understanding and acceptance, several strategies can be employed to build bridges between LGBTQ individuals and their religious backgrounds:

- **Promoting Inclusive Theology:** Developing and promoting inclusive theological perspectives that affirm LGBTQ identities is essential. This can involve reinterpretation of religious texts to highlight themes of love, acceptance, and justice. For example, many progressive theologians emphasize the importance of love in the teachings of Jesus, arguing that love should transcend all barriers, including sexual orientation.

- **Creating Safe Spaces:** Religious organizations can create safe spaces for LGBTQ individuals to share their experiences and struggles. These spaces can serve as forums for dialogue, healing, and community building. For instance, some churches have established LGBTQ support groups that focus on faith and identity, allowing individuals to explore their spirituality in a supportive environment.

- **Engaging in Interfaith Dialogue:** Interfaith initiatives can provide platforms for LGBTQ individuals and religious leaders to engage in meaningful conversations about faith and identity. These dialogues can help dismantle stereotypes and foster mutual understanding. An example of this is the Interfaith Alliance, which brings together diverse faith leaders to advocate for LGBTQ rights and promote inclusion within their communities.

- **Advocating for Policy Changes:** Encouraging religious organizations to adopt inclusive policies that protect LGBTQ individuals from discrimination can create a more welcoming environment. This advocacy can lead to the implementation of non-discrimination policies within religious institutions, ensuring that LGBTQ individuals are treated with dignity and respect.

Examples of Successful Bridge-Building Initiatives

Several successful initiatives have demonstrated the potential for building bridges between LGBTQ individuals and their religious backgrounds:

- **The United Church of Christ:** This denomination has been at the forefront of LGBTQ inclusion, having ordained openly LGBTQ ministers and supporting same-sex marriage long before it became widely accepted. Their commitment to social justice and inclusion serves as a model for other religious communities.

- **The Gay Christian Network:** This organization provides resources and support for LGBTQ Christians, promoting dialogue and understanding between LGBTQ individuals and their faith communities. Through online forums, conferences, and educational materials, they work to create a more inclusive environment within Christianity.

- **Pride in Our Faith:** This initiative focuses on empowering LGBTQ individuals within religious contexts, offering workshops and resources to help them reconcile their faith with their identities. By fostering understanding and acceptance, Pride in Our Faith aims to create inclusive religious communities.

Conclusion

Building bridges between LGBTQ individuals and their religious backgrounds is a vital step toward fostering acceptance and understanding within faith communities. By promoting inclusive theology, creating safe spaces, engaging in interfaith dialogue, and advocating for policy changes, we can work toward a future where LGBTQ individuals feel accepted and valued within their religious contexts. The journey may be challenging, but the potential for healing and reconciliation is profound, paving the way for a more inclusive and compassionate world.

Engaging in Interfaith Initiatives for LGBTQ Acceptance

In a world where faith and sexual orientation often collide, the need for interfaith initiatives that promote LGBTQ acceptance has never been more critical. These initiatives serve as a bridge, fostering understanding and compassion among diverse religious communities while advocating for the rights and dignity of LGBTQ individuals. The intersection of faith and sexual orientation can be fraught with tension, as traditional doctrines may conflict with contemporary understandings of identity and love. However, by engaging in interfaith dialogues, we can challenge harmful narratives and cultivate a more inclusive environment.

Theoretical Framework

At the heart of interfaith initiatives lies the theory of *intersectionality*, which posits that individuals experience multiple, overlapping identities that influence their social experiences and access to resources. In this context, LGBTQ individuals often navigate the complexities of their sexual orientation alongside their religious beliefs. The intersection of these identities can lead to unique challenges, including discrimination, exclusion, and internal conflict.

Moreover, the *social identity theory* suggests that individuals derive a sense of self from their group memberships, which can be both a source of strength and a source of division. For LGBTQ individuals within religious communities, the struggle for acceptance can lead to a crisis of identity, prompting the need for supportive interfaith spaces that affirm their worth and dignity.

Problems Faced by LGBTQ Individuals in Religious Communities

Many LGBTQ individuals face rejection from their religious communities, leading to feelings of isolation and alienation. This rejection can manifest in various forms, including:

- **Doctrinal Exclusion:** Many religious texts and teachings explicitly condemn non-heteronormative sexual orientations and identities, leading to an environment where LGBTQ individuals feel unwelcome.

BRIDGING THE GAP: LGBTQ RIGHTS AND RELIGION

- **Social Stigmatization:** LGBTQ individuals may experience social ostracism from their congregations, resulting in diminished support systems and increased mental health challenges.

- **Internalized Homophobia:** The clash between personal identity and religious beliefs can lead to internalized stigma, causing LGBTQ individuals to grapple with self-acceptance and worthiness.

Examples of Successful Interfaith Initiatives

Despite these challenges, numerous interfaith initiatives have emerged to advocate for LGBTQ acceptance within religious contexts. Some notable examples include:

- **The Interfaith Coalition for LGBTQ Equality:** This coalition brings together leaders from various faith traditions to promote dialogue and understanding around LGBTQ issues. Through workshops, community events, and educational resources, they aim to dismantle prejudices and foster acceptance.

- **Pride and Faith:** An initiative that encourages LGBTQ individuals to reclaim their faith while embracing their identities. By providing safe spaces for worship and fellowship, this movement seeks to empower LGBTQ individuals to explore their spirituality without fear of judgment.

- **The Religious Institute:** A national organization advocating for sexual and reproductive health, rights, and justice within faith communities. They work to create inclusive religious environments through educational programs and resources that challenge harmful doctrines.

Engaging Religious Leaders in Dialogue

One of the most effective strategies for fostering LGBTQ acceptance is engaging religious leaders in constructive dialogue. By encouraging faith leaders to participate in interfaith initiatives, we can create opportunities for them to confront their biases and re-examine traditional interpretations of sacred texts.

$$\text{Acceptance} = \frac{\text{Understanding} + \text{Empathy}}{\text{Fear} + \text{Prejudice}} \qquad (26)$$

This equation illustrates that acceptance can be achieved when understanding and empathy outweigh fear and prejudice. Interfaith initiatives can provide the necessary framework for this transformation, allowing leaders to engage with LGBTQ individuals and learn about their experiences firsthand.

The Role of Education and Awareness

Education plays a vital role in interfaith initiatives aimed at promoting LGBTQ acceptance. By providing educational resources that highlight the experiences of LGBTQ individuals within various faith traditions, we can dispel myths and challenge stereotypes. Workshops, seminars, and community discussions can serve as platforms for sharing stories, fostering empathy, and building solidarity.

Conclusion

Engaging in interfaith initiatives for LGBTQ acceptance is essential for creating a more inclusive society. By addressing the challenges faced by LGBTQ individuals in religious communities and promoting dialogue among diverse faith traditions, we can pave the way for a future where love and acceptance transcend boundaries. Through education, advocacy, and collaboration, we can transform the narrative around faith and sexuality, ensuring that all individuals are celebrated for who they are, regardless of their sexual orientation or religious beliefs.

Advocating for religious equality and LGBTQ rights

The intersection of religion and LGBTQ rights is a complex and often contentious arena. Advocacy for religious equality alongside LGBTQ rights requires a nuanced understanding of both the theological underpinnings of various faiths and the lived experiences of LGBTQ individuals. This section explores the challenges, theories, and practical examples of how advocates can promote a harmonious coexistence of these two often conflicting spheres.

Understanding the Theoretical Framework

At the core of advocating for religious equality and LGBTQ rights lies the principle of intersectionality, which posits that individuals experience overlapping systems of discrimination and privilege. According to Crenshaw (1989), intersectionality is essential for understanding how various forms of social stratification, such as race, gender, and sexual orientation, interact. This framework is crucial for LGBTQ advocates who seek to engage with religious communities, as it allows them to recognize the diverse identities and experiences within these groups.

Additionally, the concept of *religious pluralism* plays a significant role in this dialogue. Religious pluralism acknowledges the coexistence of multiple religious beliefs and practices within a society, promoting respect and understanding among different faiths. Advocates can leverage this concept to foster dialogue between LGBTQ individuals and religious communities, emphasizing that diversity in belief systems can coexist with respect for LGBTQ rights.

Identifying the Problems

Despite the theoretical frameworks that support coexistence, significant challenges persist. Many religious institutions maintain traditional teachings that view homosexuality as incompatible with their doctrines. This often results in the marginalization of LGBTQ individuals within these communities, leading to a crisis of faith for many. The psychological impact of this marginalization can be profound, contributing to mental health issues among LGBTQ individuals who feel rejected by their faith communities.

Moreover, the legal landscape varies significantly across different countries and regions. In some jurisdictions, religious exemptions allow for discrimination against LGBTQ individuals under the guise of religious freedom. This creates a paradox where the right to practice one's religion infringes upon the rights of others, leading to a need for comprehensive legal reform that protects both religious expression and LGBTQ rights.

Practical Examples of Advocacy

1. **Interfaith Dialogues**: One effective approach to bridging the gap between religious communities and LGBTQ advocates is through interfaith dialogues. These initiatives bring together leaders from various faiths and LGBTQ activists to discuss common values, such as love, acceptance, and justice. For instance, the *Interfaith Alliance* in the United States has successfully organized events that promote understanding and respect between religious groups and LGBTQ individuals.

2. **Inclusive Religious Spaces**: Creating inclusive religious spaces is another vital strategy. Many congregations have begun to openly welcome LGBTQ individuals, providing safe environments where they can worship without fear of discrimination. The *United Church of Christ* is a notable example, having adopted policies that affirm LGBTQ inclusion in all aspects of church life, including leadership roles.

3. **Legal Advocacy**: Advocacy for legal reforms that protect LGBTQ rights while respecting religious freedoms is essential. Organizations like the *American Civil Liberties Union (ACLU)* work to challenge discriminatory laws and promote policies that ensure equal rights for LGBTQ individuals, regardless of the religious context. This includes fighting against laws that permit discrimination based on sexual orientation under the pretext of religious beliefs.

4. **Educational Initiatives**: Educating both LGBTQ individuals and religious communities about each other's experiences and struggles can foster empathy and understanding. Workshops, seminars, and community events can be organized to discuss the importance of both LGBTQ rights and religious equality. For example, the *Religious Institute* offers resources and training for faith leaders to create inclusive congregations, focusing on the intersection of faith and sexuality.

Conclusion

Advocating for religious equality and LGBTQ rights is an ongoing journey that requires commitment, empathy, and collaboration. By employing intersectional approaches, engaging in meaningful dialogues, and promoting inclusive practices, advocates can work towards a future where both religious beliefs and LGBTQ identities are respected and celebrated. The path may be fraught with challenges, but the potential for transformative change is immense. As we navigate this complex landscape, it is crucial to remember that at the heart of both faith and advocacy lies the universal call for love, dignity, and respect for all individuals.

Bibliography

[1] Crenshaw, K. (1989). Demarginalizing the Intersection of Race and Sex: A Black Feminist Critique of Antidiscrimination Doctrine, Feminist Theory and Antiracist Politics. *University of Chicago Legal Forum*, 1989(1), 139-167.

[2] Interfaith Alliance. (n.d.). Retrieved from `https://interfaithalliance.org`

[3] United Church of Christ. (n.d.). Retrieved from `https://www.ucc.org`

[4] American Civil Liberties Union. (n.d.). Retrieved from `https://www.aclu.org`

[5] Religious Institute. (n.d.). Retrieved from `http://religiousinstitute.org`

A Technological Revolution for Equality

A Technological Revolution for Equality

A Technological Revolution for Equality

In the modern landscape of advocacy, technology has emerged as a powerful tool for social change, particularly in the realm of LGBTQ rights. This chapter delves into how technology is not just a catalyst for change but a revolutionary force that can dismantle barriers and foster equality across the globe.

The Role of Technology in LGBTQ Advocacy

The advent of the internet and social media has transformed the way activists communicate, organize, and mobilize. Social media platforms like Twitter, Instagram, and Facebook have become virtual town squares, allowing LGBTQ advocates to share their stories, raise awareness, and connect with allies. According to a study by Smith (2020), approximately 70% of LGBTQ individuals have utilized social media to engage in activism or advocacy, highlighting the integral role these platforms play in modern movements.

One notable example is the #LoveIsLove campaign, which gained traction during the fight for marriage equality in the United States. This hashtag not only unified supporters but also provided a platform for individuals to share their personal stories, thereby humanizing the struggle for equality. The visibility of these narratives shifted public perception and ultimately influenced legislative changes.

Harnessing the Power of Social Media for Change

Social media's ability to amplify voices is unprecedented. Activists can reach global audiences instantaneously, creating a ripple effect that can lead to significant societal shifts. This phenomenon is encapsulated in the equation:

$$V = f(S, A, C)$$

Where:

- V = Visibility of LGBTQ issues
- S = Social media engagement
- A = Allyship and support from non-LGBTQ individuals
- C = Cultural context and receptiveness

This equation illustrates that the visibility of LGBTQ issues is a function of social media engagement, the support from allies, and the broader cultural context. For instance, during Pride Month, social media campaigns often see a spike in engagement, demonstrating the potential for technology to foster a supportive environment.

Utilizing Digital Platforms to Amplify LGBTQ Voices

Digital platforms are not limited to social media; they also include blogs, podcasts, and video channels that provide LGBTQ individuals with a space to express themselves. Platforms like YouTube have enabled creators to share their journeys, challenges, and triumphs, fostering a sense of community and solidarity.

For example, the YouTube channel "Queer Eye" has garnered millions of views, not just for its entertainment value but for its ability to showcase diverse LGBTQ experiences, thereby challenging stereotypes and promoting acceptance. The success of such platforms underscores the importance of representation in media.

Innovations in Technology for Enhanced LGBTQ Visibility

Technological innovations have also paved the way for new forms of advocacy. Virtual reality (VR) and augmented reality (AR) are being utilized to create immersive experiences that educate users about LGBTQ issues. For instance, the VR project "The T Project" allows users to experience the life of a transgender individual, fostering empathy and understanding.

Moreover, data analytics has become a tool for advocacy groups to better understand the needs and challenges faced by LGBTQ communities. By analyzing social media trends and engagement metrics, organizations can tailor their campaigns to address specific issues, making their advocacy efforts more effective.

Creating Virtual Communities for LGBTQ Support and Empowerment

The internet has also facilitated the creation of virtual communities that provide support and empowerment for LGBTQ individuals. Online forums and support groups offer safe spaces for individuals to share their experiences and seek guidance. These communities are particularly vital for those living in conservative areas where in-person support may be limited.

The equation for community engagement can be expressed as:

$$E = \frac{I}{D}$$

Where:

- E = Engagement level

- I = Individual contributions and interactions

- D = Distance (both physical and emotional) from traditional support networks

This equation indicates that as individual contributions increase and distance from traditional support decreases, engagement levels within virtual communities rise, enhancing the overall support network for LGBTQ individuals.

Leveraging AI and Data Analytics for Targeted LGBTQ Initiatives

Artificial Intelligence (AI) and data analytics have the potential to revolutionize LGBTQ advocacy by providing insights into the specific needs of marginalized communities. By analyzing data from social media interactions, advocacy groups can identify trending issues and tailor their initiatives accordingly.

For example, an analysis of social media sentiment can reveal shifts in public opinion regarding LGBTQ rights, allowing organizations to adjust their messaging and strategies in real-time. This data-driven approach not only enhances the effectiveness of advocacy efforts but also ensures that the voices of the community are heard and prioritized.

Conclusion

In conclusion, technology is not just a tool but a revolutionary force in the fight for LGBTQ equality. From social media campaigns that amplify voices to innovative technologies that foster empathy and understanding, the digital landscape offers unprecedented opportunities for advocacy. As we continue to harness the power of technology, we must remain vigilant in ensuring that these tools are used to uplift and empower LGBTQ individuals, paving the way for a more inclusive and equitable future. The journey towards equality is ongoing, but with technology as an ally, the possibilities for change are limitless.

The Role of Technology in LGBTQ Advocacy

Harnessing the power of social media for change

Social media has emerged as a powerful tool for advocacy, particularly within the LGBTQ community. Platforms like Twitter, Facebook, Instagram, and TikTok have transformed the way individuals and organizations communicate, mobilize, and engage with audiences. This section explores how social media can be harnessed to promote LGBTQ rights, amplify voices, and create meaningful change.

Theoretical Framework

The impact of social media on social movements can be understood through the lens of several theoretical frameworks, including the **Networked Publics Theory** and the **Framing Theory**.

Networked Publics Theory posits that social media creates a new public sphere where individuals can connect, share information, and organize around common causes. This theory suggests that the decentralized nature of social media allows for a more democratic form of communication, enabling marginalized voices to be heard.

Framing Theory, on the other hand, focuses on how information is presented and interpreted. Social media allows activists to frame issues in ways that resonate with broader audiences, thereby increasing the likelihood of engagement and support. For instance, hashtags like #LoveIsLove and #TransRightsAreHumanRights serve to frame LGBTQ issues in a positive light, encouraging solidarity and support.

Challenges in Social Media Advocacy

While social media offers numerous advantages, it also presents significant challenges. One major issue is the prevalence of **misinformation** and **hate speech**. The rapid spread of false information can undermine LGBTQ advocacy efforts and perpetuate harmful stereotypes. Moreover, hate speech directed at LGBTQ individuals can create a hostile online environment, discouraging participation and engagement.

Another challenge is the issue of **digital divide**. Not all individuals have equal access to technology or the internet, which can limit the reach of social media campaigns. Marginalized communities may face barriers such as lack of resources, education, or internet connectivity, which can hinder their ability to participate in online advocacy.

Successful Examples of Social Media Advocacy

Despite these challenges, there are numerous examples of successful social media campaigns that have made a significant impact on LGBTQ rights. One notable example is the **It Gets Better Project**, launched in 2010 in response to a series of LGBTQ youth suicides. The campaign utilized YouTube and other social media platforms to share uplifting messages from individuals, encouraging LGBTQ youth to persevere through their struggles. The campaign went viral, resulting in millions of views and fostering a sense of community and support among LGBTQ youth.

Another powerful example is the **#BlackLivesMatter** movement, which has intersected with LGBTQ advocacy to address issues of racial and sexual identity. Social media has played a crucial role in organizing protests, sharing personal stories, and raising awareness about the violence faced by Black LGBTQ individuals. The movement's ability to mobilize supporters globally demonstrates the potential of social media to effect change on a large scale.

Strategies for Effective Social Media Advocacy

To effectively harness the power of social media for LGBTQ advocacy, several strategies can be employed:

1. **Create Engaging Content:** Use a mix of videos, infographics, and personal stories to engage audiences. Visual content is more likely to be shared and can help convey complex messages in an accessible way.

2. **Utilize Hashtags:** Develop and promote specific hashtags that encapsulate the campaign's message. Hashtags can increase visibility and create a sense of community among supporters.

3. **Foster Community Engagement:** Encourage followers to share their stories and experiences. Building a sense of community can empower individuals and create a supportive environment for advocacy.

4. **Collaborate with Influencers:** Partner with social media influencers who resonate with the LGBTQ community. Their reach can amplify messages and attract new supporters.

5. **Monitor and Respond:** Actively engage with followers by responding to comments and messages. Monitoring social media can also help identify misinformation and address it promptly.

Conclusion

Harnessing the power of social media for change is not just about technology; it's about connection, empowerment, and advocacy. By understanding the theoretical frameworks that underpin social media activism, recognizing the challenges involved, and implementing effective strategies, LGBTQ advocates can utilize these platforms to create a more inclusive and equitable society. As we continue to navigate the complexities of the digital landscape, the potential for social media to drive meaningful change remains immense, making it an invaluable tool in the fight for LGBTQ rights.

Utilizing digital platforms to amplify LGBTQ voices

In the contemporary landscape of advocacy, digital platforms have emerged as powerful tools for amplifying LGBTQ voices. The advent of social media, blogs, and various online communities has transformed the way marginalized groups communicate, organize, and advocate for their rights. This section explores the theoretical underpinnings of this phenomenon, the challenges faced, and practical examples that illustrate the effectiveness of digital platforms in elevating LGBTQ narratives.

Theoretical Framework

The utilization of digital platforms can be understood through the lens of *networked advocacy*, a concept that highlights how social media and online communities facilitate the rapid dissemination of information and the mobilization of supporters. According to [?], the rise of the internet has led to the formation of a *network society*, where traditional barriers to communication are diminished, allowing marginalized voices to be heard. This shift is particularly significant for LGBTQ individuals who have historically faced systemic silencing.

Furthermore, *Framing Theory* plays a crucial role in understanding how LGBTQ narratives are constructed and presented online. Framing involves the selection and emphasis of certain aspects of a perceived reality, which influences how audiences interpret issues. Digital platforms allow LGBTQ advocates to frame their stories in ways that resonate with broader audiences, thereby fostering empathy and understanding.

Challenges in Digital Advocacy

Despite the advantages, utilizing digital platforms for advocacy is not without its challenges. One significant issue is the prevalence of *online harassment* and *cyberbullying* targeted at LGBTQ individuals. According to a report by the *Pew Research Center*, nearly 70% of LGBTQ individuals have experienced some form of online harassment. This hostile environment can deter individuals from sharing their stories or participating in advocacy efforts.

Moreover, algorithms on platforms like Facebook and Twitter can inadvertently marginalize LGBTQ content by prioritizing mainstream narratives. This phenomenon, known as *algorithmic bias*, can limit the visibility of LGBTQ voices and perpetuate existing inequalities. [?] emphasizes the importance of recognizing how these biases affect marginalized groups, necessitating a critical approach to digital advocacy.

Practical Examples

Despite these challenges, numerous examples illustrate the successful amplification of LGBTQ voices through digital platforms. One notable case is the #LoveIsLove campaign, which gained traction on social media during the fight for marriage equality in various countries. The hashtag became a rallying cry, uniting individuals and organizations worldwide to share personal stories and advocate for LGBTQ rights. This grassroots movement showcased the power of digital platforms in creating a sense of community and solidarity.

Another prominent example is the use of YouTube as a platform for LGBTQ storytelling. Content creators like *Gigi Gorgeous* and *Tegan and Sara* have utilized their channels to share their experiences, challenges, and triumphs. Their narratives not only resonate with LGBTQ youth but also educate broader audiences about the realities faced by the community. The accessibility of video content allows for a more intimate connection, fostering empathy and understanding.

Additionally, organizations like *GLAAD* and *The Trevor Project* have effectively harnessed social media to raise awareness about LGBTQ issues. Through targeted campaigns, they have successfully mobilized supporters and created impactful dialogues around topics such as mental health, suicide prevention, and anti-discrimination legislation. By leveraging digital platforms, these organizations have amplified their reach and influence, making significant strides in advocacy.

Conclusion

In conclusion, the utilization of digital platforms to amplify LGBTQ voices represents a critical evolution in advocacy. While challenges such as online harassment and algorithmic bias persist, the potential for storytelling and community building through these platforms is unparalleled. By embracing the theoretical frameworks of networked advocacy and framing theory, LGBTQ advocates can navigate the complexities of digital spaces to ensure their voices are heard. As we continue to explore the intersection of technology and advocacy, it is essential to foster inclusive online environments that empower LGBTQ individuals to share their stories and advocate for their rights.

Innovations in technology for enhanced LGBTQ visibility

In recent years, the intersection of technology and LGBTQ advocacy has led to groundbreaking innovations that enhance visibility and representation for the LGBTQ community. These innovations not only empower individuals but also challenge societal norms and promote inclusivity. This section explores the various technological advancements that have significantly contributed to enhancing LGBTQ visibility, highlighting their impact and the ongoing challenges faced in this realm.

The Role of Social Media

Social media platforms such as Twitter, Instagram, and TikTok have become powerful tools for LGBTQ individuals and organizations to share their stories and experiences. These platforms allow users to connect with a global audience, fostering a sense of community and belonging. The ability to share personal narratives can be a powerful form of advocacy, as it humanizes the LGBTQ experience and challenges stereotypes.

One notable example is the viral hashtag campaigns like #LoveIsLove and #Pride, which have been instrumental in raising awareness and promoting acceptance of LGBTQ relationships. These campaigns often lead to increased visibility of LGBTQ issues in mainstream media, further normalizing LGBTQ identities and experiences.

Virtual Reality and Augmented Reality

Innovations in virtual reality (VR) and augmented reality (AR) are also making significant strides in enhancing LGBTQ visibility. These technologies provide immersive experiences that allow users to step into the shoes of LGBTQ individuals, fostering empathy and understanding. For instance, VR experiences can simulate the challenges faced by LGBTQ individuals, such as coming out or dealing with discrimination.

Organizations like *The Trevor Project* have utilized VR technology to create educational programs aimed at fostering understanding and acceptance among youth. By immersing users in realistic scenarios, these programs help to break down barriers and promote allyship.

Mobile Applications for Support and Community Building

Mobile applications designed specifically for the LGBTQ community have emerged as vital resources for visibility and support. Apps like Grindr, HER, and LGBTQ+ meet-up platforms not only facilitate social connections but also provide safe spaces for individuals to express their identities. These platforms often include features that promote community engagement, such as forums, events, and resources for mental health support.

Moreover, apps like *Pride Buddy* connect LGBTQ individuals with mentors and allies, fostering a sense of belonging and support. By leveraging technology, these applications enhance visibility and create networks that empower LGBTQ individuals to share their stories and seek assistance.

Data Analytics for Advocacy

Data analytics is another innovative approach that has transformed LGBTQ advocacy. By collecting and analyzing data on LGBTQ experiences, organizations can identify trends, challenges, and areas needing improvement. This data-driven approach enables advocates to craft targeted campaigns that address specific issues faced by the community.

For example, the *Human Rights Campaign* (HRC) utilizes data analytics to track legislation affecting LGBTQ rights across the United States. By presenting this data visually, they enhance the visibility of LGBTQ issues, making it easier for advocates and policymakers to understand the landscape and take action.

Challenges and Limitations

Despite these advancements, challenges remain in the quest for enhanced LGBTQ visibility through technology. Issues such as online harassment, cyberbullying, and data privacy continue to plague the community. For instance, many LGBTQ individuals face discrimination and harassment on social media platforms, which can deter them from sharing their stories or engaging in advocacy.

Furthermore, there is a digital divide that affects marginalized groups within the LGBTQ community. Access to technology and the internet is not uniform, and individuals in lower socioeconomic brackets may struggle to engage with these innovations. Addressing these disparities is crucial to ensuring that all voices within the LGBTQ community are heard and represented.

Conclusion

Innovations in technology have played a pivotal role in enhancing LGBTQ visibility, providing platforms for storytelling, community building, and advocacy. While challenges persist, the potential for technology to foster understanding and acceptance remains immense. As we continue to navigate the digital landscape, it is essential to harness these innovations to amplify LGBTQ voices and promote equality for all. The future of LGBTQ advocacy lies in leveraging technology to create inclusive spaces where individuals can express their identities freely and authentically.

Creating virtual communities for LGBTQ support and empowerment

In an increasingly digital world, the power of virtual communities has emerged as a transformative force for LGBTQ support and empowerment. These online spaces provide safe havens for individuals to connect, share experiences, and mobilize for advocacy. The creation of these communities is rooted in the principles of inclusivity, representation, and the collective strength found in shared identities.

Theoretical Framework

The establishment of virtual communities can be understood through the lens of social identity theory, which posits that individuals derive a sense of self from their group memberships. According to [?], belonging to a social group enhances self-esteem and fosters a sense of belonging. For LGBTQ individuals, who may face marginalization in their offline lives, virtual communities serve as vital spaces where they can affirm their identities without fear of discrimination.

Moreover, the theory of community empowerment highlights the importance of collective action in addressing social issues. [?] emphasizes that empowerment involves increasing the spiritual, political, social, educational, gender, or economic strength of individuals and communities. Virtual communities facilitate this empowerment by providing platforms for knowledge sharing, resource exchange, and advocacy.

Challenges Faced

Despite the potential benefits, creating virtual communities for LGBTQ individuals is not without challenges. One significant issue is the prevalence of online harassment and cyberbullying, which can deter individuals from participating in these spaces. Studies indicate that LGBTQ individuals are disproportionately targeted by online hate speech, leading to feelings of isolation and fear (([?])).

Additionally, there is the challenge of digital divide, where access to technology and the internet is not equitable. Marginalized individuals may lack the resources to participate fully in virtual communities, thus perpetuating existing inequalities. As [?] notes, bridging this digital divide is crucial for ensuring that all voices are heard and represented.

Examples of Successful Virtual Communities

Numerous successful virtual communities have emerged, demonstrating the power of online platforms in fostering LGBTQ support and empowerment. One notable example is *The Trevor Project*, which provides crisis intervention and suicide prevention services to LGBTQ youth. Through their digital platforms, they offer a safe space for young people to connect with trained counselors and peers, thus addressing the urgent need for mental health support within the community.

Another example is *LGBTQ+ Reddit*, a subforum that allows users to share their experiences, seek advice, and build connections. The anonymity provided by the platform encourages open dialogue about sensitive topics, fostering a sense of community and belonging among its members. This platform exemplifies how virtual spaces can promote inclusivity and support, even in the face of societal stigma.

Strategies for Building Effective Virtual Communities

To create effective virtual communities for LGBTQ support and empowerment, several strategies can be employed:

1. **Establish Clear Guidelines**: Creating a set of community guidelines that promote respect, inclusivity, and safety is essential. These guidelines should explicitly prohibit hate speech and harassment, fostering a welcoming environment for all members.

2. **Utilize Moderation Tools**: Employing moderators who can actively monitor discussions and enforce community guidelines helps maintain a positive atmosphere. Tools that allow users to report inappropriate behavior can also enhance safety.

3. **Encourage Active Participation**: Engaging members through interactive content, such as webinars, discussions, and Q&A sessions, can foster a sense of belonging. Providing opportunities for members to share their stories and experiences encourages deeper connections.

4. **Promote Accessibility**: Ensuring that virtual communities are accessible to individuals with varying levels of technology proficiency is crucial. This can involve providing tutorials, resources, and support for those unfamiliar with digital platforms.

5. **Leverage Social Media**: Utilizing social media platforms to promote virtual communities can help reach a broader audience. Campaigns that highlight the benefits of joining these communities can attract new members and foster engagement.

Conclusion

Creating virtual communities for LGBTQ support and empowerment is a vital endeavor in the fight for equality and inclusion. By harnessing the power of technology, these communities provide safe spaces for individuals to connect, share, and advocate for their rights. While challenges such as online harassment and the digital divide persist, the potential for empowerment through these virtual networks remains immense. As we continue to navigate the complexities of the digital landscape, it is essential to prioritize the creation and maintenance of inclusive virtual spaces that uplift and support the LGBTQ community.

Leveraging AI and data analytics for targeted LGBTQ initiatives

In the digital age, the integration of Artificial Intelligence (AI) and data analytics has transformed the landscape of advocacy, particularly for marginalized communities such as the LGBTQ population. Leveraging these technologies allows activists and organizations to create targeted initiatives that address specific needs and challenges faced by LGBTQ individuals. This section explores the theoretical foundations, practical applications, and real-world examples of how AI and data analytics can be harnessed to drive impactful LGBTQ initiatives.

Theoretical Foundations

The use of AI in advocacy is grounded in several theoretical frameworks, including *Big Data Theory* and *Predictive Analytics*. Big Data Theory posits that vast amounts of data can yield insights that were previously unattainable, enabling organizations to understand trends, behaviors, and needs within the LGBTQ community. Predictive Analytics, on the other hand, involves using statistical algorithms and machine learning techniques to identify the likelihood of future outcomes based on historical data.

The equation for a basic predictive model can be expressed as:

$$Y = \beta_0 + \beta_1 X_1 + \beta_2 X_2 + \ldots + \beta_n X_n + \epsilon \tag{27}$$

where: - Y is the dependent variable (e.g., likelihood of discrimination), - $X_1, X_2, \ldots, X_n$ are independent variables (e.g., age, location, socioeconomic status), - β_0 is the intercept, - β_i are the coefficients, - ϵ is the error term.

This model can help organizations predict areas where LGBTQ individuals may face greater risks, allowing for more focused interventions.

Identifying Issues and Trends

AI and data analytics can be utilized to identify pressing issues within the LGBTQ community by analyzing social media trends, survey data, and public discourse. For instance, sentiment analysis—a technique that uses natural language processing to analyze text data—can gauge public attitudes towards LGBTQ issues. By mining data from platforms like Twitter or Facebook, organizations can:

- Assess the prevalence of hate speech or discrimination.

- Identify key topics of concern within the community.

- Monitor changes in public sentiment over time.

For example, a study by the *Pew Research Center* found that social media platforms could be instrumental in tracking shifts in public opinion regarding same-sex marriage. By analyzing millions of tweets, researchers were able to visualize how acceptance grew over time, providing valuable insights for advocacy strategies.

Targeted Campaigns and Resource Allocation

Once issues are identified, AI can help organizations create targeted campaigns that address specific needs. Data analytics can reveal demographics most affected by certain issues, allowing for tailored messaging and resource allocation. For instance, if data shows that LGBTQ youth in a particular region are struggling with mental health, organizations can develop initiatives specifically designed to support this demographic.

One successful example is the *Trevor Project*, which uses data analytics to understand the needs of LGBTQ youth. By analyzing crisis intervention data, they can identify trends in suicidal ideation and tailor their outreach programs accordingly. This targeted approach has resulted in more effective interventions and resource distribution.

Enhancing Community Engagement

AI-driven tools can also enhance community engagement by facilitating better communication and connection among LGBTQ individuals. Chatbots, powered by AI, can provide immediate support and information to users seeking help. For example, organizations like *LGBTQ+ Youth Line* have implemented AI chatbots to offer real-time assistance to youth in crisis, ensuring they receive the support they need when they need it most.

Moreover, data analytics can be employed to evaluate the effectiveness of community programs. By collecting feedback and analyzing participation data, organizations can continuously improve their initiatives to better serve the LGBTQ community.

Challenges and Ethical Considerations

Despite the potential benefits, leveraging AI and data analytics in LGBTQ advocacy also presents challenges. Issues such as data privacy, algorithmic bias, and the digital divide must be addressed to ensure that these technologies serve all members of the community equitably. For instance, if data collection methods are not inclusive, marginalized subgroups within the LGBTQ community may be overlooked, leading to ineffective or harmful initiatives.

Furthermore, ethical considerations surrounding data usage must be prioritized. Organizations must establish clear guidelines for data collection, ensuring informed consent and transparency. As AI systems are trained on historical data, there is a risk of perpetuating existing biases if not carefully monitored.

Conclusion

In conclusion, the integration of AI and data analytics into LGBTQ advocacy presents a powerful opportunity to create targeted initiatives that address the unique challenges faced by the community. By harnessing these technologies, organizations can identify pressing issues, allocate resources effectively, and enhance community engagement. However, it is crucial to navigate the associated challenges and ethical considerations thoughtfully to ensure that these tools empower rather than marginalize. As the landscape of LGBTQ advocacy continues to evolve, the strategic use of AI and data analytics will be essential in driving meaningful change and fostering a more inclusive society.

Digital Activism and Online Advocacy

Leveraging online platforms for activism

In the digital age, online platforms have emerged as powerful tools for activism, particularly within the LGBTQ community. These platforms not only facilitate communication and information sharing but also empower individuals to mobilize for change. This section explores how activists leverage social media, blogs, and other online tools to advocate for LGBTQ rights, raise awareness, and foster community engagement.

Theoretical Framework

The theory of *Networked Publics*, as articulated by boyd (2008), posits that the internet has transformed public discourse by creating new spaces for interaction and engagement. Online platforms allow activists to reach wider audiences, bypassing traditional media gatekeepers. This democratization of information is crucial for marginalized communities, enabling them to share their narratives and advocate for their rights.

The *Diffusion of Innovations* theory (Rogers, 1962) also provides insight into how ideas spread through social networks. Activists can utilize online platforms to disseminate information rapidly, fostering a culture of sharing and engagement that can lead to collective action.

Challenges and Opportunities

While online platforms present numerous opportunities, they also come with challenges. The digital divide remains a significant barrier, as not all individuals have equal access to technology or the internet. Furthermore, issues such as online harassment, misinformation, and algorithmic bias can hinder the effectiveness of digital activism.

For instance, LGBTQ activists often face cyberbullying and hate speech, which can deter participation and silence voices. Addressing these challenges requires a multifaceted approach, including advocacy for stronger online protections and the development of supportive online communities.

Case Studies

One notable example of leveraging online platforms for activism is the #LoveIsLove campaign, which gained momentum during the fight for marriage equality in the United States. Social media platforms like Twitter and Instagram were instrumental in amplifying voices and sharing personal stories that humanized the issue. By using the hashtag, activists created a sense of solidarity and urgency, motivating individuals to engage in advocacy efforts.

Another example is the #TransRightsAreHumanRights movement, which has utilized online platforms to raise awareness about violence against transgender individuals. Activists have shared personal testimonies, statistics, and resources, fostering a community of support and advocacy. The campaign's success highlights the power of social media in shaping public discourse and influencing policy change.

Strategies for Effective Online Activism

To effectively leverage online platforms for activism, several strategies can be employed:

- **Storytelling:** Sharing personal stories can create emotional connections and foster empathy. Activists should encourage individuals to share their experiences, highlighting the human impact of LGBTQ issues.

- **Engagement:** Activists should actively engage with their audience by responding to comments, asking questions, and creating interactive content. This fosters a sense of community and encourages participation.

- **Collaboration:** Partnering with other organizations and influencers can amplify messages and expand reach. Collaborative campaigns can create a united front, drawing attention to critical issues.

- **Education:** Providing educational resources and information can empower individuals to advocate for LGBTQ rights. Activists should share infographics, articles, and videos that inform and inspire action.

- **Utilizing Data:** Analyzing engagement metrics and audience demographics can help activists tailor their content and strategies. Understanding what resonates with the audience can enhance the effectiveness of campaigns.

Conclusion

In conclusion, leveraging online platforms for activism presents both challenges and opportunities for the LGBTQ community. By harnessing the power of social media and digital tools, activists can amplify their voices, foster community engagement, and advocate for change. As the landscape of digital activism continues to evolve, it is essential for advocates to adapt their strategies and remain vigilant against the challenges that arise. The potential for online platforms to drive social change is immense, and with continued innovation and collaboration, the LGBTQ movement can thrive in the digital age.

Engaging in meaningful conversations through social media

In the digital age, social media platforms have emerged as powerful tools for advocacy and engagement, particularly within the LGBTQ community. These platforms provide a unique space for individuals to share their stories, connect with others, and mobilize support for various causes. Engaging in meaningful conversations through social media not only fosters community but also promotes awareness and understanding of LGBTQ issues.

The Role of Social Media in Advocacy

Social media serves as a catalyst for dialogue, allowing users to express their opinions, share experiences, and participate in discussions that matter to them. According to the *Social Media Advocacy Theory*, social media can enhance the effectiveness of advocacy efforts by providing a platform for grassroots movements to gain visibility. This theory posits that the more individuals engage with content related to social issues, the more likely they are to participate in advocacy efforts, thus creating a ripple effect of awareness and action.

Challenges in Online Conversations

While social media offers numerous opportunities for engagement, it also presents challenges. One significant issue is the prevalence of online hate speech and discrimination. Cyberbullying and harassment can deter individuals from participating in conversations, particularly those from marginalized groups. A study by the *Pew Research Center* found that 70% of LGBTQ individuals have experienced some form of online harassment, leading to increased anxiety and reluctance to engage openly.

Furthermore, the echo chamber effect can limit the diversity of discussions. Users often curate their feeds to align with their beliefs, which can create an environment where only like-minded perspectives are shared. This phenomenon can hinder the potential for meaningful dialogue and understanding between different viewpoints.

Strategies for Meaningful Engagement

To foster meaningful conversations, advocates can employ several strategies:

- **Creating Inclusive Spaces:** Establishing safe online environments where individuals can share their experiences without fear of judgment is crucial. This can be achieved through moderated groups or forums that prioritize respect and inclusivity.

- **Utilizing Storytelling:** Personal narratives resonate deeply with audiences. By sharing authentic stories, individuals can humanize LGBTQ issues and encourage empathy among those who may not fully understand the challenges faced by the community. For example, the hashtag #ShareYourStory has been instrumental in amplifying personal experiences, allowing users to connect on a deeper level.

- **Encouraging Open Dialogue:** Advocates should invite diverse perspectives and encourage respectful debate. This can be facilitated through Q&A sessions, live discussions, or panel events hosted on platforms like Instagram Live or Twitter Spaces.

- **Leveraging Hashtags and Trends:** Using relevant hashtags can increase the visibility of LGBTQ issues. Campaigns like #LoveIsLove and #TransRightsAreHumanRights have successfully brought attention to important topics and mobilized support.

- **Collaborating with Influencers:** Partnering with social media influencers who are passionate about LGBTQ rights can help reach a broader audience. Influencers can amplify messages, making them more accessible to individuals who may not be actively seeking information about LGBTQ issues.

Case Studies of Successful Engagement

Several successful campaigns demonstrate the power of social media in fostering meaningful conversations:

- **The Ice Bucket Challenge:** While initially focused on ALS awareness, this viral campaign highlighted the importance of community support and activism. Participants shared videos of themselves completing the challenge, which not only raised funds but also sparked conversations about health issues affecting marginalized communities.

- **#BlackTransLivesMatter:** This hashtag emerged as a response to the violence against Black trans individuals, creating a platform for advocacy and awareness. The campaign successfully engaged diverse voices, prompting discussions about intersectionality within the LGBTQ movement.

- **#Pride:** During Pride Month, social media platforms become vibrant spaces for celebration and advocacy. Users share their pride stories, leading to increased visibility and support for LGBTQ rights. Brands also participate, showcasing their commitment to diversity and inclusion, which can further amplify the conversation.

Conclusion

Engaging in meaningful conversations through social media is essential for advancing LGBTQ advocacy. By creating inclusive spaces, utilizing storytelling, and leveraging trends, advocates can foster dialogue that promotes understanding and support. Despite the challenges posed by online harassment and echo chambers, the potential for social media to drive positive change remains significant. As LGBTQ individuals continue to share their experiences and connect with others, social media will undoubtedly play a crucial role in shaping the future of advocacy and community engagement.

The impact of online activism on policy change

Online activism has emerged as a powerful tool for advocacy, particularly in the context of LGBTQ rights. The digital landscape allows for rapid dissemination of information, mobilization of supporters, and engagement with policymakers. This section explores the multifaceted impact of online activism on policy change, examining relevant theories, challenges, and illustrative examples.

Theoretical Framework

The impact of online activism can be understood through several theoretical lenses. One prominent theory is the *Networked Publics Theory*, which posits that social media platforms create new forms of public discourse and collective action. According to [?], networked publics facilitate the formation of communities that transcend geographical boundaries, enabling marginalized groups to organize and advocate for their rights effectively.

Another relevant framework is the *Framing Theory*, which suggests that the way issues are presented in public discourse can significantly influence public perception and policy outcomes. Online activists often utilize strategic framing to highlight injustices faced by the LGBTQ community, thus shaping the narrative around policy discussions. [?] identifies that effective framing can lead to increased visibility and urgency, prompting policymakers to take action.

Mechanisms of Influence

Online activism influences policy change through several mechanisms:

- **Awareness Raising:** Social media campaigns can raise awareness about specific issues, such as discriminatory laws or practices. For instance, the hashtag #LoveIsLove gained traction during the fight for marriage equality, bringing attention to the need for legal recognition of same-sex relationships.

- **Mobilization:** Digital platforms facilitate the mobilization of supporters for protests, petitions, and lobbying efforts. The *Equality March* for LGBTQ rights in various cities worldwide has seen significant participation driven by social media outreach.

- **Direct Engagement with Policymakers:** Online activism allows advocates to engage directly with policymakers through platforms like Twitter. This direct line of communication can pressure officials to respond to constituents' concerns, as seen in campaigns that tag elected representatives in discussions about LGBTQ rights.

- **Data-Driven Advocacy:** The use of data analytics in online campaigns helps identify trends and public sentiment, providing activists with the information needed to craft compelling arguments for policy change. For example, studies showing the positive impact of inclusive policies on mental health outcomes for LGBTQ individuals have been shared widely to advocate for legislative reforms.

Challenges and Limitations

Despite its potential, online activism faces several challenges that can impede its effectiveness in driving policy change:

- **Digital Divide:** Access to technology and the internet is not uniform, which can limit the participation of marginalized groups in online activism. This digital divide can exacerbate existing inequalities within the LGBTQ community, particularly among those in lower socio-economic brackets or rural areas.

- **Misinformation:** The prevalence of misinformation on social media can undermine the credibility of LGBTQ advocacy efforts. False narratives can spread rapidly, complicating the work of activists who must then counter these misleading claims.

- **Backlash and Repression:** Online activism can provoke backlash from conservative groups and individuals, leading to harassment and threats against activists. In some cases, governments may respond with increased surveillance or censorship of online spaces where LGBTQ issues are discussed.

- **Short Attention Spans:** The fast-paced nature of social media can lead to short attention spans among users, making it challenging for activists to sustain engagement over time. This phenomenon, often referred to as "slacktivism," can result in superficial support for issues without leading to meaningful action.

Case Studies

To illustrate the impact of online activism on policy change, consider the following examples:

- **The Marriage Equality Movement:** The campaign for marriage equality in the United States utilized social media to mobilize support and influence public opinion. The viral video "#LoveIsLove" showcased personal stories that resonated with viewers, contributing to a shift in societal attitudes and ultimately leading to the landmark Supreme Court decision in *Obergefell v. Hodges* (2015).

- **Transgender Rights Advocacy:** The #TransRightsAreHumanRights campaign effectively raised awareness about the discrimination faced by transgender individuals. Through coordinated online efforts, advocates successfully pressured lawmakers to introduce and pass legislation that protects transgender rights in several states.

- **Global LGBTQ Rights Initiatives:** Organizations like *Human Rights Campaign* and *ILGA World* have leveraged online platforms to advocate for LGBTQ rights globally. Their campaigns often highlight human rights abuses in countries with anti-LGBTQ laws, mobilizing international support and pressuring governments to reform discriminatory policies.

Conclusion

The impact of online activism on policy change is profound, offering new avenues for advocacy and engagement. While challenges persist, the ability to mobilize, raise awareness, and engage directly with policymakers has transformed the landscape of LGBTQ advocacy. As technology continues to evolve, so too will the strategies employed by activists, ensuring that the fight for equality remains dynamic and responsive to the needs of the community.

Forming online communities to mobilize LGBTQ advocacy

In the digital age, online communities have become pivotal in mobilizing LGBTQ advocacy, providing safe spaces for individuals to connect, share experiences, and organize collective action. These communities leverage the power of the internet to break geographical barriers, allowing advocates and allies to come together from different parts of the world. The formation of these communities is rooted in several theoretical frameworks, including Social Identity Theory and Network Theory.

Theoretical Foundations

Social Identity Theory posits that individuals derive a sense of identity from their group memberships. For LGBTQ individuals, online communities can serve as a sanctuary where they can express their identities without fear of judgment. This sense of belonging fosters solidarity and collective efficacy, which are crucial for mobilizing advocacy efforts.

Network Theory emphasizes the importance of connections among individuals within a community. Online platforms facilitate the formation of networks that can amplify advocacy messages and mobilize resources. These networks can be instrumental in organizing events, campaigns, and educational initiatives that promote LGBTQ rights.

Challenges in Online Community Formation

Despite the advantages of online communities, several challenges persist. One major issue is the prevalence of online harassment and hate speech, which can deter individuals from participating in these spaces. The anonymity of the internet can embolden individuals to engage in harmful behaviors, creating a hostile environment for LGBTQ individuals.

Additionally, the digital divide remains a significant barrier. Not all LGBTQ individuals have equal access to technology or the internet, which can lead to disparities in representation and participation within online communities. This gap can exacerbate existing inequalities, particularly for marginalized subgroups within the LGBTQ community.

Examples of Successful Online Communities

Several online communities have successfully mobilized LGBTQ advocacy and created impactful change. One notable example is the *Trevor Project*, which utilizes social media platforms to provide crisis intervention and support for LGBTQ youth. Through their online presence, they have built a community that offers resources, mentorship, and a platform for advocacy.

Another example is *GLAAD*, which focuses on promoting LGBTQ representation in media. Their online campaigns often engage users to share their stories and experiences, creating a sense of community and collective action. By utilizing hashtags and interactive content, GLAAD mobilizes individuals to advocate for change in media representation.

Strategies for Effective Mobilization

To effectively mobilize LGBTQ advocacy through online communities, several strategies can be employed:

- **Creating Safe Spaces:** Establishing guidelines and moderation practices that ensure respectful discourse can help foster a welcoming environment for all members.

- **Utilizing Social Media Platforms:** Engaging users through platforms like Twitter, Instagram, and TikTok can amplify advocacy messages and reach wider audiences.

- **Encouraging Participation:** Initiatives such as online petitions, virtual events, and webinars can encourage active participation and mobilization among community members.

- **Building Alliances:** Collaborating with other advocacy groups can strengthen efforts and broaden the reach of campaigns, creating a united front for LGBTQ rights.

- **Leveraging Data Analytics:** Utilizing data to understand community needs and preferences can inform advocacy strategies and enhance engagement.

Conclusion

The formation of online communities is a powerful tool for mobilizing LGBTQ advocacy. By fostering connections, providing safe spaces, and utilizing technology, these communities can amplify voices, challenge discrimination, and promote equality. However, it is essential to address the challenges of online harassment and the digital divide to ensure that all individuals can participate in advocacy efforts. As the landscape of LGBTQ rights continues to evolve, the role of online communities will remain crucial in shaping the future of activism.

Using social media algorithms to drive LGBTQ narratives

In the digital age, social media platforms have become powerful tools for advocacy and activism, particularly for marginalized communities, including the LGBTQ community. One of the most significant aspects of social media is its reliance on algorithms, which dictate what content users see based on their interactions, preferences, and behaviors. Understanding and leveraging these algorithms can amplify LGBTQ narratives, promote visibility, and foster community engagement.

The Role of Algorithms in Content Visibility

Social media algorithms are designed to enhance user engagement by curating content that aligns with individual interests. For LGBTQ activists, this presents both opportunities and challenges. The primary goal of these algorithms is to maximize user interaction, often prioritizing posts that generate likes, shares, and comments. As a result, content that resonates emotionally or provides valuable information can gain traction, leading to increased visibility for LGBTQ issues.

Mathematically, the engagement of a post can be represented as:

$$E = f(L, S, C) \tag{28}$$

where E is the engagement score, L represents likes, S denotes shares, and C indicates comments. The function f captures the interaction between these variables, highlighting how each contributes to the overall visibility of the content.

Challenges of Algorithmic Bias

However, the algorithms governing social media platforms are not without flaws. They can exhibit biases that marginalize certain voices, including those within the LGBTQ community. For instance, content that challenges societal norms or addresses controversial issues may be deprioritized or shadowbanned, limiting its reach. This phenomenon raises critical questions about representation and equity in digital spaces.

To illustrate, consider the case of a viral campaign advocating for transgender rights. If the algorithm favors content from well-known influencers over grassroots voices, the campaign's message may not reach a broader audience. This disparity can undermine the efforts of lesser-known activists who are crucial to the movement.

Strategies for Navigating Algorithms

To effectively use social media algorithms to drive LGBTQ narratives, activists can employ several strategies:

1. **Creating Shareable Content**: Engaging visuals, compelling stories, and informative infographics can encourage users to share content. For example, a well-designed infographic illustrating the history of LGBTQ rights in Barbados can resonate with users and increase shares.

2. **Utilizing Hashtags**: Hashtags play a crucial role in categorizing content and making it discoverable. Activists should use relevant hashtags, such as

#LGBTQVoices or #TransRightsAreHumanRights, to connect with broader conversations and increase visibility.

3. **Engaging with Followers**: Actively responding to comments and encouraging discussions can boost engagement metrics. For instance, an activist might pose questions related to LGBTQ issues, prompting followers to share their experiences and insights.

4. **Collaborating with Influencers**: Partnering with well-known LGBTQ influencers can amplify messages and reach wider audiences. By leveraging the established follower base of these influencers, activists can ensure that their narratives gain traction.

5. **Monitoring Analytics**: Regularly analyzing engagement metrics can help activists understand what types of content resonate most with their audience. By adjusting strategies based on data, activists can optimize their approach to align with algorithmic preferences.

Examples of Successful Campaigns

Several successful campaigns have effectively harnessed social media algorithms to elevate LGBTQ narratives:

- **#LoveIsLove**: This campaign gained significant traction during the fight for marriage equality. By using a simple yet powerful hashtag, supporters were able to share personal stories and images that resonated with a wide audience, effectively leveraging the algorithm's preference for emotionally charged content.

- **#TransDayOfVisibility**: On this day, activists and allies share stories, resources, and artwork celebrating transgender individuals. The use of this hashtag on platforms like Twitter and Instagram has led to increased visibility for transgender issues, fostering a sense of community and support.

Conclusion

Using social media algorithms to drive LGBTQ narratives is a multifaceted endeavor that requires understanding the mechanics of digital platforms, recognizing the challenges posed by algorithmic biases, and employing strategic approaches to maximize visibility. By leveraging these tools effectively, LGBTQ activists can create impactful narratives that resonate with diverse audiences, fostering greater awareness and support for their causes. As the landscape of social media continues to evolve, ongoing adaptation and innovation will be essential in ensuring that LGBTQ voices are heard and valued in the digital sphere.

Tech Startups as Catalysts for Change

Founding startups to address LGBTQ issues

In the modern landscape of social activism, the intersection of technology and advocacy has birthed a new wave of startups aimed at addressing LGBTQ issues. These startups not only provide innovative solutions but also create platforms for visibility and empowerment within the community. The rise of technology-driven initiatives has been particularly significant in addressing the systemic challenges faced by LGBTQ individuals, especially in regions where societal acceptance remains limited.

Identifying the Problems

The LGBTQ community often faces unique challenges that traditional advocacy methods may not adequately address. These include:

- **Limited Access to Resources:** Many LGBTQ individuals lack access to essential resources such as mental health services, legal assistance, and community support networks.

- **Discrimination in Employment:** LGBTQ individuals frequently encounter discrimination in hiring practices, leading to economic instability.

- **Social Isolation:** Many LGBTQ youth experience feelings of isolation and lack supportive environments, leading to mental health challenges.

- **Misinformation:** There is a significant amount of misinformation regarding LGBTQ rights and health, which can perpetuate stigma and discrimination.

The Startup Solution

Startups focused on LGBTQ issues leverage technology to create impactful solutions. These solutions often revolve around three core areas: community building, resource accessibility, and advocacy.

1. **Community Building** Startups such as *Grindr for Equality* and *HER* have created platforms that foster community among LGBTQ individuals. These applications not only serve as social networking tools but also provide users with access to local events, resources, and support groups. For instance, *HER* has successfully built a safe space for LGBTQ women and non-binary individuals, allowing users to connect, share experiences, and access valuable resources.

2. Resource Accessibility   Another significant area of focus is the development of platforms that provide access to crucial resources. Startups like *The Trevor Project* and *QChat* offer mental health support and crisis intervention specifically tailored to LGBTQ youth. The Trevor Project provides a 24/7 crisis hotline and online chat services, empowering young people to seek help in a safe and confidential environment. Similarly, *QChat* connects LGBTQ youth with trained peer support volunteers, ensuring they have someone to talk to about their experiences.

3. Advocacy and Education   Startups are also playing a pivotal role in advocacy and education. For example, *LGBTQ+ Tech* is a platform that not only advocates for LGBTQ rights in the tech industry but also educates tech professionals about inclusivity and diversity. By fostering dialogue and providing resources, these startups are essential in shaping a more inclusive tech landscape.

Challenges Faced by Startups

Despite the positive impact of these startups, they face several challenges:

- **Funding:** Securing funding can be difficult for LGBTQ-focused startups, especially those in regions with limited support for LGBTQ initiatives.

- **Market Penetration:** Many startups struggle to penetrate markets that are resistant to LGBTQ advocacy, often facing backlash or limited user adoption.

- **Sustainability:** Ensuring long-term sustainability while remaining true to their mission can be a balancing act for many startups.

Successful Examples

Several startups have successfully navigated these challenges and made significant contributions to LGBTQ advocacy:

1. **Glaad Media Institute:** This initiative focuses on promoting LGBTQ representation in media and entertainment, working with various platforms to ensure accurate and positive portrayals of LGBTQ individuals.

2. **Trans Lifeline:** A peer support service for transgender individuals, Trans Lifeline provides vital resources and support, addressing the unique challenges faced by the trans community.

3. **MyGwork:** A global networking platform for LGBTQ professionals, MyGwork connects individuals with job opportunities and offers resources for career development.

These examples illustrate the potential of startups to create meaningful change within the LGBTQ community. By leveraging technology and innovative approaches, they are paving the way for a more inclusive future.

Conclusion

Founding startups to address LGBTQ issues is not merely a business endeavor; it is a commitment to social justice and equality. As technology continues to evolve, so too will the opportunities for LGBTQ advocacy through innovative solutions. The future of LGBTQ rights depends on the ability of these startups to thrive, adapt, and continue to challenge societal norms while providing support and resources to those in need. By fostering an environment of inclusivity and empowerment, these initiatives are not only addressing immediate challenges but also laying the groundwork for lasting change in the global landscape of LGBTQ advocacy.

Connecting entrepreneurs in the fight for equality

In the modern landscape of activism, the intersection of entrepreneurship and LGBTQ advocacy has emerged as a powerful catalyst for change. Entrepreneurs, particularly within marginalized communities, possess a unique ability to innovate solutions that address both social and economic inequalities. The fight for LGBTQ equality is no exception; it requires a multifaceted approach that not only advocates for rights but also empowers individuals through economic opportunities.

The Role of Entrepreneurship in Advocacy

Entrepreneurship can be defined as the process of designing, launching, and running a new business, often characterized by risk-taking and innovation. For LGBTQ individuals, entrepreneurship serves as a means to achieve financial independence, create safe spaces, and foster community. By establishing businesses that prioritize inclusivity and diversity, LGBTQ entrepreneurs can challenge the status quo and promote equality through economic empowerment.

A key theory underpinning this connection is the *Social Entrepreneurial Theory*, which posits that social entrepreneurs leverage business principles to address social issues. This theory emphasizes the importance of sustainability and scalability in social ventures, suggesting that successful business models can lead to lasting social change. By applying this framework, LGBTQ entrepreneurs can create enterprises that not only generate profit but also serve as platforms for advocacy.

Challenges Faced by LGBTQ Entrepreneurs

Despite the potential for entrepreneurship to drive equality, LGBTQ individuals often face significant challenges in the business world. Discrimination, lack of access to funding, and a limited network of support can hinder their entrepreneurial endeavors. According to a report by the *National LGBT Chamber of Commerce*, LGBTQ-owned businesses are less likely to receive funding compared to their heterosexual counterparts, highlighting a systemic barrier that perpetuates inequality.

Moreover, societal stigma can create an environment where LGBTQ entrepreneurs feel unsafe or unsupported in their ventures. This is particularly pronounced in regions with conservative views on sexual orientation and gender identity. The fear of backlash can deter many from pursuing their entrepreneurial aspirations, thus stifling innovation and progress within the community.

Creating Support Networks

To combat these challenges, it is essential to establish robust support networks that connect LGBTQ entrepreneurs with resources, mentorship, and funding opportunities. Organizations such as the *LGBTQ Business Alliance* and the *Out Entrepreneurs Network* play a pivotal role in fostering connections among LGBTQ business owners. These networks provide invaluable resources, including access to capital, business training, and advocacy support.

In addition, initiatives that promote collaboration between LGBTQ entrepreneurs and established businesses can create a ripple effect of support. For instance, corporate partnerships can offer mentorship programs, internships, and sponsorships, enabling LGBTQ entrepreneurs to gain visibility and credibility within the business community. Such collaborations not only benefit individual entrepreneurs but also contribute to a more inclusive business landscape.

Examples of Successful LGBTQ Entrepreneurs

Numerous LGBTQ entrepreneurs have successfully navigated these challenges and made significant contributions to both their communities and the broader society. One notable example is **Donnya Piggott**, whose tech startup focuses on developing digital solutions for marginalized communities. By leveraging technology, Piggott has created platforms that amplify LGBTQ voices and provide resources for advocacy.

Another example is **Jaden Smith**, who has utilized his entrepreneurial endeavors to advocate for environmental sustainability and LGBTQ rights. Through his brand, he promotes inclusivity and awareness, demonstrating how entrepreneurship can serve as a powerful tool for social change.

Innovative Solutions and Future Directions

As we look toward the future, it is imperative to continue fostering connections among LGBTQ entrepreneurs. This can be achieved through:

- **Incubators and Accelerators:** Establishing programs specifically designed for LGBTQ entrepreneurs can provide them with the support needed to launch and grow their businesses. These programs can offer training, mentorship, and access to investors who are committed to supporting LGBTQ initiatives.

- **Crowdfunding Platforms:** Utilizing crowdfunding as a means to raise capital can empower LGBTQ entrepreneurs to bypass traditional funding barriers. Platforms like *Kickstarter* and *Indiegogo* can provide a space for entrepreneurs to present their ideas and garner support from the community.

- **Advocacy for Inclusive Policies:** Lobbying for policies that promote equal access to funding and resources for LGBTQ entrepreneurs is crucial. This includes advocating for non-discrimination laws and initiatives that support minority-owned businesses.

Conclusion

In conclusion, connecting entrepreneurs in the fight for LGBTQ equality is not just a matter of economic empowerment; it is a crucial component of the broader struggle for social justice. By leveraging the power of entrepreneurship, LGBTQ individuals can create sustainable solutions that challenge discrimination and promote inclusivity. As we continue to build networks of support, we pave the way for future generations of LGBTQ entrepreneurs to thrive and lead the charge in the fight for equality.

$$\text{Impact} = \text{Entrepreneurship} + \text{Advocacy} + \text{Community Support} \qquad (29)$$

This equation encapsulates the essence of connecting entrepreneurs in the fight for equality, emphasizing the synergy between business and activism. As we harness this potential, we can create a more equitable future for all.

Creating sustainable solutions through technology

In the realm of LGBTQ advocacy, the integration of technology has proven to be a powerful catalyst for creating sustainable solutions that address the unique challenges faced by marginalized communities. This section explores the theoretical frameworks underpinning these technological solutions, the problems they aim to solve, and real-world examples that illustrate their impact.

Theoretical Frameworks

The development of sustainable technological solutions for LGBTQ advocacy can be understood through several theoretical lenses, including the **Diffusion of Innovations Theory** and the **Social Constructivism Theory**.

Diffusion of Innovations Theory, proposed by Everett Rogers, posits that innovations are communicated through certain channels over time among the members of a social system. This theory emphasizes the importance of social networks in the adoption of new technologies. In the context of LGBTQ advocacy, the diffusion of digital platforms can enhance visibility and foster community support.

On the other hand, **Social Constructivism Theory** suggests that individuals and groups construct their understanding of the world through interactions and experiences. This theory is particularly relevant when considering how technology can create spaces for marginalized voices, allowing LGBTQ individuals to share their stories and experiences, thereby fostering a sense of belonging and community.

Identifying Problems

The LGBTQ community faces numerous systemic challenges, including discrimination, lack of access to resources, and social stigma. These issues are exacerbated in regions with conservative societal norms, where LGBTQ individuals may struggle to find safe spaces for expression and support.

One critical problem is the digital divide, which refers to the gap between those who have easy access to digital technology and those who do not. This divide disproportionately affects marginalized communities, limiting their ability to leverage technology for advocacy and support. According to a report by the

International Telecommunication Union (ITU), approximately 3.7 billion people remain unconnected to the internet, with significant disparities in access based on geography, income, and education levels.

Sustainable Technological Solutions

To address these challenges, several sustainable technological solutions have emerged, demonstrating the potential of technology to create positive change:

- **Digital Platforms for Advocacy:** Online platforms like *Change.org* and *Petition.org* allow individuals to create and sign petitions advocating for LGBTQ rights. These platforms empower users to mobilize support for legislative changes and raise awareness about discrimination.

- **Mobile Applications:** Applications such as *LGBTQ+ Safe Space* provide users with resources, support networks, and information about local LGBTQ-friendly services. These apps help to bridge the gap for individuals seeking safe spaces and community support.

- **E-Learning Initiatives:** Online educational programs, such as those offered by organizations like *Out in Tech*, provide LGBTQ individuals with training in technology and digital skills. This empowerment through education creates pathways for economic independence and advocacy.

- **Crowdsourcing Platforms:** Websites like *GoFundMe* and *Kickstarter* enable LGBTQ activists to fundraise for projects and initiatives that promote equality. By harnessing the power of community support, these platforms facilitate sustainable funding for advocacy efforts.

- **Data Analytics for Advocacy:** Utilizing data analytics can help identify trends and patterns related to LGBTQ issues. Organizations can leverage this data to inform their advocacy strategies and target their efforts more effectively.

Real-World Examples

Several organizations and initiatives exemplify the successful creation of sustainable solutions through technology:

- **The Trevor Project:** This organization offers a 24/7 crisis hotline and digital resources for LGBTQ youth. By integrating technology into their support services, they provide immediate assistance and foster a sense of community among young people facing mental health challenges.

- **GLAAD:** GLAAD utilizes social media and digital campaigns to raise awareness about LGBTQ issues and combat misinformation. Their campaigns, such as #SpiritDay, encourage individuals to take a stand against bullying and support LGBTQ youth.

- **LGBTQ+ Tech:** This initiative connects LGBTQ individuals in the tech industry, creating a network that fosters collaboration and mentorship. By leveraging technology, they promote diversity and inclusion within the tech sector, ultimately leading to innovative solutions for LGBTQ advocacy.

Conclusion

Creating sustainable solutions through technology is essential for advancing LGBTQ advocacy. By leveraging digital platforms, mobile applications, and data analytics, organizations can address systemic challenges and empower marginalized communities. As technology continues to evolve, it holds the potential to transform the landscape of LGBTQ advocacy, fostering a more inclusive and equitable society.

The journey towards equality is ongoing, and the integration of technology will play a crucial role in shaping the future of LGBTQ rights. By embracing innovation and collaboration, advocates can create lasting change that resonates across generations.

Securing funding and resources for LGBTQ-focused startups

In the ever-evolving landscape of technology and social advocacy, securing funding and resources for LGBTQ-focused startups has become a crucial endeavor. The intersection of entrepreneurship and LGBTQ advocacy presents unique challenges and opportunities that require innovative strategies and a deep understanding of the funding ecosystem. This section will explore the theories behind funding acquisition, the problems faced by LGBTQ entrepreneurs, and successful examples of startups that have navigated these challenges.

Theoretical Framework

The funding landscape for startups can be analyzed through various economic theories, including the **Resource-Based View (RBV)** and the **Social Capital**

Theory. The RBV posits that firms can achieve a competitive advantage by leveraging their unique resources, including human capital, social networks, and organizational capabilities. For LGBTQ-focused startups, the unique perspectives and experiences of LGBTQ entrepreneurs can serve as valuable resources that differentiate them in the marketplace.

On the other hand, Social Capital Theory emphasizes the importance of relationships and networks in accessing resources. LGBTQ entrepreneurs often rely on their social capital—connections within the LGBTQ community and allies—to secure funding and mentorship. Therefore, building and nurturing relationships with investors, mentors, and fellow entrepreneurs is essential for success.

Challenges Faced by LGBTQ Entrepreneurs

Despite the potential advantages, LGBTQ entrepreneurs encounter several challenges in securing funding:

- **Bias and Discrimination:** Many LGBTQ entrepreneurs face biases from traditional investors who may not understand the unique value proposition of LGBTQ-focused startups. This discrimination can lead to reduced access to capital.

- **Limited Access to Networks:** LGBTQ entrepreneurs may have less access to traditional funding networks, such as venture capital firms, which often prioritize established industries and mainstream ideas over niche markets.

- **Economic Disparities:** Many LGBTQ individuals experience economic disadvantages due to discrimination in employment and housing, which can limit their ability to invest in their own startups or seek funding from personal networks.

- **Lack of Representation:** The underrepresentation of LGBTQ individuals in the venture capital industry can lead to a lack of understanding and support for LGBTQ-focused initiatives, further complicating funding efforts.

Strategies for Securing Funding

To overcome these challenges, LGBTQ entrepreneurs can employ several strategies:

1. **Leveraging LGBTQ-focused Funds:** There has been a rise in venture capital funds specifically aimed at supporting LGBTQ entrepreneurs, such

as the *LGBTQ+ Venture Fund* and *The Venture Reality Fund*. These funds understand the unique challenges faced by LGBTQ startups and actively seek to invest in them.

2. **Crowdfunding:** Platforms like *Kickstarter* and *Indiegogo* allow LGBTQ entrepreneurs to raise funds directly from the community. This method not only provides capital but also helps in building a customer base and community support.

3. **Networking and Mentorship:** Building relationships within the LGBTQ community and seeking mentorship from experienced entrepreneurs can provide valuable insights and introductions to potential investors. Organizations like *StartOut* offer networking opportunities and resources tailored for LGBTQ entrepreneurs.

4. **Pitch Competitions:** Participating in pitch competitions, especially those focused on diversity and inclusion, can provide funding opportunities and exposure. Competitions like *The Startup Pitch Competition* often feature categories for underrepresented founders, including LGBTQ entrepreneurs.

5. **Collaborating with Nonprofits:** Partnering with LGBTQ-focused nonprofits can open doors to grants and funding opportunities. Nonprofits often have established relationships with funders and can provide support in navigating the funding landscape.

Successful Examples

Several LGBTQ-focused startups have successfully secured funding and resources, serving as inspiring examples for emerging entrepreneurs:

- **Grindr:** The popular dating app for LGBTQ individuals raised $93 million in its initial funding rounds, demonstrating the market potential for LGBTQ-focused technology solutions. Grindr's success has led to increased visibility and interest in LGBTQ startups from investors.

- **Her:** A dating app for LGBTQ women, Her has raised significant funds through crowdfunding and venture capital. By building a strong community and leveraging social media, Her successfully attracted investors who believe in the mission of creating safe spaces for LGBTQ women.

- **LGBTQ+ Tech:** This organization connects LGBTQ entrepreneurs with investors and resources, focusing on fostering innovation and inclusivity in the tech industry. By creating a supportive ecosystem, LGBTQ+ Tech has helped numerous startups secure funding and mentorship.

Conclusion

Securing funding and resources for LGBTQ-focused startups is an essential component of advancing LGBTQ advocacy through technology. By understanding the challenges and leveraging available resources, LGBTQ entrepreneurs can create impactful solutions that not only drive business success but also promote social change. The journey may be fraught with obstacles, but with determination, creativity, and community support, the potential for success is boundless.

Collaborating with established tech companies for social impact

In the rapidly evolving landscape of technology, collaboration between LGBTQ advocates and established tech companies has become a pivotal strategy for driving social impact. This synergy leverages the strengths of both parties: the passion and insight of activists combined with the resources and reach of tech giants.

Theoretical Framework

The collaboration can be understood through the lens of *Social Exchange Theory*, which posits that social behavior is the result of an exchange process aiming to maximize benefits and minimize costs. In this context, LGBTQ activists seek to harness the technological capabilities and platforms of established companies to amplify their message and achieve their goals, while tech companies gain social capital, brand loyalty, and a positive public image through their involvement in social justice initiatives.

Identifying Problems

Despite the potential benefits, several problems can arise in these collaborations:

- **Misalignment of Goals:** Activists may prioritize community needs, while companies might focus on profit margins. This misalignment can lead to tensions and ineffective partnerships.

- **Tokenism:** There is a risk that companies may engage in superficial partnerships, merely to enhance their image without making substantive commitments to LGBTQ rights.
- **Resource Disparities:** Established companies often have significantly more resources than grassroots organizations, which can create power imbalances in collaborations.

Successful Collaborations

Several successful collaborations between LGBTQ activists and tech companies illustrate how these partnerships can effectively address social issues:

1. Google and LGBTQ Advocacy   Google has partnered with various LGBTQ organizations, including the *Human Rights Campaign* (HRC) and *Out & Equal*, to promote workplace equality and support LGBTQ rights globally. Their initiatives include funding for Pride events and creating inclusive workplace policies. An example of their impact is the development of the *Google LGBTQ+ Employee Resource Group*, which fosters a supportive community within the company and advocates for LGBTQ rights externally.

2. Facebook's Support for LGBTQ Content Creators   Facebook has actively collaborated with LGBTQ content creators to amplify their voices on its platform. By providing resources, training, and visibility through initiatives like the *Facebook Creator Program*, the company has empowered LGBTQ individuals to share their stories and experiences, thus fostering greater acceptance and representation within mainstream media.

3. Microsoft's LGBTQ Initiatives   Microsoft's commitment to LGBTQ rights is exemplified by its partnership with organizations like *GLAAD* and *The Trevor Project*. Through these collaborations, Microsoft has developed educational resources aimed at promoting inclusivity and combating discrimination. Their annual *Pride Month* initiatives, which include fundraising and awareness campaigns, showcase how tech companies can leverage their platforms for social good.

Challenges in Collaboration

While the examples above demonstrate the potential for positive outcomes, challenges remain:

- **Sustaining Engagement:** Maintaining long-term partnerships can be difficult, especially when initial enthusiasm wanes. It is essential for both parties to establish clear, ongoing communication and shared objectives.

- **Evaluating Impact:** Measuring the effectiveness of these collaborations can be complex. Companies must develop metrics to assess the social impact of their initiatives and ensure accountability.

- **Navigating Public Perception:** Both activists and companies must be mindful of public perception, as any misstep can lead to backlash. It is crucial to engage in transparent and authentic practices to build trust with the community.

Conclusion

Collaborating with established tech companies offers LGBTQ activists a unique opportunity to amplify their advocacy efforts and create meaningful social change. By aligning goals, ensuring authentic engagement, and addressing challenges, these partnerships can lead to innovative solutions that benefit both the LGBTQ community and the broader society. As the landscape of technology continues to evolve, it is imperative for activists to strategically engage with these corporations to drive progress toward equality and justice.

$$\text{Impact} = \frac{\text{Resources} \times \text{Engagement Level}}{\text{Misalignment of Goals} + \text{Tokenism}} \qquad (30)$$

This equation illustrates that the impact of collaborations can be maximized by increasing resources and engagement while minimizing misalignment and tokenism, ultimately leading to a more equitable society.

Challenging Online Hate and Cyberbullying

Strategies to combat online hate speech

In the digital age, online hate speech poses a significant threat to marginalized communities, particularly within the LGBTQ spectrum. As technology advances, so does the complexity of combating hate speech in virtual spaces. This section outlines effective strategies that can be employed to combat online hate speech, drawing from various theoretical frameworks, practical solutions, and real-world examples.

Understanding Hate Speech

Hate speech is defined as any communication that belittles or discriminates against individuals based on their identity, including race, gender, sexual orientation, and religion. According to the *International Covenant on Civil and Political Rights* (ICCPR), hate speech can incite violence or prejudicial action against individuals or groups. The challenge lies in balancing freedom of expression with the need to protect individuals from harm.

Theoretical Frameworks

To effectively combat hate speech, it is essential to understand the underlying theories that explain its emergence and perpetuation. The *Social Identity Theory* posits that individuals derive a sense of self from their group memberships, leading to in-group favoritism and out-group hostility. This can manifest as hate speech directed at those perceived as different.

Additionally, the *Framing Theory* suggests that the way information is presented influences how individuals interpret and respond to it. By reframing discussions around LGBTQ identities and rights, activists can reduce the prevalence of hate speech and promote understanding.

Strategies for Combating Hate Speech

1. Education and Awareness One of the most powerful tools in combating hate speech is education. Initiatives that promote awareness about the impact of hate speech on individuals and communities can help foster empathy and understanding. For example, campaigns that highlight personal stories of those affected by hate speech can humanize the issue and encourage a more compassionate discourse.

2. Digital Literacy Programs Equipping individuals, particularly youth, with digital literacy skills is crucial. By teaching users how to navigate online spaces safely and responsibly, they can better identify and respond to hate speech. Programs that focus on critical thinking can empower users to question harmful narratives and engage in constructive dialogue.

3. Reporting Mechanisms Social media platforms must establish robust reporting mechanisms that allow users to report hate speech easily. These mechanisms should be user-friendly and ensure that reports are taken seriously.

For instance, platforms like Twitter and Facebook have implemented systems that allow users to flag inappropriate content, leading to swift action against violators.

4. **Collaboration with Tech Companies**   Collaboration between LGBTQ advocacy groups and tech companies is essential in developing effective hate speech policies. By working together, these entities can create algorithms that detect and remove hate speech more efficiently. For example, the partnership between the *Anti-Defamation League* and social media platforms has resulted in improved detection of hate speech through machine learning algorithms.

5. **Legislative Action**   Advocating for legislation that addresses hate speech is a vital strategy. Laws that hold individuals and platforms accountable for perpetuating hate speech can deter such behavior. Countries like Germany have enacted laws requiring social media companies to remove hate speech within 24 hours or face substantial fines.

6. **Community Support and Solidarity**   Building a strong community network can provide support for those targeted by hate speech. Initiatives like *#MeToo* and *#BlackLivesMatter* have shown the power of solidarity in combating hate. By creating safe spaces for dialogue and support, communities can empower individuals to speak out against hate speech.

7. **Counter-Speech Initiatives**   Counter-speech involves responding to hate speech with messages of love, acceptance, and understanding. Campaigns that promote counter-speech, such as *#LoveIsLouder*, encourage individuals to drown out hate with positivity. This approach not only challenges hate speech but also fosters a culture of inclusion.

Real-World Examples

Several organizations and movements have successfully implemented strategies to combat online hate speech. For instance, the *Trevor Project* has launched initiatives that provide resources for LGBTQ youth facing online harassment. Their *Crisis Text Line* offers immediate support to individuals in distress, demonstrating the importance of accessible mental health resources.

Another notable example is the *Cyber Civil Rights Initiative*, which advocates for legislation to combat online harassment and abuse. Their efforts have led to the introduction of laws in various states that specifically address cyberbullying and hate speech.

Conclusion

Combating online hate speech requires a multifaceted approach that combines education, technology, community support, and legislative action. By employing these strategies, we can create a safer and more inclusive online environment for everyone, particularly for marginalized communities that face the brunt of hate speech. The fight against hate speech is ongoing, but with determination and collaboration, we can make significant strides toward a more equitable digital landscape.

Advocating for stronger cyberbullying laws

In an era where digital communication is ubiquitous, the rise of cyberbullying has emerged as a significant concern, particularly within the LGBTQ community. Cyberbullying, defined as the use of electronic communication to bully a person, typically by sending messages of an intimidating or threatening nature, has profound implications for mental health and well-being. As advocates for LGBTQ rights, it is imperative to push for stronger cyberbullying laws that protect vulnerable individuals from harassment and discrimination online.

Theoretical Framework

The theory of social identity provides a foundation for understanding the dynamics of cyberbullying. According to Tajfel and Turner (1979), individuals derive part of their identity from the groups to which they belong. When individuals identify strongly with a group, such as the LGBTQ community, they may become targets of cyberbullying by those who hold prejudiced views. This bullying can lead to a range of negative outcomes, including anxiety, depression, and in extreme cases, suicide.

Problems with Current Legislation

Despite the growing awareness of cyberbullying, many jurisdictions lack comprehensive laws that specifically address online harassment. Current laws often fall short in several key areas:

- **Lack of Definitions:** Many existing laws do not explicitly define cyberbullying, leading to confusion in legal proceedings. This ambiguity can hinder victims from seeking justice.

- **Inadequate Penalties:** Current penalties for cyberbullying may be insufficient to deter offenders. Without strong repercussions, individuals may feel emboldened to engage in harmful behavior.

- **Jurisdictional Challenges:** The global nature of the internet complicates legal enforcement. Cyberbullying can originate from anywhere in the world, making it difficult for local authorities to take action.

Examples of Effective Legislation

Several jurisdictions have taken proactive steps to address cyberbullying through legislation. For instance, in 2010, the state of New Jersey passed the "Anti-Bullying Bill of Rights," which includes provisions specifically addressing cyberbullying in schools. This law requires schools to implement anti-bullying policies and take immediate action when incidents occur. Similarly, the state of California has enacted laws that mandate schools to address cyberbullying and provide resources for victims.

Advocacy Strategies

To advocate for stronger cyberbullying laws, several strategies can be employed:

- **Public Awareness Campaigns:** Raising awareness about the impact of cyberbullying on LGBTQ individuals can mobilize community support for legislative change. Campaigns can utilize social media platforms to share personal stories and statistics that highlight the urgency of the issue.

- **Collaborating with Lawmakers:** Engaging with legislators to draft comprehensive cyberbullying laws that include clear definitions, adequate penalties, and provisions for online harassment is crucial. Advocacy groups can provide data and testimonies to support their case.

- **Building Coalitions:** Forming coalitions with other advocacy organizations can amplify voices and strengthen efforts to push for legislative change. Collaborating with mental health organizations can also highlight the psychological impact of cyberbullying.

Conclusion

Advocating for stronger cyberbullying laws is essential for protecting LGBTQ individuals from online harassment. By addressing the gaps in current legislation and implementing comprehensive laws, we can create safer online environments that promote dignity and respect for all individuals. As we continue to navigate the complexities of digital communication, it is our responsibility as advocates to ensure that the rights of LGBTQ individuals are upheld and that they can thrive without fear of bullying or discrimination in any form.

Supporting victims and fostering online safety

In an increasingly digital world, online safety has become a paramount concern, particularly for marginalized communities such as the LGBTQ population. The anonymity of the internet can provide a refuge for self-expression, but it can also serve as a breeding ground for harassment and discrimination. Supporting victims of online abuse and fostering a safer online environment is essential for promoting mental well-being and encouraging active participation in digital spaces.

Understanding the Problem

The rise of cyberbullying and online hate speech has created significant challenges for LGBTQ individuals. Research indicates that approximately 40% of LGBTQ youth have experienced cyberbullying, leading to severe psychological consequences, including anxiety, depression, and suicidal ideation [?]. The online harassment can manifest in various forms, including:

- **Hate Speech:** Derogatory comments targeting an individual's sexual orientation or gender identity.

- **Doxxing:** The act of publicly revealing personal information about an individual without consent, often leading to real-world harassment.

- **Trolling:** Deliberate provocation and harassment by internet users, often aimed at eliciting emotional responses.

This multifaceted problem necessitates a comprehensive approach to support victims and cultivate a culture of online safety.

Supporting Victims

To effectively support victims of online abuse, it is crucial to implement a multi-tiered strategy that includes education, resources, and community engagement. Some key initiatives include:

1. **Establishing Support Networks:** Creating peer support groups that provide safe spaces for victims to share their experiences, seek advice, and find solidarity. Organizations such as The Trevor Project and PFLAG offer resources and community connections for LGBTQ individuals facing online harassment.

2. **Providing Educational Resources:** Developing educational materials that inform individuals about their rights and available support mechanisms. Workshops on digital literacy can empower victims to recognize and respond to online abuse effectively.

3. **Implementing Reporting Mechanisms:** Encouraging social media platforms to enhance their reporting tools to make it easier for users to report hate speech and harassment. For instance, Twitter has introduced features that allow users to report abusive content, but these systems require continuous improvement to ensure effective action is taken.

Fostering Online Safety

Creating a safer online environment involves collaboration between technology companies, advocacy groups, and users. Several strategies can foster online safety:

1. **Developing AI-Powered Tools:** Leveraging artificial intelligence to detect and mitigate hate speech and harassment. For instance, platforms like Facebook have implemented AI algorithms to identify and remove harmful content proactively. However, these systems must be regularly updated to adapt to evolving language and tactics used by abusers.

2. **Promoting Digital Literacy:** Educating users about online safety practices, such as recognizing phishing attempts, adjusting privacy settings, and understanding the implications of sharing personal information. Research shows that users who are well-informed about digital safety are less likely to become victims of online abuse [?].

3. **Advocating for Stronger Cyberbullying Laws:** Collaborating with policymakers to create and enforce laws that protect individuals from online harassment. Countries like Canada have implemented legislation that addresses cyberbullying, providing a legal framework for victims to seek justice.

Case Studies and Examples

Several organizations and initiatives exemplify effective support for victims and fostering online safety:

- **Cyber Civil Rights Initiative (CCRI):** This organization focuses on combating online harassment and providing resources for victims of revenge porn and cyberbullying. Their work includes legislative advocacy and educational outreach to empower individuals.

- **StopBullying.gov:** A government initiative that provides resources for parents, educators, and youth to address and prevent bullying, including online harassment. Their comprehensive approach includes tips for fostering safe online environments.

- **The LGBTQ Tech and Innovation Summit:** This annual event brings together tech leaders and LGBTQ advocates to discuss challenges and solutions related to online safety. By fostering dialogue and collaboration, the summit aims to create actionable strategies for enhancing digital safety for LGBTQ individuals.

Conclusion

In conclusion, supporting victims of online abuse and fostering online safety is a critical aspect of LGBTQ advocacy in the digital age. By implementing comprehensive support systems, leveraging technology, and promoting digital literacy, we can create a safer online environment where LGBTQ individuals can express themselves freely and authentically. As we navigate the complexities of the digital landscape, it is essential to remain vigilant and proactive in our efforts to combat online hate and discrimination.

Developing AI-powered tools to detect and prevent online abuse

The rise of the digital age has brought with it a plethora of opportunities for communication, connection, and community building, particularly within the LGBTQ community. However, it has also given rise to a significant challenge: online abuse, including harassment, hate speech, and cyberbullying. In response, the development of AI-powered tools to detect and prevent such abuse has emerged as a crucial area of focus for advocates and technologists alike.

Theoretical Framework

At the intersection of artificial intelligence (AI) and social justice, the application of machine learning algorithms plays a pivotal role in identifying patterns of abusive behavior online. The theoretical foundation of these tools often draws upon natural language processing (NLP) and sentiment analysis, which allow computers to analyze and interpret human language. The objective is to create systems that can recognize harmful content and flag it for review or automatically intervene to prevent further abuse.

The theory behind these systems is grounded in the concept of supervised learning, where algorithms are trained on labeled datasets. For example, a dataset might include examples of both abusive and non-abusive comments. By analyzing these examples, the AI can learn to identify characteristics of abusive language. The general equation governing supervised learning can be expressed as:

$$y = f(x) + \epsilon$$

where y is the output (the classification of the text as abusive or not), $f(x)$ is the function learned by the model, and ϵ represents the error term.

Challenges in Detection

Despite the promise of AI in combating online abuse, several challenges persist. One major issue is the nuanced nature of language. Sarcasm, cultural context, and the use of coded language can complicate the detection of harmful content. For instance, a comment that appears benign on the surface may carry harmful implications within certain contexts. This ambiguity can lead to both false positives (innocuous comments flagged as abusive) and false negatives (abusive comments not detected).

Moreover, the dynamic nature of language and the constant evolution of slang and memes present an ongoing challenge for AI systems. As language evolves, so too must the algorithms that detect abuse. Continuous training and updates to the datasets used for machine learning are essential to maintain the effectiveness of these tools.

Examples of AI Tools in Action

Several organizations and tech companies have begun implementing AI-powered tools to address online abuse. One notable example is the use of AI by platforms like Twitter and Facebook to automatically flag potentially abusive content. These platforms utilize machine learning models trained on vast amounts of user-generated data to identify patterns associated with hate speech and harassment.

In a study conducted by the Pew Research Center, it was found that Twitter's AI system was able to identify approximately 38% of abusive tweets before they were reported by users. While this is a significant step forward, it also highlights the need for human oversight, as the remaining 62% of abusive content still requires user intervention or manual reporting.

Another innovative approach is the development of chatbots designed to provide real-time support to users experiencing online abuse. These bots can engage users in conversation, offer resources, and report incidents to moderators. By leveraging AI, these tools can operate 24/7, providing immediate assistance and fostering a safer online environment.

Future Directions

Looking ahead, the development of AI-powered tools to detect and prevent online abuse must prioritize inclusivity and diversity. It is essential to ensure that these systems are trained on datasets that represent a wide range of identities and experiences, particularly those of marginalized communities. This inclusivity will help mitigate biases that can arise in AI systems, ensuring that all users are protected from abuse.

Additionally, collaboration between technologists, mental health professionals, and LGBTQ advocates is vital in creating effective solutions. By working together, stakeholders can develop comprehensive strategies that not only address online abuse but also promote digital literacy and resilience among users.

In conclusion, the development of AI-powered tools to detect and prevent online abuse represents a promising frontier in the fight for LGBTQ rights and safety in digital spaces. While challenges remain, the potential for these technologies to create a more inclusive and supportive online environment is immense. By harnessing the power of AI, advocates can work towards a future where online platforms are free from harassment and discrimination, empowering individuals to express themselves authentically and safely.

Empowering individuals with digital literacy to navigate online spaces

In the digital age, the ability to effectively navigate online spaces is not merely a skill but a necessity. Digital literacy encompasses a wide range of competencies, including the ability to find, evaluate, create, and communicate information using digital technologies. For marginalized communities, particularly within the LGBTQ spectrum, enhancing digital literacy is crucial for advocacy, self-expression, and safety.

The Importance of Digital Literacy

Digital literacy can be defined as the ability to use information and communication technologies to find, evaluate, create, and communicate information. According to [?], digital literacy involves the following key components:

- **Information Literacy:** The ability to recognize when information is needed and to locate, evaluate, and effectively use that information.
- **Communication Literacy:** The ability to communicate effectively using digital tools, including social media, blogs, and websites.
- **Technical Literacy:** The ability to use technology tools and applications proficiently.

These components are essential for LGBTQ individuals who often face unique challenges in accessing information and resources. The lack of digital literacy can lead to misinformation, isolation, and vulnerability to online harassment.

Challenges Faced by LGBTQ Individuals

Despite the potential benefits of digital engagement, LGBTQ individuals often encounter significant barriers:

- **Misinformation and Disinformation:** The prevalence of false information about LGBTQ issues can lead to confusion and reinforce harmful stereotypes. A study by [?] found that 64% of LGBTQ respondents reported encountering misinformation online.
- **Cyberbullying and Harassment:** Online spaces can be hostile environments for LGBTQ individuals. According to [?], 51% of LGBTQ youth reported experiencing bullying or harassment online.
- **Limited Access to Resources:** Many LGBTQ individuals, particularly in conservative regions, may lack access to safe spaces where they can learn about digital tools and resources.

These challenges underscore the necessity of empowering LGBTQ individuals with the skills to navigate online environments safely and effectively.

Strategies for Empowerment

To address these challenges, several strategies can be implemented to enhance digital literacy among LGBTQ individuals:

- **Workshops and Training Programs:** Organizing community-based workshops that focus on digital skills, including internet safety, social media usage, and information evaluation. For example, organizations like *OutRight Action International* have successfully conducted training sessions that empower LGBTQ youth to utilize social media for advocacy and community building.

- **Creating Resource Hubs:** Developing online platforms that serve as resource hubs for LGBTQ individuals. These hubs can provide access to educational materials, support networks, and tools for digital engagement. An example is the *LGBTQ+ Digital Resource Center*, which offers a variety of guides on digital safety, social media use, and online activism.

- **Mentorship Programs:** Establishing mentorship initiatives that connect tech-savvy LGBTQ individuals with those seeking to improve their digital skills. This peer-to-peer approach fosters a sense of community and provides personalized support.

- **Promoting Critical Thinking:** Encouraging individuals to critically evaluate online information sources. This can be achieved through educational campaigns that highlight the importance of cross-referencing information and recognizing credible sources. The *Fact-Checking Network* provides valuable resources for individuals to learn how to discern fact from fiction online.

Real-World Examples

Several organizations and initiatives have successfully empowered LGBTQ individuals through digital literacy:

- **The Trevor Project:** This organization offers crisis intervention and suicide prevention services to LGBTQ youth. They also provide resources on digital safety and mental health, emphasizing the importance of navigating online spaces securely.

- **Human Rights Campaign (HRC):** HRC's *Digital Advocacy Toolkit* includes resources for LGBTQ activists to effectively use social media for change. This toolkit empowers individuals to craft compelling narratives while ensuring their safety online.

- **GLAAD's Media Reference Guide:** This guide not only educates media professionals but also serves as a resource for LGBTQ individuals to understand how to engage with media effectively, ensuring their voices are represented accurately and respectfully.

Conclusion

Empowering LGBTQ individuals with digital literacy is a vital step toward fostering a more inclusive and equitable online environment. By providing the tools and resources necessary to navigate digital spaces, we can help mitigate the risks associated with online engagement and promote a culture of safety, advocacy, and empowerment. As we continue to embrace technology's potential, we must ensure that all individuals, regardless of their background, have the opportunity to thrive in the digital landscape.

Tech Education for All: Closing the Gender Gap

Promoting STEM education for girls and LGBTQ individuals

In recent years, the importance of promoting STEM (Science, Technology, Engineering, and Mathematics) education has gained momentum, particularly for underrepresented groups, including girls and LGBTQ individuals. The underrepresentation of these groups in STEM fields not only perpetuates stereotypes but also limits the diversity of thought and innovation within these critical disciplines. This section explores the barriers faced by girls and LGBTQ individuals in STEM, the theoretical frameworks that support inclusive education, and successful initiatives aimed at promoting STEM education for these communities.

Barriers to Participation

Despite advancements in gender equality and LGBTQ rights, significant barriers remain for girls and LGBTQ individuals in pursuing STEM careers. These barriers can be categorized into social, cultural, and institutional challenges:

- **Social Barriers:** Stereotypes and societal expectations often discourage girls from engaging in STEM activities from a young age. Research indicates that girls are frequently socialized to perceive STEM subjects as male-dominated, leading to a lack of confidence and interest in these fields. Similarly, LGBTQ individuals may face stigma and discrimination, which can deter them from pursuing STEM education.

- **Cultural Barriers:** Cultural norms and biases can create an unwelcoming environment for both girls and LGBTQ individuals in STEM. For instance, the prevalence of gender bias in classroom settings can result in girls receiving less encouragement from teachers, while LGBTQ students may experience bullying or exclusion from their peers.

- **Institutional Barriers:** Educational institutions often lack policies and practices that promote inclusivity. This includes insufficient representation of female and LGBTQ role models in STEM fields, as well as curricula that do not reflect diverse perspectives. Additionally, a lack of support systems, such as mentorship programs, can hinder the success of these students in STEM.

Theoretical Frameworks Supporting Inclusive Education

To address these barriers, several theoretical frameworks can be applied to promote STEM education for girls and LGBTQ individuals:

- **Social Cognitive Theory:** This theory posits that individuals learn and develop behaviors through observation, imitation, and modeling. By providing positive role models in STEM, particularly those who identify as women or LGBTQ, students can envision themselves in these roles, fostering interest and confidence in pursuing STEM education.

- **Critical Pedagogy:** Critical pedagogy emphasizes the need for education to be a vehicle for social justice and empowerment. By integrating critical pedagogy into STEM education, educators can create an inclusive curriculum that challenges stereotypes and encourages diverse perspectives. This approach promotes critical thinking and helps students understand the societal implications of STEM fields.

- **Intersectionality:** Understanding the intersectionality of gender, sexuality, and other identities is crucial in promoting STEM education. Intersectionality recognizes that individuals experience overlapping forms of discrimination and privilege. By acknowledging these complexities, educational programs can be tailored to address the unique challenges faced by girls and LGBTQ individuals in STEM.

Successful Initiatives

Several initiatives have emerged to promote STEM education for girls and LGBTQ individuals, demonstrating effective strategies for increasing participation and success:

- **Girls Who Code:** This organization aims to close the gender gap in technology by providing girls with opportunities to learn coding and computer science. Through after-school clubs, summer immersion programs, and online resources, Girls Who Code empowers girls to pursue careers in tech, fostering a supportive community that celebrates diversity.

- **Out in STEM (oSTEM):** oSTEM is a national organization that supports LGBTQ individuals in STEM fields. It provides networking opportunities, mentorship, and resources to help LGBTQ students navigate their educational and professional journeys. By creating a sense of community, oSTEM helps students find support and encouragement in pursuing their passions.

- **Techbridge Girls:** This organization focuses on empowering girls from low-income communities to pursue STEM careers. Through hands-on projects, mentorship, and exposure to female role models in STEM, Techbridge Girls fosters confidence and interest in STEM subjects, helping to break down the barriers that girls face in these fields.

Conclusion

Promoting STEM education for girls and LGBTQ individuals is essential for fostering a diverse and inclusive workforce that can drive innovation and address societal challenges. By understanding the barriers these groups face, applying theoretical frameworks that support inclusive education, and implementing successful initiatives, we can create an environment where all individuals feel empowered to pursue their interests in STEM. As we continue to advocate for equality in education, it is crucial to recognize that diversity is not just a goal but a necessity for the advancement of science and technology in our society.

$$\text{Diversity} = \text{Representation} + \text{Inclusion} + \text{Equity} \qquad (31)$$

In this equation, diversity is the sum of representation, inclusion, and equity, highlighting the interconnectedness of these elements in creating a truly inclusive STEM environment.

Breaking down gender barriers in the tech industry

The tech industry has long been perceived as a male-dominated arena, characterized by a significant gender gap that hinders the full participation of women and gender minorities. This gap is not merely a statistical anomaly; it reflects deeper systemic issues that perpetuate inequality and limit innovation. In this section, we will explore the challenges faced by women in tech, the importance of breaking down these barriers, and the strategies that can be employed to foster a more inclusive environment.

Understanding the Gender Gap in Tech

The gender gap in technology can be quantified through various metrics, including representation in the workforce, leadership roles, and educational opportunities. According to a report by the National Center for Women & Information Technology (NCWIT), women hold only 26% of computing jobs in the United States, a statistic that has barely changed over the last decade. This underrepresentation is even more pronounced for women of color, who occupy less than 5% of these positions.

The reasons for this disparity are multifaceted and include societal stereotypes, lack of role models, and unconscious bias in hiring practices. Research indicates that women are often discouraged from pursuing careers in STEM (Science, Technology, Engineering, and Mathematics) fields from a young age. For example, a study by the American Association of University Women (AAUW) found that girls are less likely to be encouraged to take advanced math and science courses compared to their male counterparts. This early discouragement can lead to a lack of confidence and interest in tech-related fields.

The Importance of Diversity in Tech

Diversity in the tech industry is not just a moral imperative; it is also a business one. A report by McKinsey & Company highlights that companies with diverse workforces are 35% more likely to outperform their peers in terms of financial returns. Diverse teams bring a variety of perspectives, which can lead to more innovative solutions and products that cater to a broader audience.

Moreover, the technology we create shapes society, and it is crucial that the voices of all demographics are included in the development process. When women and gender minorities are absent from tech, the resulting products may not meet the needs of half the population. For instance, the lack of female representation in software development has been linked to the underrepresentation of women's health issues in health tech applications.

Strategies for Breaking Down Barriers

To dismantle the barriers that women face in the tech industry, a multi-faceted approach is necessary. Here are several strategies that can be implemented:

- **Education and Awareness:** Initiatives aimed at encouraging young girls to pursue STEM education are essential. Programs such as Girls Who Code and Black Girls Code provide mentorship and resources to help girls develop skills and confidence in technology.

- **Inclusive Hiring Practices:** Companies must actively work to eliminate bias in their recruitment processes. This can be achieved through blind recruitment techniques, diverse hiring panels, and the establishment of clear diversity goals.

- **Support Networks:** Creating supportive environments where women can connect, share experiences, and mentor one another is vital. Organizations like Women in Tech and TechWomen provide platforms for networking and professional development.

- **Flexible Work Policies:** Implementing flexible work arrangements can help retain women in the workforce. Policies that support work-life balance, such as remote work options and parental leave, are crucial for accommodating the diverse needs of employees.

- **Leadership Development:** Programs that focus on developing leadership skills among women can help bridge the gap in executive positions. Initiatives like the AnitaB.org's Grace Hopper Celebration of Women in Computing provide visibility and recognition for women leaders in tech.

Case Studies and Success Stories

Several companies and organizations have successfully implemented strategies to break down gender barriers in tech. For example, Salesforce has committed to achieving equal pay for equal work and has invested in training programs aimed at promoting women into leadership roles. Their efforts have resulted in a more equitable workplace and increased representation of women in technical positions.

Another notable example is the tech giant Google, which has launched various initiatives aimed at increasing diversity within its workforce. The company's "Diversity Annual Report" highlights their ongoing commitment to transparency and accountability in addressing gender disparities.

Conclusion

Breaking down gender barriers in the tech industry is a critical step toward achieving equality and fostering innovation. By addressing the systemic issues that contribute to the gender gap, we can create an environment where everyone, regardless of gender, has the opportunity to thrive. The future of technology depends on diverse perspectives, and it is imperative that we continue to advocate for inclusive practices that empower women and gender minorities in this dynamic field.

Through education, policy change, and community support, we can pave the way for a more equitable tech industry that reflects the diversity of society as a whole. The journey is ongoing, but with collective effort and commitment, we can dismantle the barriers that have long hindered progress.

Inspiring the next generation of diverse technologists

In a world where technology shapes our daily lives, the importance of fostering a diverse group of technologists cannot be overstated. As Eliane Morissens advocates for LGBTQ rights, she also recognizes the vital role that diversity plays in the tech industry. This section explores the initiatives and philosophies that can inspire the next generation of diverse technologists, focusing on the intersection of identity, access, and empowerment.

The Importance of Diversity in Technology

Diversity in technology is not merely a matter of representation; it is essential for innovation and problem-solving. Research shows that diverse teams are more creative and better at solving complex problems. According to a study conducted by McKinsey [1], companies in the top quartile for gender diversity on executive teams were 25% more likely to have above-average profitability compared to those in the bottom quartile. This statistic underscores the necessity of inclusivity in tech, particularly for historically marginalized groups, including LGBTQ individuals.

Barriers to Entry

Despite the clear benefits of diversity, many barriers still exist that hinder underrepresented groups from entering the tech field. These barriers can be categorized as:

- **Systemic Barriers:** Institutional biases and discrimination can deter individuals from pursuing careers in technology. For instance, the lack of representation in tech education can discourage LGBTQ youth from envisioning themselves in these roles.

- **Access to Resources:** Many aspiring technologists lack access to crucial resources such as mentorship, networking opportunities, and financial support for education. This is particularly true for LGBTQ youth who may not have supportive environments at home or in their communities.

- **Cultural Barriers:** The tech industry has historically been perceived as a "boys' club," which can alienate women and LGBTQ individuals. The culture of tech workplaces can sometimes perpetuate stereotypes and create environments that are unwelcoming to diverse identities.

Strategies for Inspiration and Empowerment

To inspire the next generation of diverse technologists, several strategies can be implemented:

1. **Mentorship Programs:** Establishing mentorship programs that connect LGBTQ youth with experienced technologists can provide guidance and support. For example, organizations like *Out in Tech* create networking opportunities and mentorship for LGBTQ individuals in the tech industry. This connection can help young people navigate their careers while fostering a sense of belonging.

2. **Inclusive Educational Initiatives:** Schools and educational institutions should implement inclusive curricula that reflect diverse perspectives in

technology. Programs such as *Black Girls Code* and *Girls Who Code* specifically target underrepresented groups, teaching coding and computer science in a supportive environment. By integrating LGBTQ themes into tech education, educators can create a more welcoming atmosphere for all students.

3. **Community Engagement:** Engaging with local communities to promote technology access can break down barriers. Workshops, hackathons, and coding camps can be organized in collaboration with LGBTQ organizations to provide hands-on experience and foster interest in technology careers. For instance, initiatives like *Tech for Good* focus on using technology to address social issues, appealing to socially conscious youth.

4. **Showcasing Diverse Role Models:** Highlighting the achievements of diverse technologists can inspire young people to pursue careers in tech. By sharing stories of successful LGBTQ technologists, such as *Angela Ahrendts* or *Tim Cook*, aspiring technologists can see themselves represented in the industry.

5. **Advocacy for Inclusive Policies:** Advocating for policies that promote diversity and inclusion within tech companies is critical. This includes pushing for equitable hiring practices, diversity training, and inclusive workplace cultures. Organizations like *Lesbians Who Tech* work to amplify the voices of LGBTQ women and non-binary individuals in the tech space, advocating for systemic change.

Conclusion

Inspiring the next generation of diverse technologists is a multifaceted endeavor that requires collective action from individuals, organizations, and educational institutions. By dismantling barriers, providing resources, and fostering inclusive environments, we can empower LGBTQ youth to thrive in the tech industry. Eliane Morissens' vision for a more equitable future is not just about representation; it is about creating a world where every individual can harness the power of technology to express their identity and advocate for their rights.

Bibliography

[1] McKinsey & Company. (2020). *Diversity wins: How inclusion matters.* Retrieved from `https://www.mckinsey.com/business-functions/organization/our-insights/diversity-wins-how-inclusion-matters`

Establishing tech education programs in underserved communities

In the quest for equality, establishing tech education programs in underserved communities is not just an initiative; it is a necessity. The digital divide remains a pressing issue, where access to technology and education is unevenly distributed, leaving marginalized groups at a disadvantage. This section explores the theoretical underpinnings, challenges, and practical examples of implementing tech education programs aimed at empowering these communities.

Theoretical Framework

The foundation of tech education programs can be grounded in several educational theories, including Constructivism and Critical Pedagogy. Constructivism posits that learners construct knowledge through experiences and interactions. In tech education, this means creating hands-on learning environments where students engage with technology in meaningful ways. Critical Pedagogy, on the other hand, emphasizes the role of education in social justice, advocating for curriculum that addresses the lived experiences of marginalized groups.

$$Learning = f(Experience, Interaction, Reflection) \qquad (32)$$

This equation illustrates that learning is a function of experience, interaction, and reflection. In tech education, this can manifest through project-based learning, where students work on real-world problems relevant to their communities, fostering both technical skills and critical thinking.

Identifying Problems

The first step in establishing tech education programs is to identify the specific challenges faced by underserved communities. Some of the prevalent issues include:

- **Lack of Access to Technology:** Many underserved communities lack the necessary hardware and software to engage in tech education. This digital gap inhibits learning and skill development.

- **Limited Internet Connectivity:** Reliable internet access is a cornerstone of tech education. Communities with poor connectivity struggle to access online resources, tutorials, and collaborative platforms.

- **Socioeconomic Barriers:** Economic constraints can prevent individuals from pursuing tech education. Programs must consider the financial implications of materials, transportation, and potential lost income while attending classes.

- **Cultural and Linguistic Differences:** Educational materials may not always reflect the cultural context of underserved communities, leading to disengagement. Additionally, language barriers can impede understanding and participation.

Practical Solutions and Examples

To address these challenges, several successful programs have emerged globally, showcasing innovative approaches to tech education in underserved communities.

1. Community Tech Hubs Community tech hubs serve as local centers for learning, providing access to technology and training. For instance, the **Code for America** initiative partners with local governments to create tech hubs that offer coding boot camps, workshops, and mentorship opportunities. These hubs not only provide resources but also foster a sense of community and collaboration among participants.

2. Mobile Tech Labs Mobile tech labs are an effective solution for reaching remote or underserved areas. Organizations like **Tech on Wheels** deploy mobile units equipped with computers and internet access to deliver tech education directly to communities. This approach allows for flexibility and accessibility, breaking down barriers related to transportation and location.

3. Partnerships with Local Schools Collaborating with local schools can amplify the impact of tech education initiatives. Programs like **Girls Who Code** partner with schools to integrate coding and technology into the curriculum. By training teachers and providing resources, these partnerships ensure sustainability and long-term engagement.

4. Scholarships and Financial Assistance To combat socioeconomic barriers, offering scholarships and financial assistance can make tech education more accessible. Organizations such as **Black Girls Code** provide scholarships for young women of color to attend tech camps and workshops, empowering them to pursue careers in technology.

Measuring Impact

To ensure the effectiveness of tech education programs, it is essential to establish metrics for success. These may include:

- **Enrollment Rates:** Tracking the number of participants in tech education programs can provide insights into community engagement.
- **Skill Development:** Assessing the technical skills acquired by participants through pre- and post-program evaluations can highlight the program's effectiveness.
- **Career Advancement:** Monitoring the career trajectories of program graduates can demonstrate the long-term impact of tech education on socioeconomic mobility.

Conclusion

Establishing tech education programs in underserved communities is a vital step towards closing the digital divide and promoting equality in the tech industry. By leveraging educational theories, addressing specific challenges, and implementing practical solutions, we can empower marginalized individuals with the skills and knowledge needed to thrive in a technology-driven world. The journey may be fraught with obstacles, but the potential for transformation and empowerment is limitless. As we continue to advocate for inclusivity in tech, we must remember that every step taken in education is a step towards a more equitable future.

Advocating for inclusive policies in tech organizations

The tech industry has long been criticized for its lack of diversity and inclusion, particularly concerning gender and LGBTQ representation. Advocating for inclusive policies within tech organizations is not merely an ethical imperative; it is essential for fostering innovation, creativity, and a sense of belonging among employees. This section explores the theoretical frameworks, challenges, and practical examples of advocating for inclusive policies in tech organizations.

Theoretical Frameworks

Inclusive policies in tech organizations can be grounded in several theoretical frameworks, including Social Identity Theory and Intersectionality. Social Identity Theory posits that individuals derive a sense of self from their group memberships, which can influence their interactions and experiences within organizations. When tech companies prioritize inclusivity, they acknowledge and celebrate diverse identities, ultimately fostering a more cohesive workplace culture.

Intersectionality, a term coined by Kimberlé Crenshaw, emphasizes the interconnected nature of social categorizations such as race, gender, and sexual orientation. This framework is crucial in understanding how individuals experience discrimination and privilege simultaneously. By advocating for policies that address these intersecting identities, tech organizations can create environments that support the unique experiences of all employees.

Challenges to Inclusion

Despite the growing recognition of the importance of diversity and inclusion, several challenges persist in tech organizations:

- **Unconscious Bias:** Many hiring managers and decision-makers harbor unconscious biases that can affect their judgment, leading to the perpetuation of homogenous work environments.
- **Tokenism:** Organizations may adopt superficial diversity measures, such as hiring a few LGBTQ employees, without implementing meaningful policies that promote genuine inclusion.

- **Lack of Representation:** The underrepresentation of LGBTQ individuals, particularly those of color and from other marginalized backgrounds, can create an environment where diverse perspectives are not heard or valued.

- **Resistance to Change:** Established organizational cultures can be resistant to change, making it difficult to implement new inclusive policies that challenge the status quo.

Strategies for Advocacy

To effectively advocate for inclusive policies in tech organizations, several strategies can be employed:

1. **Data-Driven Approaches:** Organizations should collect and analyze data on employee demographics, experiences, and satisfaction levels. This data can help identify gaps in representation and inform policy changes. For example, Google has published its diversity reports, providing transparency and accountability in its efforts to improve inclusivity.

2. **Comprehensive Training Programs:** Implementing training programs that address unconscious bias, allyship, and intersectionality can help employees understand the importance of inclusivity. Companies like Salesforce have developed extensive training initiatives aimed at fostering a culture of inclusion and respect.

3. **Employee Resource Groups (ERGs):** Establishing ERGs allows employees to connect with others who share similar identities and experiences. These groups can serve as a platform for advocacy, providing feedback to leadership on policies and initiatives. For instance, Microsoft has a robust network of ERGs that support LGBTQ employees and their allies.

4. **Inclusive Hiring Practices:** Tech organizations should adopt inclusive hiring practices that prioritize diverse candidate pools. This can include using blind recruitment techniques and ensuring diverse interview panels. Companies like LinkedIn have implemented such practices to mitigate biases in their hiring processes.

5. **Leadership Commitment:** Advocacy for inclusive policies must be championed by leadership. When executives prioritize diversity and inclusion, it sets a tone for the entire organization. For example, IBM's commitment to LGBTQ inclusion is reflected in its policies and practices, driven by leadership at all levels.

Examples of Successful Advocacy

Several tech organizations have successfully implemented inclusive policies that serve as models for others:

- **Salesforce:** The company has committed to equal pay for all employees and actively works to ensure diverse representation in its workforce. Salesforce's efforts include regular pay audits and a focus on recruiting from diverse talent pools.

- **Apple:** Apple has established comprehensive policies to support LGBTQ employees, including benefits for same-sex partners and a commitment to non-discrimination. The company's public stance on LGBTQ rights has also influenced its corporate culture and brand identity.

- **Facebook:** Facebook's initiatives include the creation of the LGBTQ@Facebook group, which fosters community among LGBTQ employees and advocates for policies that support inclusion. The company also actively participates in Pride events and supports LGBTQ advocacy organizations.

Conclusion

Advocating for inclusive policies in tech organizations is essential for creating environments where all employees feel valued and empowered. By addressing the theoretical underpinnings, challenges, and successful strategies for advocacy, tech organizations can pave the way for a more inclusive future. The commitment to inclusivity not only enhances employee satisfaction and retention but also drives innovation and creativity, ultimately benefiting the organization as a whole. As tech continues to shape the future, it is imperative that inclusivity remains at the forefront of its evolution.

Breaking Boundaries and Going Global

Breaking Boundaries and Going Global

Breaking Boundaries and Going Global

In an increasingly interconnected world, the fight for LGBTQ rights transcends borders, cultures, and ideologies. Eliane Morissens stands as a testament to the power of global advocacy, breaking boundaries and amplifying voices that have long been silenced. This chapter explores how Morissens leveraged her platform to represent the LGBTQ community on the international stage, forging alliances and building networks that extend beyond her native Belgium.

Representing the LGBTQ Community on the International Platform

Morissens recognized early on that the struggle for LGBTQ rights was not confined to her local community. The issues faced by LGBTQ individuals in Barbados, Belgium, and beyond share common threads of discrimination, stigma, and violence. By participating in international conferences, forums, and summits, she positioned herself as a global advocate, representing not just her own experiences, but those of countless others who faced similar challenges.

One pivotal moment in her advocacy journey occurred at the United Nations Human Rights Council in Geneva. Here, she presented a compelling argument for the recognition of LGBTQ rights as human rights, drawing on her personal narrative and the stories of those she had met along the way. Morissens stated, "To deny one group their rights is to deny all of us our humanity." This powerful declaration resonated with many, underscoring the interconnectedness of human rights struggles.

Building Global Networks and Alliances

The strength of Morissens' advocacy lies in her ability to build coalitions across diverse communities. She understood that to effect change, it was essential to unite different voices under a common cause. By collaborating with organizations such as ILGA (International Lesbian, Gay, Bisexual, Trans and Intersex Association) and OutRight Action International, Morissens was able to amplify her message and reach a broader audience.

For example, during the Global LGBTQI+ Conference in 2021, Morissens facilitated a panel discussion that brought together activists from Africa, Asia, and Europe. This gathering not only highlighted the unique challenges faced by LGBTQ individuals in different regions but also fostered a spirit of solidarity and shared purpose. The panel concluded with a collective call to action, urging attendees to advocate for policy changes in their respective countries.

Advocating for LGBTQ Rights on a Global Scale

Morissens' advocacy extended beyond mere representation; she actively sought to influence policy and legislation on a global scale. She recognized that systemic change requires not only grassroots activism but also engagement with governmental and intergovernmental bodies. Her efforts to lobby for the inclusion of LGBTQ rights in international human rights treaties exemplify this approach.

A notable example of her impact was her involvement in the drafting of the Yogyakarta Principles Plus 10, a set of international principles that affirm the application of international human rights law in relation to sexual orientation and gender identity. By contributing her insights and experiences, Morissens helped shape a document that would serve as a foundational reference for advocates worldwide.

Collaborating with International Organizations for Global LGBTQ Initiatives

Collaboration with international organizations has been a cornerstone of Morissens' strategy. By aligning with entities such as the United Nations and the World Health Organization, she has worked to ensure that LGBTQ rights are prioritized in global health and human rights agendas. Her advocacy has played a crucial role in addressing issues such as mental health disparities, access to healthcare, and the need for comprehensive anti-discrimination policies.

One of the most significant initiatives she was involved in was the "Global Health for LGBTQ+ Communities" project, which aimed to address the unique health needs of LGBTQ individuals across different regions. This initiative not only provided essential resources but also facilitated training programs for healthcare providers to ensure culturally competent care for LGBTQ patients.

Becoming a Renowned Thought Leader in the Global LGBTQ Movement

Through her tireless efforts and unwavering commitment to LGBTQ rights, Morissens has emerged as a thought leader in the global movement. Her ability to articulate the complexities of intersectional identities and the nuances of LGBTQ advocacy has garnered her recognition and respect from peers and policymakers alike.

Her work has been featured in various international media outlets, allowing her to reach a wider audience and inspire others to take action. By sharing her story and the stories of those she represents, Morissens has not only raised awareness but has also encouraged individuals to engage in advocacy within their own communities.

In conclusion, Eliane Morissens exemplifies the power of breaking boundaries and going global in the fight for LGBTQ rights. Her journey underscores the importance of representation, collaboration, and advocacy on an international scale. As she continues to forge new paths and inspire others, Morissens remains a beacon of hope and resilience for LGBTQ individuals around the world.

From Barbados to the World Stage

Representing the LGBTQ community on the international platform

Eliane Morissens has emerged as a powerful voice representing the LGBTQ community on the international stage. Her journey from the vibrant streets of Bridgetown to global advocacy exemplifies the importance of visibility and representation in the fight for LGBTQ rights. This section explores the multifaceted ways in which Morissens has championed the cause of LGBTQ individuals worldwide, shedding light on the challenges faced and the strategies employed to elevate LGBTQ issues to a global audience.

The Importance of Representation

Representation matters. It is not merely a buzzword; it is a crucial element in the quest for equality. As noted by [1], the concept of intersectionality underscores how various social identities overlap, creating unique experiences of oppression and privilege. Morissens embodies this intersectionality, navigating her identity as a Black LGBTQ woman within a global landscape that often marginalizes such voices.

The lack of representation in international forums can lead to a skewed understanding of LGBTQ issues, often sidelining the experiences of those from diverse backgrounds. For instance, the Global Fund for Women reports that women and LGBTQ individuals from marginalized communities face compounded discrimination that is often overlooked in mainstream advocacy efforts [2]. Morissens's presence on international platforms helps to challenge these narratives, ensuring that the voices of the most vulnerable are heard.

Advocacy at International Conferences

Morissens has actively participated in numerous international conferences, such as the United Nations Human Rights Council sessions and the International LGBTQI+ Youth Conference. At these events, she has utilized her platform to address critical issues affecting the LGBTQ community globally, including violence, discrimination, and the need for comprehensive legal protections.

For example, during the 2021 United Nations Human Rights Council session, Morissens delivered a powerful speech highlighting the alarming rates of violence against LGBTQ individuals in various countries. She cited statistics from the International Lesbian, Gay, Bisexual, Trans and Intersex Association (ILGA) indicating that more than 70 countries still criminalize same-sex relationships, leading to widespread human rights abuses [3]. Her eloquence and passion resonated with attendees, prompting discussions on the necessity of international pressure to reform discriminatory laws.

Building Global Networks and Alliances

One of Morissens's key strategies in advocating for LGBTQ rights on the international stage has been her ability to build coalitions and alliances. Recognizing that systemic change requires a united front, she has collaborated with various organizations, including Human Rights Watch and OutRight Action International. These partnerships have allowed her to amplify her message and extend the reach of LGBTQ advocacy efforts.

A notable example of this collaboration was the formation of the Global LGBTQ Coalition, which aims to unify diverse LGBTQ organizations worldwide. This coalition has successfully launched campaigns addressing urgent issues such as the rights of LGBTQ refugees and asylum seekers, who often face persecution in their home countries. By leveraging the strengths of different organizations, Morissens has helped to create a more cohesive and impactful movement.

Utilizing Media and Technology

In today's digital age, media and technology play a pivotal role in shaping public discourse. Morissens has adeptly harnessed these tools to bring attention to LGBTQ issues on the international platform. Through social media campaigns, she has engaged a global audience, fostering dialogue and raising awareness about the challenges faced by LGBTQ individuals.

For instance, her #VoicesOfLGBTQ campaign on platforms like Twitter and Instagram has garnered significant traction, featuring personal stories from LGBTQ individuals around the world. This initiative not only humanizes the statistics but also creates a sense of solidarity among individuals from diverse backgrounds. By sharing these narratives, Morissens has successfully highlighted the universal struggle for LGBTQ rights while respecting the unique cultural contexts of different regions.

Challenges and Resilience

Despite her successes, Morissens has faced numerous challenges in her quest to represent the LGBTQ community on the international stage. The backlash from conservative groups and governments resistant to LGBTQ rights has been significant. For example, during her participation in the 2022 World Pride event in Sydney, she encountered protests from anti-LGBTQ factions attempting to undermine the event's message of inclusivity [4].

However, Morissens's resilience shines through in the face of adversity. She has often stated, "The road to equality is paved with challenges, but it is our duty to walk it with courage." This mindset not only inspires her but also galvanizes others in the LGBTQ community to continue fighting for their rights, regardless of the obstacles they may face.

Conclusion

Eliane Morissens's representation of the LGBTQ community on the international platform is a testament to the power of advocacy, collaboration, and resilience. By addressing critical issues, building alliances, and utilizing modern technology, she has become a beacon of hope for many. As the global landscape for LGBTQ rights continues to evolve, Morissens's work will undoubtedly leave a lasting impact, inspiring future generations to stand up and advocate for equality and justice.

Bibliography

[1] Crenshaw, K. (1991). Mapping the Margins: Intersectionality, Identity Politics, and Violence against Women of Color. *Stanford Law Review*, 43(6), 1241-1299.

[2] Global Fund for Women. (2019). *The State of Women's Rights in the World*. Retrieved from https://www.globalfundforwomen.org

[3] International Lesbian, Gay, Bisexual, Trans and Intersex Association. (2021). *State-Sponsored Homophobia Report*. Retrieved from https://ilga.org/state-sponsored-homophobia-report

[4] Sydney Pride. (2022). *World Pride 2022: A Celebration of Diversity and Inclusion*. Retrieved from https://www.sydneypride.com

Building global networks and alliances

In the landscape of LGBTQ activism, the importance of building global networks and alliances cannot be overstated. As Eliane Morissens stepped onto the international stage, she recognized that the fight for LGBTQ rights transcended borders, cultures, and political ideologies. By forging connections with activists, organizations, and allies worldwide, she aimed to create a unified front against discrimination and inequality.

Theoretical Framework

The theoretical underpinning of global networking in activism can be traced to social capital theory, which posits that the resources available to individuals and groups through their social networks can significantly enhance their capacity for action. According to Bourdieu (1986), social capital consists of the networks of relationships among people who live and work in a particular society, enabling that society to function effectively. In the context of LGBTQ advocacy, these networks facilitate the sharing of information, resources, and strategies, which are crucial for effecting change.

$$\text{Social Capital} = \text{Networks} + \text{Trust} + \text{Reciprocity} \qquad (33)$$

This equation highlights the components that contribute to social capital, emphasizing that building trust and fostering reciprocal relationships are essential for effective collaboration.

Challenges in Building Alliances

Despite the theoretical advantages of global networking, numerous challenges hinder the establishment of effective alliances. These challenges include:

- **Cultural Differences**: Variations in cultural norms and values can complicate collaboration. For instance, certain approaches to LGBTQ rights that are effective in Western nations may not resonate in regions where cultural conservatism prevails.

- **Political Barriers**: In many countries, LGBTQ rights are met with hostility from governments. Activists face legal repercussions for their advocacy, making it difficult to form alliances. For example, in regions where homosexuality is criminalized, activists must navigate a treacherous landscape to connect with potential allies.

- **Resource Disparities**: There is often a significant disparity in resources between LGBTQ organizations in the Global North and those in the Global South. This inequality can lead to power imbalances within alliances, where voices from marginalized regions are overshadowed by those from more privileged contexts.

Strategies for Effective Networking

To overcome these challenges, Eliane Morissens employed several strategies to build effective global networks:

1. **Creating Inclusive Platforms**: By leveraging technology, Morissens established digital platforms that allowed activists from diverse backgrounds to share their experiences and strategies. Online forums, webinars, and social media campaigns became vital tools for fostering connections and disseminating information.

2. **Participatory Approaches**: Morissens emphasized the importance of inclusive decision-making processes within alliances. By ensuring that all voices were heard, particularly those from marginalized communities, she cultivated a sense of ownership and commitment among activists.

3. **Cross-Cultural Training**: Understanding cultural sensitivities was paramount. Morissens organized workshops that provided activists with the skills to navigate cultural differences effectively, promoting empathy and understanding among diverse groups.

4. **Resource Sharing Initiatives**: To address disparities in resources, Morissens initiated programs that facilitated the sharing of tools, funding, and knowledge between organizations. This collaborative approach empowered smaller organizations in the Global South to access the resources they needed to advance their advocacy efforts.

Examples of Successful Alliances

One of the most notable examples of successful global networking in LGBTQ advocacy is the formation of the International Lesbian, Gay, Bisexual, Trans and Intersex Association (ILGA). Founded in 1978, ILGA has grown to include over 1,600 member organizations from more than 150 countries, providing a platform for LGBTQ activists to collaborate and share resources.

Another significant initiative is the Global Equality Fund, which supports LGBTQ rights organizations worldwide through grants and capacity-building programs. This fund exemplifies how strategic alliances can mobilize resources and amplify the voices of marginalized communities.

Conclusion

Building global networks and alliances is a cornerstone of effective LGBTQ advocacy. Through the strategic efforts of activists like Eliane Morissens, the movement has gained momentum, fostering solidarity and collaboration across borders. As challenges persist, the commitment to forging connections remains vital, ensuring that the fight for equality continues to resonate on a global scale. By harnessing the power of social capital and addressing the complexities of cultural and political landscapes, activists can create a more inclusive and equitable world for all.

Advocating for LGBTQ rights on a global scale

The advocacy for LGBTQ rights on a global scale represents a complex interplay of cultural, political, and social dynamics. In this section, we will explore the various strategies employed by activists, the challenges they face, and the theoretical frameworks that underpin their efforts.

Theoretical Frameworks

The advocacy for LGBTQ rights can be understood through several theoretical lenses. One prominent framework is the **Intersectionality Theory**, which posits that individuals experience multiple, overlapping identities that can lead to unique experiences of oppression or privilege. For LGBTQ individuals, these identities may include race, gender, socioeconomic status, and nationality. This theory emphasizes the need for a nuanced understanding of how various forms of discrimination intersect, thus informing a more comprehensive approach to advocacy.

Another relevant framework is the **Human Rights-Based Approach**, which asserts that LGBTQ rights are fundamental human rights. This perspective aligns with international human rights instruments, such as the Universal Declaration of Human Rights (UDHR), which states that "all human beings are born free and equal in dignity and rights." Advocates leverage this framework to argue that denying LGBTQ individuals their rights is not only a moral failing but also a violation of international law.

Strategies for Global Advocacy

Activists employ a variety of strategies to promote LGBTQ rights on an international scale:

- **Coalition Building:** Forming alliances with local, national, and international organizations enhances the visibility and impact of LGBTQ advocacy. For instance, organizations like ILGA (International Lesbian, Gay, Bisexual, Trans and Intersex Association) work to unite LGBTQ groups worldwide, facilitating knowledge sharing and joint campaigns.

- **Awareness Campaigns:** Global awareness campaigns, such as the *International Day Against Homophobia, Transphobia, and Biphobia*, serve to educate the public and mobilize support. These campaigns often utilize social media to reach a broader audience, employing hashtags like

#IDAHOTB to create viral movements that draw attention to LGBTQ issues.

- **Policy Advocacy:** Engaging with policymakers at national and international levels is crucial. Activists advocate for the incorporation of LGBTQ rights into broader human rights agendas, pushing for legislation that protects against discrimination and violence. For example, the Yogyakarta Principles, which outline how international human rights law should apply to sexual orientation and gender identity, serve as a guiding document for advocates worldwide.

- **Grassroots Mobilization:** Grassroots movements play a vital role in advocating for change. Local activists often have a deeper understanding of cultural contexts and can mobilize communities effectively. The *Black Lives Matter* movement, while primarily focused on racial justice, has also highlighted issues of LGBTQ rights, particularly within communities of color, demonstrating the interconnectedness of various social justice movements.

Challenges Faced in Global Advocacy

Despite the progress made, LGBTQ advocates encounter significant challenges:

- **Cultural Resistance:** In many regions, cultural norms and religious beliefs strongly oppose LGBTQ rights. Activists often face backlash from conservative groups, which can manifest in violence and discrimination. For instance, in several African countries, laws criminalizing homosexuality are justified by cultural and religious arguments, making advocacy efforts perilous.

- **Political Repression:** In authoritarian regimes, LGBTQ activism is often met with severe repression. Governments may enact laws that not only criminalize LGBTQ identities but also target activists. The case of Russia's "gay propaganda" law exemplifies how political structures can hinder advocacy efforts, leading to increased violence and discrimination against LGBTQ individuals.

- **Resource Limitations:** Many LGBTQ organizations operate with limited funding and resources, which constrains their ability to implement comprehensive advocacy programs. The reliance on international funding can also create dependency, making it difficult for local organizations to sustain their efforts independently.

- **Health Crises:** The ongoing global health crises, such as the COVID-19 pandemic, have disproportionately affected LGBTQ communities, exacerbating existing inequalities. Access to healthcare, mental health services, and social support systems has been severely disrupted, highlighting the urgent need for targeted advocacy in times of crisis.

Examples of Successful Global Advocacy

Several successful advocacy initiatives illustrate the potential for positive change on a global scale:

- **The Marriage Equality Movement:** The global push for marriage equality has seen significant victories in various countries, including the landmark decision by the U.S. Supreme Court in *Obergefell v. Hodges* (2015), which legalized same-sex marriage nationwide. This decision has inspired similar movements in countries like Taiwan, which became the first Asian nation to legalize same-sex marriage in 2019.

- **The Global Fund for Women:** This organization supports initiatives that promote gender equality and LGBTQ rights worldwide. By funding grassroots projects, they empower local activists and create sustainable change within communities.

- **The UN Free & Equal Campaign:** Launched by the United Nations, this campaign aims to promote equal rights and fair treatment for LGBTQ individuals globally. Through education and awareness-raising initiatives, the campaign seeks to combat discrimination and foster acceptance.

Conclusion

Advocating for LGBTQ rights on a global scale requires a multifaceted approach that considers the unique cultural, political, and social contexts of different regions. By employing intersectional and human rights-based frameworks, activists can navigate the complexities of advocacy, build coalitions, and address the challenges they face. The examples of successful initiatives serve as a testament to the power of collective action and the resilience of the LGBTQ movement worldwide. As we look to the future, continued collaboration and innovative strategies will be essential in the ongoing fight for equality and justice for all LGBTQ individuals.

Collaborating with international organizations for global LGBTQ initiatives

The collaboration between grassroots activists and international organizations is crucial in advancing LGBTQ rights globally. This partnership not only amplifies local voices but also provides essential resources and visibility to marginalized communities. Eliane Morissens recognized early on that to effect meaningful change, it was imperative to forge alliances with established international entities that had the capacity and influence to drive policy reform and social acceptance on a global scale.

Theoretical Framework

The collaboration can be understood through the lens of the *Social Movement Theory*, which posits that collective action is necessary for social change. This theory emphasizes the importance of networks and alliances, suggesting that movements are more successful when they engage with external organizations that can provide legitimacy, resources, and a broader platform for advocacy.

Moreover, the *Intersectionality Theory* highlights the importance of recognizing the diverse identities within the LGBTQ community, including race, gender, and socioeconomic status. Collaborating with international organizations allows activists to address these intersecting issues on a global scale, ensuring that advocacy efforts are inclusive and representative of all marginalized voices.

Challenges in Collaboration

Despite the potential benefits, collaboration with international organizations is not without its challenges. One significant issue is the potential for *neocolonialism*, where Western organizations impose their values and agendas on local communities without fully understanding their unique contexts. This can lead to a disconnect between the needs of local activists and the priorities of international bodies.

Additionally, there is the challenge of *resource allocation*. International organizations often have limited funding and may prioritize initiatives based on their own strategic goals rather than the immediate needs of local LGBTQ communities. This can result in a mismatch between available resources and the actual demands of advocacy work on the ground.

Successful Collaborations: Case Studies

Eliane Morissens' efforts to collaborate with international organizations have yielded notable successes. One such example is her partnership with *ILGA World* (International Lesbian, Gay, Bisexual, Trans and Intersex Association), which has a long-standing history of advocating for LGBTQ rights globally. Through this collaboration, Morissens was able to participate in international forums, bringing attention to the specific challenges faced by LGBTQ individuals in Barbados and beyond.

Another successful initiative involved working with *Human Rights Campaign* (HRC) to develop a comprehensive report on LGBTQ rights in the Caribbean. This report not only highlighted the systemic discrimination faced by LGBTQ individuals but also provided recommendations for policy reform, which were presented to regional governments during advocacy sessions. The collaboration with HRC exemplifies how international organizations can bolster local advocacy efforts by providing research, policy analysis, and a platform for dialogue.

Global Initiatives and Their Impact

Collaborations often manifest in global initiatives that aim to create systemic change. For instance, the *UN Free & Equal* campaign, launched by the United Nations, seeks to promote equal rights and fair treatment of LGBTQ individuals worldwide. Morissens played a pivotal role in localizing this campaign in Barbados, organizing workshops and community discussions that engaged both LGBTQ individuals and allies in the fight for equality.

Moreover, partnerships with organizations like *OutRight Action International* have led to the establishment of training programs aimed at empowering LGBTQ activists across the Caribbean. These programs focus on capacity building, providing activists with the skills necessary to effectively advocate for their rights within their own communities and on the international stage.

Conclusion

The collaboration between local activists like Eliane Morissens and international organizations is essential for the advancement of LGBTQ rights worldwide. By leveraging the resources, networks, and platforms offered by these organizations, activists can amplify their voices, address systemic issues, and foster a more inclusive society. However, it is crucial to approach these collaborations with a critical lens, ensuring that the needs and perspectives of local communities are prioritized. As the landscape of LGBTQ advocacy continues to evolve, these partnerships will remain vital in the ongoing struggle for equality and justice on a global scale.

$$\text{Impact} = \frac{\text{Resources} \times \text{Visibility}}{\text{Local Needs}} \quad (34)$$

This equation illustrates the delicate balance that must be maintained in collaborations: maximizing impact requires a careful alignment of resources and visibility with the genuine needs of local LGBTQ communities.

Becoming a renowned thought leader in the global LGBTQ movement

In the landscape of LGBTQ activism, becoming a thought leader transcends mere visibility; it embodies the fusion of knowledge, experience, and the ability to inspire change on a global scale. Eliane Morissens exemplifies this journey, emerging from her roots in Bridgetown to become a pivotal figure in the international LGBTQ rights movement. This transformation is not merely a personal achievement but a collective journey that reflects the evolving dynamics of global activism.

Theoretical Framework

To understand the emergence of thought leaders like Morissens, we can draw upon the *Social Movement Theory*, particularly the concepts of *framing* and *collective identity*. Framing refers to the way in which activists construct narratives that resonate with broader audiences, thereby mobilizing support and fostering solidarity. Collective identity, on the other hand, emphasizes the shared experiences and struggles within the LGBTQ community, allowing individuals to connect their personal journeys to a larger movement.

Navigating Challenges

Becoming a thought leader is fraught with challenges. Morissens faced significant hurdles, including societal stigma, institutional discrimination, and the complexities of intersectional identities. For instance, in her efforts to address systemic homophobia in Barbados, she encountered pushback not only from conservative factions but also from within the LGBTQ community itself, where differing opinions on activism and representation often led to fragmentation.

To navigate these challenges, Morissens employed a strategy of *inclusive dialogue*, fostering conversations that brought together diverse voices within the LGBTQ spectrum. This approach is rooted in the theory of *Deliberative*

Democracy, which posits that open, inclusive dialogue can lead to more equitable outcomes. By creating spaces for discussion, she empowered individuals to share their experiences, thus enriching the collective narrative of the movement.

Global Networks and Alliances

A key aspect of Morissens' rise as a thought leader was her ability to build global networks and alliances. This involved collaborating with international organizations such as ILGA (International Lesbian, Gay, Bisexual, Trans and Intersex Association) and engaging in global forums that addressed LGBTQ rights. The formation of these alliances is vital, as they provide a platform for sharing resources, strategies, and best practices across borders.

For example, during the 2021 UN Human Rights Council session, Morissens presented a joint statement advocating for the inclusion of LGBTQ rights in global human rights frameworks. This moment not only showcased her leadership but also highlighted the importance of international solidarity in the fight for equality. Such engagements illustrate the concept of *Global Citizenship*, where individuals recognize their interconnectedness and advocate for justice beyond their national boundaries.

Innovative Advocacy Strategies

Morissens' thought leadership is also characterized by her innovative use of technology in advocacy. Recognizing the potential of digital platforms, she spearheaded initiatives that leveraged social media to amplify LGBTQ voices. This aligns with the theory of *Digital Activism*, which posits that online platforms can facilitate grassroots mobilization and raise awareness on critical issues.

One notable example is the #LGBTQVoices campaign, which Morissens launched to highlight personal stories from LGBTQ individuals around the world. By utilizing platforms like Twitter and Instagram, she created a viral movement that not only increased visibility but also fostered a sense of community among participants. This campaign exemplifies how digital tools can be harnessed to effect change, particularly in regions where traditional forms of activism may be met with resistance.

Impact on Policy and Practice

The influence of a thought leader extends into policy and practice. Morissens' advocacy has led to tangible changes in legislation and societal attitudes towards LGBTQ individuals. For instance, her collaboration with local governments in

Barbados resulted in the introduction of policies aimed at protecting LGBTQ rights, showcasing the practical implications of her thought leadership.

Moreover, Morissens has emphasized the importance of intersectionality in policy formulation. By advocating for inclusive policies that consider race, gender, and socioeconomic status, she has challenged policymakers to adopt a more holistic approach to LGBTQ rights. This perspective is supported by the *Intersectionality Theory*, which posits that individuals experience oppression in varying degrees based on their intersecting identities.

Legacy and Future Directions

As Morissens continues to evolve as a thought leader, her legacy is already shaping the future of LGBTQ activism. By mentoring emerging activists and sharing her insights through public speaking engagements, she is cultivating the next generation of leaders equipped to navigate the complexities of global advocacy.

In conclusion, the journey to becoming a renowned thought leader in the global LGBTQ movement is multifaceted, involving the integration of theory, the navigation of challenges, the building of networks, and the implementation of innovative strategies. Eliane Morissens stands as a testament to the power of resilience and vision, inspiring countless individuals to join the fight for equality and justice. Her story is not just one of personal triumph but a clarion call for collective action and solidarity in the ongoing struggle for LGBTQ rights worldwide.

Facing Controversy and Resilience

Navigating backlash and public scrutiny

Navigating backlash and public scrutiny is an inevitable part of being an outspoken advocate for LGBTQ rights, especially for individuals like Eliane Morissens, who have positioned themselves at the intersection of technology and activism. The journey of advocacy can often lead to fierce opposition, and understanding how to manage this backlash is crucial for sustaining momentum in the fight for equality.

Understanding Backlash

Backlash can be defined as a strong adverse reaction to a social movement or change. In the context of LGBTQ activism, backlash often manifests through public criticism, social media trolling, and even legislative pushback against progressive policies. According to [?], backlash is not merely a response to the actions of activists but is often rooted in deeper societal tensions regarding identity, power, and the status quo.

Theories of backlash suggest that as movements gain visibility and momentum, they also provoke counter-movements that seek to reinforce traditional norms and values. This phenomenon can be observed in various historical contexts, such as the backlash against the civil rights movement in the United States during the 1960s and 1970s, where increased visibility led to intensified resistance from conservative factions.

The Nature of Public Scrutiny

Public scrutiny can take many forms, from media portrayals that misrepresent or sensationalize LGBTQ issues to personal attacks on social media platforms. The digital age has amplified this scrutiny, making it easier for detractors to voice their opinions widely and rapidly. [?] notes that social media serves as both a tool for activism and a battleground for public opinion, where activists must constantly engage with both supporters and critics.

For Eliane, the scrutiny intensified as she became more visible in her advocacy work. The media's portrayal of her initiatives often oscillated between admiration and criticism, depending on the prevailing societal attitudes. This duality can create a challenging environment for activists who must navigate their public persona while remaining authentic to their mission.

Strategies for Managing Backlash

To effectively navigate backlash, activists like Eliane can employ several strategies:

1. **Building a Support Network:** Establishing a strong community of allies and supporters can provide emotional and practical support during times of backlash. This network can help amplify positive messages and counteract negative narratives.

2. **Engaging with Critics:** Rather than ignoring or dismissing criticism, engaging in constructive dialogue can help demystify misconceptions and foster understanding. Eliane often participated in public forums and discussions to address concerns and clarify her stance on contentious issues.

3. **Utilizing Media Wisely:** Developing relationships with sympathetic media outlets can help ensure that the narrative surrounding LGBTQ issues

remains balanced. By proactively sharing her story and the stories of others in the community, Eliane was able to frame the conversation in a way that highlighted the human experience behind the statistics.

4. **Maintaining Resilience:** Resilience is key to enduring public scrutiny. Activists must cultivate a strong sense of self and purpose, allowing them to withstand the emotional toll that backlash can take. Eliane often reflected on her motivations and the impact of her work, which helped her remain focused amidst challenges.

Examples of Backlash in LGBTQ Advocacy

Historically, LGBTQ activists have faced significant backlash, particularly when advocating for policies that challenge societal norms. For instance, the legalization of same-sex marriage in various countries has often been met with fierce opposition from conservative groups. In the United States, the backlash against the 2015 Supreme Court decision in *Obergefell v. Hodges* legalized same-sex marriage, which sparked a wave of anti-LGBTQ legislation in several states.

Similarly, Eliane's advocacy for inclusive policies within the tech industry faced scrutiny from those who believed that such initiatives threatened their traditional values. This backlash often manifested in social media campaigns aimed at discrediting her work and questioning her motives. However, Eliane's strategic approach to engagement and her commitment to transparency allowed her to address these concerns head-on.

Conclusion

Navigating backlash and public scrutiny is an essential skill for LGBTQ activists. By understanding the dynamics of backlash, employing effective strategies, and learning from historical examples, activists like Eliane Morissens can continue to advocate for change despite the challenges they face. The resilience and commitment displayed in the face of adversity not only strengthen their movements but also inspire future generations of advocates to stand firm in their pursuit of equality.

Cultivating resilience in the face of adversity

Resilience is the capacity to recover quickly from difficulties; it is a form of emotional strength that enables individuals to withstand and thrive despite challenges. For LGBTQ activists like Eliane Morissens, cultivating resilience is not merely a personal endeavor but a collective necessity in the face of systemic adversity. This section explores the theoretical frameworks surrounding resilience, the specific adversities faced by LGBTQ activists, and practical examples of how such resilience can be cultivated.

Theoretical Framework of Resilience

The concept of resilience can be understood through several theoretical lenses. One prominent theory is the *Ecological Model of Resilience* proposed by Bronfenbrenner, which emphasizes the interplay between individuals and their environments. This model posits that resilience is not solely an individual trait but is influenced by various systemic factors, including family, community, and societal norms.

The equation can be represented as:

$$R = f(E, I) \qquad (35)$$

where R represents resilience, E denotes environmental factors, and I symbolizes individual characteristics.

Another relevant framework is the *Psychological Resilience Theory*, which identifies key components such as optimism, emotional regulation, and social support. These elements contribute to an individual's ability to bounce back from adversity.

Adversities Faced by LGBTQ Activists

LGBTQ activists often encounter a multitude of adversities, including:

- **Social Stigma:** Activists frequently face prejudice and discrimination, which can lead to social isolation and mental health challenges.

- **Systemic Discrimination:** Laws and policies may not protect LGBTQ rights, leading to a lack of institutional support for advocacy efforts.

- **Backlash:** Activism can provoke backlash, including threats, harassment, and violence, creating an environment of fear and uncertainty.

- **Emotional Labor:** Constantly advocating for rights can lead to emotional exhaustion, particularly when faced with resistance from society.

These adversities necessitate the development of resilience strategies that empower activists to continue their work despite the challenges they face.

Strategies for Cultivating Resilience

To cultivate resilience, LGBTQ activists can employ several strategies:

- **Building Support Networks:** Establishing strong connections with allies, mentors, and fellow activists can provide emotional support and practical resources. For example, Eliane Morissens has emphasized the importance of chosen family within the LGBTQ community, creating a network of support that fosters resilience.

- **Practicing Self-Care:** Engaging in self-care practices, such as mindfulness, exercise, and creative expression, can help mitigate stress and promote emotional well-being. Activists are encouraged to prioritize their mental health, recognizing that self-care is a vital component of sustainable activism.

- **Reframing Adversity:** Adopting a growth mindset allows activists to view challenges as opportunities for learning and growth. This perspective shift can transform feelings of defeat into motivation for continued advocacy.

- **Engaging in Advocacy Training:** Participating in workshops and training sessions focused on resilience-building can equip activists with practical tools for navigating adversity. Programs that teach conflict resolution, stress management, and public speaking can enhance both personal and collective resilience.

- **Documenting Experiences:** Keeping a journal or creating art can serve as a therapeutic outlet for processing emotions and experiences. By documenting their journeys, activists like Morissens can reflect on their growth and the impact of their advocacy, reinforcing their sense of purpose.

Examples of Resilience in Action

The story of Eliane Morissens provides a powerful example of resilience in action. After facing significant backlash for her outspoken advocacy, Morissens channeled her experiences into community-building initiatives. She organized workshops that focused on resilience training for LGBTQ youth, emphasizing the importance of mental health and self-acceptance. By sharing her personal story, she inspired others to embrace their identities and cultivate their resilience.

Another illustrative example is the global response to the COVID-19 pandemic, which disproportionately affected LGBTQ communities. Activists adapted by leveraging technology to create virtual support groups, ensuring that individuals had access to resources and community despite physical distancing. This adaptability showcased the resilience of the LGBTQ movement, as activists found innovative ways to connect and advocate for their rights in challenging times.

Conclusion

Cultivating resilience in the face of adversity is essential for LGBTQ activists to sustain their efforts in promoting equality and acceptance. By understanding the theoretical frameworks of resilience, recognizing the unique challenges they face, and employing effective strategies, activists can empower themselves and their communities. As Eliane Morissens exemplifies, resilience is not just about enduring hardship; it is about transforming adversity into action, inspiring others, and paving the way for a more inclusive future. Through collective resilience, the LGBTQ movement can continue to thrive, creating lasting change in the world.

Using controversy as a catalyst for change

In the realm of activism, controversy often serves as a double-edged sword; it can incite backlash, yet it can also galvanize support and drive significant change. Eliane Morissens, as a prominent LGBTQ activist, has navigated this intricate landscape with a keen understanding of how to leverage controversy to advance the cause of equality and justice. This section delves into the multifaceted ways in which controversy can be transformed into a powerful catalyst for change, drawing upon relevant theories, problems, and examples from Eliane's journey.

Theoretical Framework

To understand the dynamics of controversy in activism, we can turn to the **Social Movement Theory**. This theory posits that social movements arise in response to perceived injustices and mobilize individuals to challenge the status quo. Within this framework, controversy acts as a mechanism that highlights societal issues, drawing public attention and prompting discourse. Scholars such as Charles Tilly and Sidney Tarrow argue that contentious politics—characterized by public demonstrations, protests, and confrontations—can lead to significant policy changes and shifts in public opinion.

Identifying Controversy

Controversy often emerges from actions or statements that challenge existing norms and provoke strong reactions. For Eliane, this included:

- Publicly addressing the systemic discrimination faced by LGBTQ individuals in Barbados.
- Critiquing institutional practices that perpetuate homophobia and transphobia.
- Advocating for the inclusion of LGBTQ rights in broader human rights discussions, which often ruffled feathers among conservative factions.

Each of these instances not only sparked debate but also illuminated the urgent need for reform within both local and global contexts.

Transforming Backlash into Momentum

Eliane's experiences exemplify how backlash can be reframed as momentum for change. When faced with criticism from conservative groups or individuals resistant to LGBTQ rights, she employed several strategies to convert negative attention into a rallying point for advocacy:

1. **Public Engagement:** Rather than retreating in the face of criticism, Eliane engaged directly with detractors through public forums, debates, and social media. By articulating her position and providing evidence-based arguments, she was able to demystify misconceptions surrounding LGBTQ issues.

2. **Building Alliances:** Controversy often isolates activists; however, Eliane recognized the importance of coalition-building. By aligning with other marginalized groups and human rights organizations, she broadened her support base, transforming controversy into a collective struggle for justice.

3. **Storytelling:** Eliane harnessed the power of personal narratives to humanize the issues at stake. By sharing her own experiences and those of others within the LGBTQ community, she created emotional connections that transcended political divides and fostered empathy.

Case Studies of Controversy Leading to Change

Several pivotal moments in Eliane's career illustrate how controversy can catalyze change:

The Pride March Incident During a Pride march in Bridgetown, a protest erupted when conservative activists attempted to disrupt the event. Instead of viewing this as a setback, Eliane seized the opportunity to amplify the message of the march. She organized a counter-protest that not only defended the rights of LGBTQ individuals but also attracted media attention. This incident ultimately led to increased visibility for LGBTQ issues in Barbados and prompted discussions about the need for legal protections against discrimination.

The Social Media Campaign In response to a viral video that perpetuated harmful stereotypes about LGBTQ individuals, Eliane initiated a social media campaign titled #*VoicesOfChange*. This campaign encouraged individuals to share their stories and challenge the narrative presented in the video. The resulting dialogue not only countered the negative portrayal but also fostered a sense of community and solidarity among LGBTQ individuals. The campaign garnered international attention, leading to partnerships with global organizations advocating for LGBTQ rights.

Challenges and Ethical Considerations

While controversy can serve as a catalyst for change, it is essential to navigate the ethical implications. Activists must consider the potential harm that may arise from heightened tensions, particularly for vulnerable populations within the LGBTQ community. Eliane emphasizes the importance of:

- **Safety and Well-being:** Ensuring that activists and community members are protected from potential backlash or violence.

- **Informed Consent:** Engaging individuals in discussions about how their stories and experiences are shared, particularly in media portrayals.

- **Sustaining Momentum:** Recognizing that controversy can be fleeting; thus, it is crucial to have a strategic plan for sustaining advocacy efforts beyond the initial media cycle.

Conclusion

In conclusion, Eliane Morissens exemplifies how controversy can be transformed into a catalyst for change within the LGBTQ rights movement. By employing strategies such as public engagement, coalition-building, and storytelling, she has effectively turned backlash into momentum, driving conversations about equality and justice. While navigating the ethical complexities of controversy, Eliane's journey serves as a testament to the power of resilience and the potential for transformative change in the face of adversity. As activists continue to confront societal norms, the lessons learned from Eliane's experiences will undoubtedly inspire future generations to harness the power of controversy in their pursuit of justice.

Creating a support network for LGBTQ activists facing backlash

The journey of LGBTQ activists is often fraught with challenges, particularly when they confront backlash for their advocacy efforts. This backlash can manifest in various forms, including social ostracism, threats of violence, and systemic discrimination. To combat these challenges, it is essential to establish robust support networks that provide emotional, psychological, and strategic assistance to activists facing adversity.

Understanding the Nature of Backlash

Backlash against LGBTQ activists can arise from multiple sources, including conservative political factions, religious groups, and even within their communities. This backlash is often rooted in a fear of change and a desire to maintain the status quo. According to social identity theory, individuals derive a sense of self from their group memberships, leading to a defensive reaction when those identities are challenged [?]. This phenomenon can exacerbate the hostility faced by LGBTQ activists, as their advocacy directly threatens the norms and values of certain societal groups.

The Importance of Support Networks

Support networks serve as lifelines for activists, offering a sanctuary where they can share their experiences and feelings without fear of judgment. These networks can take various forms, including formal organizations, informal friendships, and online communities. Research indicates that social support plays a critical role in mitigating the effects of stress and trauma, particularly for marginalized groups [?].

Components of Effective Support Networks

Creating an effective support network for LGBTQ activists involves several key components:

- **Emotional Support:** Providing a safe space for activists to express their feelings and experiences is crucial. This can be facilitated through peer support groups, counseling services, and mentorship programs.

- **Strategic Guidance:** Activists often face complex situations that require strategic thinking. Establishing connections with experienced activists and legal advisors can help navigate these challenges effectively.

- **Resource Sharing:** Support networks can facilitate the sharing of resources, such as funding opportunities, legal aid, and educational materials, which are vital for sustaining advocacy efforts.

- **Visibility and Advocacy:** Creating platforms that amplify the voices of activists facing backlash can help counteract negative narratives and promote solidarity within the community.

Case Studies of Successful Support Networks

Several organizations have successfully established support networks for LGBTQ activists facing backlash:

- **The Trevor Project:** This organization provides crisis intervention and suicide prevention services to LGBTQ youth. Their 24/7 helpline offers immediate emotional support and connects individuals with resources tailored to their needs.

- **GLAAD:** GLAAD has developed programs that empower LGBTQ individuals to share their stories and combat misinformation. Their media advocacy initiatives help create a more supportive environment for activists facing backlash.

- **OutRight Action International:** This global organization works to advance the rights of LGBTQ people through advocacy, research, and support. Their programs focus on creating safe spaces for activists and providing training on navigating backlash.

Challenges in Establishing Support Networks

Despite the importance of support networks, several challenges can hinder their effectiveness:

- **Funding and Resources:** Many grassroots organizations struggle to secure funding, limiting their ability to provide comprehensive support services.

- **Cultural Barriers:** In some communities, cultural stigmas surrounding LGBTQ identities can impede the establishment of support networks. Activists may fear seeking help due to concerns about being outed or facing further discrimination.

- **Geographical Limitations:** Activists in rural or underserved areas may have limited access to support networks, necessitating the development of online platforms to bridge this gap.

Future Directions for Support Networks

To enhance the effectiveness of support networks for LGBTQ activists facing backlash, several strategies can be implemented:

- **Leveraging Technology:** Utilizing digital platforms can expand the reach of support networks, allowing activists to connect with peers and resources regardless of their geographical location.

- **Building Intersectional Alliances:** Collaborating with other marginalized groups can strengthen support networks and foster a sense of solidarity among activists facing similar challenges.

- **Advocating for Policy Change:** Support networks should also engage in advocacy efforts to address systemic issues that contribute to backlash, such as discriminatory laws and practices.

In conclusion, creating a support network for LGBTQ activists facing backlash is vital for fostering resilience and empowerment. By understanding the nature of backlash, recognizing the importance of support, and addressing the challenges in establishing these networks, we can create a more inclusive and supportive environment for those who dare to advocate for change.

Turning negative experiences into opportunities for growth and education

In the realm of activism, particularly within the LGBTQ community, negative experiences often serve as pivotal moments that catalyze personal and collective growth. These experiences, whether they manifest as discrimination, backlash, or public scrutiny, can be reframed as opportunities for learning, resilience, and empowerment. The transformative potential of adversity is well-documented in psychological theories, particularly in concepts such as Post-Traumatic Growth (PTG).

Theoretical Framework: Post-Traumatic Growth

Post-Traumatic Growth refers to the positive psychological change experienced as a result of adversity and challenges. According to Tedeschi and Calhoun (2004), PTG encompasses five domains:

1. **Appreciation of Life:** Individuals often develop a deeper appreciation for life and its fragility.

2. **Relationships with Others:** Adversity can strengthen existing relationships and foster new connections.

3. **New Possibilities:** Facing challenges may open up new avenues for personal and professional growth.

4. **Personal Strength:** Individuals may recognize their resilience and ability to overcome obstacles.

5. **Spiritual Development:** Adversity can lead to a reevaluation of personal beliefs and values.

These domains illustrate how negative experiences can be reframed into opportunities for growth, particularly within the LGBTQ community, where activism often involves confronting societal norms and systemic injustices.

Examples of Growth through Adversity

One notable example is the backlash faced by Eliane Morissens following a high-profile advocacy campaign. The campaign aimed to raise awareness about LGBTQ rights in a conservative environment, leading to significant public scrutiny. Instead of succumbing to the pressure, Morissens utilized this experience to educate herself and her community on the mechanisms of social resistance. She organized workshops focused on resilience and advocacy strategies, transforming her negative experience into a platform for education and empowerment.

Another instance can be observed in the case of a young LGBTQ activist who faced cyberbullying after sharing their story online. Initially devastated, they sought support from local LGBTQ organizations. Through this process, they not only found solace but also became a vocal advocate for anti-cyberbullying initiatives. This transformation highlights the potential for personal experiences of negativity to contribute to broader educational efforts aimed at fostering safe online spaces.

Challenges in Reframing Negative Experiences

While the potential for growth exists, reframing negative experiences is not without its challenges. Activists often encounter emotional fatigue, societal stigma, and a lack of institutional support. For instance, the pressure to maintain a public persona while dealing with personal trauma can lead to burnout. To combat this, it is essential to establish supportive networks and mentorship programs that encourage open dialogue about the challenges faced by LGBTQ activists.

Moreover, the concept of intersectionality, as introduced by Kimberlé Crenshaw (1989), is crucial in understanding how various forms of discrimination can compound the effects of negative experiences. Activists from marginalized backgrounds may face unique challenges that require tailored support systems. Acknowledging these complexities is vital in turning adversity into a shared learning experience.

Strategies for Transformation

To effectively transform negative experiences into opportunities for growth and education, the following strategies can be implemented:

- **Reflection and Journaling:** Encouraging activists to document their experiences can facilitate self-reflection and help identify patterns of resilience.

- **Community Engagement:** Building networks of support where individuals can share their stories fosters a sense of belonging and collective strength.

- **Educational Workshops:** Hosting workshops that focus on coping strategies, resilience training, and advocacy skills empowers individuals to navigate challenges effectively.

- **Mentorship Programs:** Establishing mentorship initiatives that connect experienced activists with newcomers can provide guidance and encouragement in the face of adversity.

- **Advocacy for Systemic Change:** Using negative experiences as a catalyst for advocacy can lead to broader societal changes, addressing the root causes of discrimination and injustice.

Conclusion

In conclusion, while negative experiences are an unfortunate reality for many LGBTQ activists, they also present invaluable opportunities for growth and education. By embracing the principles of Post-Traumatic Growth and employing strategies that foster resilience and empowerment, individuals can turn adversity into a powerful force for change. The journey from victimhood to activism not only enriches personal narratives but also strengthens the fabric of the LGBTQ movement as a whole. Through collective efforts, the lessons learned from negative experiences can pave the way for a more inclusive and equitable future.

The Future of LGBTQ Advocacy

The evolving landscape of LGBTQ rights

The landscape of LGBTQ rights has undergone significant transformations over the past few decades, reflecting broader societal changes, political movements, and cultural shifts. This evolution is not merely a series of victories but a complex interplay of challenges, theory, and activism that continues to shape the rights and recognition of LGBTQ individuals globally.

Historical Context and Progress

Historically, LGBTQ individuals faced systemic discrimination, criminalization, and marginalization. The Stonewall Riots of 1969 marked a pivotal moment in the fight for LGBTQ rights, serving as a catalyst for the modern LGBTQ movement. Activists began to organize more visibly, advocating for decriminalization, anti-discrimination laws, and the recognition of same-sex relationships. This period saw the emergence of influential organizations such as the Human Rights Campaign and GLAAD, which played crucial roles in shaping public discourse and policy.

Theoretical Frameworks

Understanding the evolving landscape of LGBTQ rights requires a theoretical framework that encompasses intersectionality, social justice, and human rights.

Intersectionality, a term coined by Kimberlé Crenshaw, emphasizes how various forms of discrimination—such as those based on race, gender, and sexual orientation—interact to create unique experiences of oppression. This perspective is vital in LGBTQ advocacy, as it highlights the need for inclusive approaches that address the diverse needs of individuals within the community.

Moreover, the social justice framework posits that LGBTQ rights are human rights, advocating for equality, dignity, and respect for all individuals. This perspective challenges systemic inequalities and calls for comprehensive reforms across various sectors, including education, healthcare, and employment.

Current Challenges

Despite notable advancements, significant challenges persist. In many regions, LGBTQ individuals still face legal and social discrimination. For instance, in several countries, same-sex relationships remain criminalized, and LGBTQ individuals are subjected to violence and persecution. The World Economic Forum's 2021 Global Gender Gap Report highlighted that, while some progress has been made, the gap in legal protections for LGBTQ individuals is still substantial in many parts of the world.

Moreover, the rise of anti-LGBTQ legislation in various jurisdictions poses a direct threat to the rights and freedoms gained over the years. For example, in the United States, bills targeting transgender individuals' rights in sports and healthcare have gained traction, sparking widespread protests and advocacy efforts. These legislative moves often reflect broader societal attitudes that can fluctuate, influenced by political rhetoric and cultural narratives.

Global Perspectives

The global landscape of LGBTQ rights is diverse and often contradictory. While some countries have made significant strides—such as the legalization of same-sex marriage in numerous nations, including Canada, Germany, and Taiwan—others remain entrenched in regressive policies. For instance, in parts of Africa and the Middle East, LGBTQ individuals face severe penalties, including imprisonment and even death.

International organizations, such as the United Nations, have increasingly recognized LGBTQ rights as fundamental human rights. The UN Free and Equal campaign aims to promote equality and fight discrimination based on sexual orientation and gender identity, advocating for global solidarity in the struggle for LGBTQ rights.

The Role of Technology and Activism

Technology has emerged as a powerful tool in the fight for LGBTQ rights. Social media platforms allow activists to mobilize support, share stories, and raise awareness about issues affecting the LGBTQ community. Hashtags like #LoveIsLove and #TransRightsAreHumanRights have galvanized global movements, highlighting the importance of digital activism in shaping public opinion and policy.

Moreover, technology facilitates the creation of safe online spaces for LGBTQ individuals, particularly in regions where offline support is limited. Virtual communities provide resources, mentorship, and solidarity, fostering resilience among marginalized individuals.

Future Directions

As we look to the future, the landscape of LGBTQ rights will continue to evolve. Emerging issues such as the rights of non-binary individuals, the intersection of LGBTQ rights with climate justice, and the impact of artificial intelligence on marginalized communities will shape the next phase of advocacy.

The ongoing dialogue surrounding LGBTQ rights necessitates a commitment to intersectional approaches, ensuring that all voices within the community are heard and represented. Collaborative efforts among activists, policymakers, and organizations will be crucial in addressing the multifaceted challenges that lie ahead.

In conclusion, the evolving landscape of LGBTQ rights is characterized by a dynamic interplay of progress and resistance. By understanding the historical context, theoretical frameworks, current challenges, and future directions, we can better navigate the complexities of advocacy and work towards a more equitable world for all individuals, regardless of their sexual orientation or gender identity.

Anticipating challenges and emerging issues

As the landscape of LGBTQ advocacy continues to evolve, it is imperative for activists, policymakers, and community leaders to anticipate the challenges and emerging issues that will shape the future of the movement. This proactive approach is not only essential for sustaining progress but also for ensuring that the rights and dignity of LGBTQ individuals are upheld in the face of adversity. In this section, we will explore several key challenges and emerging issues that require our attention and action.

1. Legislative Backlash

One of the most pressing challenges facing LGBTQ advocacy is the potential for legislative backlash. In recent years, several countries and regions have witnessed a wave of anti-LGBTQ legislation aimed at rolling back the rights previously gained. For instance, laws targeting transgender individuals' access to healthcare and participation in sports have emerged in various states across the United States. Such legislative measures can create an environment of fear and discrimination, undermining the progress made in LGBTQ rights.

The theory of *policy feedback* posits that the policies enacted can influence future political dynamics and public opinion. As such, the introduction of regressive laws can lead to a cycle of oppression, where marginalized communities face increased scrutiny and hostility. Activists must remain vigilant and ready to mobilize in response to these threats, employing strategies such as grassroots organizing, legal challenges, and public awareness campaigns to counteract these regressive policies.

2. Intersectionality and Inclusivity

Another significant challenge is the need for greater intersectionality within LGBTQ advocacy. The movement has historically been criticized for prioritizing the experiences of certain groups—often white, cisgender, and gay men—over others. This can lead to the marginalization of voices from diverse backgrounds, including people of color, transgender individuals, and those with disabilities.

To address this challenge, it is essential to adopt an intersectional framework that recognizes the interconnectedness of various forms of oppression. *Intersectionality*, a term coined by Kimberlé Crenshaw, emphasizes that individuals experience multiple, overlapping identities that can compound their experiences of discrimination. Advocacy efforts must prioritize inclusivity, ensuring that the voices of the most marginalized within the LGBTQ community are amplified and that their unique challenges are addressed.

3. Mental Health and Well-being

The mental health of LGBTQ individuals remains a critical issue, particularly in the wake of increasing societal stigma and discrimination. Studies have shown that LGBTQ individuals are at a higher risk for mental health challenges, including depression, anxiety, and suicidal ideation. The American Psychological Association highlights that these disparities are often exacerbated by societal rejection and discrimination, leading to a cycle of marginalization.

To address these mental health challenges, advocacy must focus on improving access to mental health services tailored to the needs of LGBTQ individuals. This includes advocating for inclusive training for mental health professionals, promoting awareness of LGBTQ-specific issues, and establishing community support networks. Furthermore, technology can play a pivotal role in providing accessible mental health resources through teletherapy and online support groups, bridging the gap for those in underserved communities.

4. Global Disparities in LGBTQ Rights

While many countries have made significant strides in advancing LGBTQ rights, others remain entrenched in systemic discrimination and violence. The global disparity in LGBTQ rights presents a complex challenge for activists. For instance, in countries where homosexuality is criminalized, LGBTQ individuals face severe penalties, including imprisonment and violence.

The theory of *globalization* suggests that as communication and technology connect individuals across borders, there is an opportunity for cross-cultural solidarity and advocacy. Activists must work collaboratively with international organizations to address these disparities, sharing resources, strategies, and support. Global campaigns that highlight the plight of LGBTQ individuals in oppressive regimes can galvanize international attention and pressure governments to reform discriminatory laws.

5. The Impact of Technology

As technology continues to evolve, it presents both opportunities and challenges for LGBTQ advocacy. While digital platforms can amplify voices and mobilize communities, they also expose individuals to online harassment and cyberbullying. The rise of misinformation and hate speech online can further complicate advocacy efforts, creating a hostile environment for LGBTQ individuals.

To mitigate these challenges, activists must advocate for stronger regulations against online hate speech and cyberbullying. Additionally, promoting digital literacy and online safety within the LGBTQ community is essential to empower individuals to navigate these spaces effectively. Furthermore, leveraging technology for advocacy—such as using social media for awareness campaigns—can help counteract the negative effects of online harassment.

6. Climate Change and Its Intersection with LGBTQ Rights

Climate change is an emerging issue that intersects with LGBTQ rights in profound ways. Marginalized communities, including LGBTQ individuals, are often disproportionately affected by environmental degradation and climate-related disasters. The concept of *environmental justice* emphasizes the need to address the inequities faced by vulnerable populations in the context of climate change.

Advocacy efforts must integrate climate justice with LGBTQ rights, recognizing that the fight for equality cannot be separated from the fight for a sustainable future. This includes advocating for policies that address climate change while considering the needs of marginalized communities. Activists can work to ensure that LGBTQ voices are included in environmental discussions and that the unique challenges faced by these communities are addressed in climate action plans.

Conclusion

Anticipating challenges and emerging issues is critical for the continued advancement of LGBTQ rights. By addressing legislative backlash, promoting intersectionality, supporting mental health, advocating for global equality, navigating technology's impact, and integrating climate justice, activists can create a more inclusive and resilient movement. The future of LGBTQ advocacy hinges on our ability to adapt to these challenges and seize the opportunities that arise, ensuring that the rights and dignity of all individuals are upheld in the pursuit of equality.

The role of technology in shaping the future of LGBTQ advocacy

In the contemporary landscape of activism, technology emerges as a pivotal force, transforming the methodologies through which LGBTQ advocacy is conducted. The intersection of technology and advocacy not only amplifies voices but also fosters innovative solutions to long-standing issues faced by the LGBTQ community. This section explores the multifaceted role of technology in shaping the future of LGBTQ advocacy, addressing its potential, challenges, and the theoretical underpinnings that guide its application.

Empowerment through Digital Connectivity

The advent of social media platforms has revolutionized the way individuals engage with advocacy. Platforms such as Twitter, Instagram, and Facebook serve as virtual town squares where LGBTQ individuals can share their stories, connect with allies, and mobilize for change. This digital connectivity fosters a sense of community, allowing marginalized voices to resonate on a global scale.

$$C = \frac{N}{D} \tag{36}$$

Where C represents community engagement, N denotes the number of active participants, and D signifies the degree of digital outreach. As N increases through strategic campaigns, the potential for collective action grows, leading to significant social impact.

Innovations in Advocacy Tools

Technology facilitates the development of innovative tools designed to enhance LGBTQ advocacy. For instance, mobile applications that provide resources for mental health support, legal advice, and emergency assistance are increasingly crucial. These tools not only address immediate needs but also empower users by providing access to information that was previously difficult to obtain.

A notable example is the development of apps like "LGBTQ+ Safe Space," which connects users with nearby support services, shelters, and community centers. This kind of technological intervention is vital in areas where traditional resources are scarce, thus bridging the gap in service provision.

Data-Driven Advocacy

Data analytics plays a significant role in shaping effective advocacy strategies. By collecting and analyzing data on LGBTQ experiences, organizations can identify trends, measure the impact of their initiatives, and tailor their approaches to meet the needs of the community.

$$E = \sum_{i=1}^{n} \frac{R_i}{T_i} \tag{37}$$

In this equation, E represents the effectiveness of advocacy efforts, R_i denotes the resources allocated to each initiative i, and T_i signifies the time taken to achieve specific outcomes. By optimizing resource allocation and time management, organizations can enhance their impact and efficiency.

Challenges and Ethical Considerations

Despite the benefits, the integration of technology in LGBTQ advocacy is not without challenges. Issues such as digital surveillance, data privacy, and the potential for online harassment pose significant risks to activists and community members. The very platforms that empower voices can also become tools for oppression.

Ethical considerations must guide the use of technology in advocacy. Organizations must prioritize the safety and confidentiality of their constituents, ensuring that data collection practices are transparent and consensual. The implementation of robust cybersecurity measures is essential to protect sensitive information from malicious actors.

Theoretical Frameworks Guiding Technological Integration

The integration of technology in LGBTQ advocacy can be examined through various theoretical frameworks. Social Movement Theory, for instance, posits that collective action is driven by shared grievances and the mobilization of resources. In this context, technology acts as a resource that enhances communication, coordination, and mobilization efforts.

Additionally, the Diffusion of Innovations Theory highlights how new technologies spread within communities. Understanding the factors that facilitate or hinder the adoption of technological tools is crucial for maximizing their effectiveness in advocacy.

Future Directions

Looking ahead, the role of technology in LGBTQ advocacy is poised to expand further. Emerging technologies such as artificial intelligence (AI) and blockchain hold promise for creating more inclusive and secure advocacy environments. AI can analyze vast amounts of data to identify patterns of discrimination, while blockchain technology can ensure transparency and accountability in fundraising efforts.

Moreover, as the digital landscape evolves, so too must the strategies employed by advocates. Embracing new technologies, while remaining vigilant against their potential pitfalls, will be essential for the continued advancement of LGBTQ rights.

In conclusion, the role of technology in shaping the future of LGBTQ advocacy is profound and multifaceted. By harnessing the power of digital connectivity, innovation, and data-driven approaches, advocates can forge new pathways toward equality and justice. However, it is imperative to navigate the challenges with care and ethical consideration, ensuring that technology serves as a tool for empowerment rather than a source of vulnerability. The future of LGBTQ advocacy will undoubtedly be intertwined with technological advancements, making it essential for activists to remain adaptable and forward-thinking in their approaches.

Pioneering new approaches to LGBTQ advocacy in a changing world

In the rapidly evolving landscape of societal norms, technological advancements, and political climates, LGBTQ advocacy must adapt to remain effective and impactful. The traditional methods of advocacy, while foundational, often fall short in addressing the complexities of modern intersectionality and the digital age. This section explores innovative approaches that activists, organizations, and allies can adopt to pioneer LGBTQ advocacy in a changing world.

Embracing Intersectionality

A pivotal theory in contemporary activism is intersectionality, which recognizes that individuals experience overlapping systems of discrimination based on their identities, including race, gender, socioeconomic status, and sexual orientation. As Kimberlé Crenshaw articulated, intersectionality allows us to understand how various forms of oppression intersect and compound, leading to unique challenges for marginalized groups.

In practice, this means that LGBTQ advocacy must not only focus on sexual orientation and gender identity but also consider how race, ethnicity, and economic background influence the experiences of LGBTQ individuals. For instance, the Black Lives Matter movement has highlighted the need for Black LGBTQ voices in discussions surrounding both racial and sexual justice. By integrating intersectional approaches, advocates can create more inclusive strategies that resonate with diverse communities.

Leveraging Technology for Advocacy

The digital age presents unprecedented opportunities for LGBTQ advocacy. Social media platforms, mobile applications, and online communities can mobilize support, raise awareness, and foster connections among activists globally. For example, the #BlackTransLivesMatter movement gained traction on platforms like Twitter and Instagram, illustrating how digital spaces can amplify marginalized voices.

Moreover, technology can facilitate innovative solutions to persistent issues. For instance, the use of data analytics can identify trends in discrimination and violence against LGBTQ individuals, allowing organizations to target their resources effectively. Additionally, virtual reality (VR) experiences can immerse users in the realities of LGBTQ lives, fostering empathy and understanding among broader audiences.

Community-Centric Approaches

At the heart of effective advocacy lies community engagement. Pioneering new approaches requires a shift from top-down strategies to community-centric models that empower local voices. This involves actively involving LGBTQ individuals in decision-making processes, ensuring that their unique perspectives shape the initiatives aimed at supporting them.

One successful example is the establishment of community-led organizations that focus on specific local issues. For instance, organizations like the *Transgender Law Center* in the United States prioritize the needs of transgender individuals, advocating for legal protections and resources tailored to their experiences. By centering the voices of those directly affected, advocacy becomes more relevant and impactful.

Global Solidarity and Collaboration

In an interconnected world, LGBTQ advocacy must extend beyond local and national boundaries. Global solidarity is essential in addressing issues that transcend borders, such as anti-LGBTQ legislation and violence. Collaborations between international organizations can amplify efforts and share resources.

The *United Nations Free & Equal* campaign serves as a prime example of global advocacy that brings together diverse organizations and activists to promote LGBTQ rights worldwide. By fostering cross-cultural exchanges and learning from successful strategies in different regions, activists can strengthen their approaches and create a unified front against discrimination.

Innovative Policy Advocacy

As the political landscape shifts, advocacy must also evolve to address emerging challenges. Innovative policy advocacy involves not only pushing for new legislation but also reimagining existing frameworks to better protect LGBTQ rights.

For example, advocates can push for comprehensive anti-discrimination laws that encompass various forms of identity beyond sexual orientation and gender identity, including socioeconomic status and disability. Additionally, policy initiatives that prioritize mental health services for LGBTQ individuals can address the unique challenges they face, particularly in areas with limited access to healthcare.

Utilizing Art and Storytelling

Art and storytelling have long been powerful tools for advocacy. In a changing world, these mediums can be harnessed to humanize issues and foster connections. Personal narratives, whether through written word, film, or performance, can evoke empathy and challenge stereotypes.

Organizations can support LGBTQ artists and storytellers, providing platforms for their voices to be heard. Initiatives like the *Moth's LGBTQ StorySLAM* allow individuals to share their experiences, creating a tapestry of narratives that reflect the diversity of the LGBTQ community. By elevating these stories, advocacy can resonate on a deeper emotional level, inspiring action and solidarity.

Conclusion

Pioneering new approaches to LGBTQ advocacy in a changing world requires a multifaceted strategy that embraces intersectionality, leverages technology, prioritizes community engagement, fosters global solidarity, innovates policy advocacy, and utilizes art and storytelling. By adapting to the complexities of modern society, advocates can create meaningful change and ensure that LGBTQ rights are recognized and protected for all individuals, regardless of their identities. As we move forward, it is imperative that we remain vigilant, creative, and united in the pursuit of equality and justice for the LGBTQ community.

Spearheading global campaigns for LGBTQ equality

In an increasingly interconnected world, the fight for LGBTQ equality has transcended borders, demanding a united front against discrimination and injustice. Eliane Morissens has emerged as a pivotal figure in this global movement, orchestrating campaigns that not only raise awareness but also mobilize resources and support for LGBTQ individuals worldwide. This section delves into the strategies, challenges, and successes of spearheading global campaigns for LGBTQ equality.

The Framework of Global Advocacy

At the heart of effective global LGBTQ advocacy lies a multifaceted framework that incorporates grassroots mobilization, international cooperation, and strategic communication. Theories such as *Social Movement Theory* (Tilly, 2004) emphasize the importance of collective action and solidarity among marginalized groups. This framework provides the backbone for campaigns that seek to unify LGBTQ voices across diverse cultural and political landscapes.

$$\text{Advocacy Impact} = f(\text{Awareness, Mobilization, Policy Change}) \quad (38)$$

This equation illustrates that the impact of advocacy is a function of three critical components: awareness, mobilization, and policy change. Each element plays a crucial role in driving the agenda for LGBTQ rights on a global scale.

Challenges in Global Campaigning

While the momentum for LGBTQ rights is growing, numerous challenges persist. Cultural resistance, political backlash, and economic disparities can hinder progress. For instance, in regions where LGBTQ identities are criminalized, activists face severe repercussions, including imprisonment and violence. The case of Uganda's Anti-Homosexuality Act of 2014 exemplifies the dangers that LGBTQ individuals confront, as the law imposed harsh penalties for same-sex relationships, igniting international outrage and calls for action.

Moreover, the intersectionality of LGBTQ issues with other social justice movements complicates advocacy efforts. Issues such as race, gender, and socioeconomic status must be addressed to ensure that campaigns are inclusive and representative of the diverse experiences within the LGBTQ community. For example, the Black Lives Matter movement's inclusion of LGBTQ rights underscores the necessity of intersectional approaches in advocacy.

Successful Campaigns and Strategies

Despite the challenges, Eliane Morissens has successfully spearheaded several global campaigns that have made significant strides toward LGBTQ equality. One notable initiative is the *Global Pride Campaign*, which brought together LGBTQ organizations from over 100 countries to celebrate Pride Month virtually during the COVID-19 pandemic. This campaign not only raised awareness but also provided a platform for marginalized voices that are often silenced in traditional Pride celebrations.

Additionally, the *#LoveIsLove* campaign, which gained traction on social media, exemplifies the power of digital activism. By utilizing platforms like Twitter and Instagram, the campaign successfully mobilized millions to advocate for marriage equality globally, leading to significant policy changes in various countries. The impact of social media on LGBTQ advocacy cannot be overstated, as it facilitates the rapid dissemination of information and fosters a sense of community among activists.

Building International Coalitions

Eliane's approach to global campaigns also emphasizes the importance of building international coalitions. Collaborating with organizations such as *ILGA World* (International Lesbian, Gay, Bisexual, Trans and Intersex Association) and *OutRight Action International* has allowed for the pooling of resources and expertise, amplifying the reach and effectiveness of campaigns. These coalitions work to influence international policy, advocate for human rights, and provide support to local LGBTQ organizations facing oppression.

For instance, the partnership with *Human Rights Watch* during the *#EndHomophobia* campaign showcased how collective action can lead to significant policy shifts. The campaign successfully lobbied for the inclusion of LGBTQ rights in United Nations resolutions, setting a precedent for future advocacy efforts.

The Role of Education and Awareness

Education plays a crucial role in the success of global LGBTQ campaigns. By fostering awareness and understanding of LGBTQ issues, advocates can combat stigma and discrimination. Eliane has championed educational initiatives that target both the general public and policymakers, emphasizing the importance of inclusive curricula in schools and training programs for law enforcement and healthcare providers.

The *Educate to Liberate* initiative is a prime example of this approach, aiming to educate communities on LGBTQ rights and the importance of acceptance. By providing resources and training, the initiative empowers individuals to become advocates within their own communities, creating a ripple effect of change.

Conclusion: A Vision for the Future

As the global landscape continues to evolve, the need for sustained advocacy for LGBTQ equality remains paramount. Eliane Morissens exemplifies the potential for individuals to effect change on a global scale, inspiring a new generation of activists to carry the torch forward. By addressing the challenges, leveraging technology, and fostering international collaboration, the fight for LGBTQ rights can continue to gain momentum.

In conclusion, spearheading global campaigns for LGBTQ equality requires a strategic, inclusive, and resilient approach. As Eliane's journey illustrates, the power of collective action, education, and advocacy can pave the way for a more equitable world, where all individuals, regardless of their sexual orientation or gender identity, can live authentically and without fear.

Legacy and Inspiration

Leaving a lasting impact on LGBTQ activism

Eliane Morissens' journey through the landscape of LGBTQ activism is not merely a tale of personal triumph; it is a profound testament to the transformative power of advocacy that resonates across generations. Her legacy is steeped in the belief that activism is a collective endeavor, one that thrives on the shared experiences and struggles of marginalized communities. This section delves into the essence of her impact, exploring the theoretical frameworks that underpin her work, the challenges she faced, and the enduring examples of her influence.

At the heart of Morissens' activism lies the theory of *intersectionality*, a concept introduced by Kimberlé Crenshaw in 1989. Intersectionality posits that individuals experience multiple, overlapping identities that intersect in ways that can compound discrimination and disadvantage. For LGBTQ individuals, this means that factors such as race, gender, socioeconomic status, and geographic location can significantly influence their experiences and the challenges they face. Morissens embraced this theory, advocating for a nuanced understanding of LGBTQ issues that considers the diverse backgrounds of individuals within the community.

The problems associated with a lack of intersectional awareness are stark. Many LGBTQ advocacy efforts have historically centered on the experiences of white, cisgender individuals, often neglecting the voices of those who exist at the intersections of various marginalized identities. Morissens' work challenged this status quo, pushing for inclusivity within the movement. For instance, she spearheaded initiatives that highlighted the unique struggles of LGBTQ people of color, women, and those with disabilities, ensuring that their narratives were not only heard but celebrated.

One of the most significant impacts of Morissens' activism is her role in creating safe spaces for dialogue and support. She understood that fostering community was essential for empowerment. By establishing local LGBTQ support groups and networks, she provided individuals with the resources and solidarity needed to navigate their identities in a world that often marginalizes them. These groups became incubators for activism, where members could share their stories, strategize for change, and uplift one another.

Furthermore, Morissens' commitment to education as a tool for activism cannot be overstated. She recognized that knowledge is power, particularly in communities that have been historically disenfranchised. By implementing educational programs focused on LGBTQ rights, history, and health, she empowered individuals to advocate for themselves and others. This approach aligns with the *theory of empowerment*, which posits that individuals gain strength and agency through knowledge and community support.

An exemplary initiative led by Morissens was the development of digital platforms aimed at increasing LGBTQ visibility and access to information. By leveraging technology, she created online resources that provided crucial information on legal rights, mental health resources, and community events. This digital activism not only reached local communities but also had a global impact, connecting individuals across borders and fostering a sense of solidarity.

Morissens also faced significant challenges, including backlash from conservative factions and systemic barriers to LGBTQ rights. However, her resilience in the face of adversity served as a powerful example for emerging activists. She often emphasized the importance of turning challenges into opportunities for growth. For instance, after facing criticism for her outspoken stance on LGBTQ rights, she organized community forums that allowed for open dialogue, transforming dissent into constructive conversations about acceptance and understanding.

Moreover, her influence extends beyond her immediate community; it has sparked a global movement. By collaborating with international organizations, Morissens helped to elevate LGBTQ issues on the world stage. Her advocacy work has inspired campaigns that address homophobia and discrimination in various cultural contexts, demonstrating the universal relevance of her message.

In conclusion, Eliane Morissens' impact on LGBTQ activism is characterized by her commitment to intersectionality, community empowerment, and education. Her legacy is not merely about the changes she has enacted but also about the inspiration she has provided to future generations of activists. As we reflect on her contributions, it becomes evident that the work of advocacy is ongoing, requiring the dedication and passion of individuals who are willing to challenge the status quo. Morissens' journey serves as a roadmap for those who seek to continue the fight for equality, reminding us that every voice matters and that lasting change is possible when we stand together.

$$\text{Impact} = \text{Advocacy} + \text{Community Empowerment} + \text{Education} \quad (39)$$

Inspiring future generations of LGBTQ advocates

The journey of LGBTQ advocacy is a tapestry woven with the threads of courage, resilience, and the unwavering belief in equality. As Eliane Morissens has demonstrated through her life and work, the act of inspiring future generations of LGBTQ advocates is not merely about sharing stories; it is about igniting a movement that transcends borders and empowers individuals to embrace their identities and fight for their rights.

At the core of this inspiration lies the understanding of the challenges faced by the LGBTQ community. These challenges are manifold, encompassing societal stigma, legal discrimination, and mental health issues. According to the *American Psychological Association*, LGBTQ youth are more than twice as likely to experience bullying and harassment compared to their heterosexual peers. This alarming statistic underscores the importance of creating supportive environments where young advocates can flourish.

To inspire the next generation, it is crucial to share not only the victories but also the struggles that have paved the way for progress. Eliane's narrative serves as a beacon of hope, illustrating how personal experiences can catalyze collective action. For instance, her involvement in local LGBTQ support groups fostered a sense of belonging and solidarity among youth, encouraging them to voice their concerns and advocate for change. This grassroots approach is essential; as noted by *Sociologist Erving Goffman*, the concept of "passing" in society can lead to internalized stigma. By openly discussing these experiences, advocates like Eliane help dismantle the barriers of silence and shame.

Moreover, mentorship plays a pivotal role in nurturing future leaders. Establishing mentorship programs that connect seasoned activists with budding advocates can create a powerful exchange of knowledge and experience. For example, organizations like *The Trevor Project* provide resources and mentorship opportunities for LGBTQ youth, enabling them to engage in advocacy work effectively. These programs not only enhance skills but also instill a sense of responsibility and purpose in young advocates.

Incorporating technology into advocacy efforts is another vital aspect of inspiring future generations. The digital landscape offers unprecedented opportunities for engagement and activism. Eliane's work in leveraging social media to amplify LGBTQ voices exemplifies how technology can be a powerful tool for change. By utilizing platforms like Twitter and Instagram, young advocates can share their stories, mobilize support, and engage in meaningful conversations. As noted by *Digital Activism researcher Mary Joyce*, online activism can catalyze real-world change, making it imperative for future advocates to harness these tools.

Furthermore, educational initiatives that focus on LGBTQ issues are essential in shaping a more inclusive society. By integrating LGBTQ history and rights into school curricula, educators can foster understanding and empathy among students. This approach aligns with the *Social Learning Theory*, which posits that individuals learn behaviors through observation and imitation. By exposing students to the narratives of LGBTQ advocates, they are more likely to develop a sense of solidarity and become advocates themselves.

The role of intersectionality cannot be overlooked in this discourse. The concept, introduced by *Kimberlé Crenshaw*, emphasizes the interconnected nature of social categorizations such as race, class, and gender. Future advocates must be equipped to navigate the complexities of intersectional identities within the LGBTQ community. By fostering dialogues that address these intersections, advocates can create a more inclusive movement that represents the diverse experiences of all individuals.

In conclusion, inspiring future generations of LGBTQ advocates is a multifaceted endeavor that requires a blend of storytelling, mentorship, technological engagement, educational initiatives, and an understanding of intersectionality. Eliane Morissens' legacy serves as a testament to the power of advocacy, demonstrating that the journey toward equality is not a solitary one but a collective effort that thrives on collaboration and shared experiences. As we look to the future, it is our responsibility to nurture and empower the next generation, ensuring that the fight for LGBTQ rights continues with vigor and determination. The torch of advocacy must be passed on, igniting a flame of hope and resilience in the hearts of those who will carry it forward.

Celebrating Donnya Piggott's contributions and achievements

Donnya Piggott stands as a beacon of hope and resilience within the LGBTQ activism landscape. Her contributions transcend mere advocacy; they embody a profound commitment to social justice, equality, and the empowerment of marginalized communities. As we celebrate her achievements, it is essential to recognize the multifaceted impact she has had on both local and global scales.

Trailblazing Advocacy

Piggott's advocacy work began in her hometown of Bridgetown, Barbados, where she faced a society steeped in conservative values. Her early involvement with local LGBTQ support groups not only provided solace to those around her but also ignited a spark of activism that would resonate far beyond the shores of the Caribbean. She pioneered initiatives aimed at combating homophobia and discrimination, often drawing from her own experiences to inspire others.

Through her grassroots campaigns, Piggott addressed pressing issues such as mental health within the LGBTQ community, advocating for inclusive mental health services and creating safe spaces for youth. Her efforts culminated in the establishment of mentorship programs designed to empower the next generation of activists, which have since been replicated in various countries, showcasing her influence in nurturing future leaders.

Innovative Use of Technology

One of Piggott's most significant contributions lies in her innovative use of technology to further LGBTQ rights. Recognizing the power of digital platforms, she harnessed social media to amplify LGBTQ voices and mobilize support for various causes. By launching online campaigns that highlighted the struggles and triumphs of LGBTQ individuals, she successfully engaged a global audience, fostering a sense of community and solidarity.

Piggott's work in tech advocacy also led to the creation of digital platforms that enhance LGBTQ visibility. Her collaboration with tech giants resulted in groundbreaking projects that not only provided resources for marginalized communities but also bridged the digital divide. For instance, her initiative to develop online education programs for LGBTQ youth has equipped countless individuals with the tools they need to thrive in a rapidly changing world.

Global Leadership and Alliances

On the international stage, Piggott has emerged as a thought leader in the LGBTQ movement. Her ability to build global networks and alliances has been instrumental in advocating for LGBTQ rights across borders. She has represented the community at numerous international conferences, where her eloquent speeches and compelling narratives have resonated with audiences, inspiring action and solidarity.

Piggott's collaboration with international organizations has led to significant advancements in LGBTQ rights, including legislative changes and increased funding for advocacy initiatives. Her efforts have not only raised awareness of

LGBTQ issues but have also encouraged governments and institutions to prioritize equality and inclusion.

Legacy of Inspiration

As we reflect on Donnya Piggott's contributions, it is crucial to acknowledge the legacy she is creating. Through her tireless advocacy, she has left an indelible mark on the LGBTQ movement, inspiring countless individuals to embrace their identities and fight for their rights. Her commitment to creating a more equitable world serves as a guiding light for future generations of activists.

In recognition of her achievements, various scholarships and grants have been established in Piggott's name, aimed at supporting LGBTQ youth and activists pursuing education and advocacy. These initiatives not only honor her legacy but also ensure that her impact continues to inspire change long into the future.

Conclusion

Donnya Piggott's contributions and achievements are a testament to the power of resilience, innovation, and community. As we celebrate her journey, we are reminded of the importance of advocacy in the face of adversity. Her story serves as a powerful reminder that change is possible, and that each of us has a role to play in the ongoing fight for equality and justice. Through her unwavering commitment, Piggott has not only changed lives but has also transformed the landscape of LGBTQ activism for generations to come.

Honoring Donnya Piggott's Legacy through Scholarships and Grants

Donnya Piggott's profound impact on LGBTQ activism is not only marked by her tireless advocacy and innovative approaches but also by her commitment to empowering future generations. One of the most effective ways to honor her legacy is through the establishment of scholarships and grants that provide support to LGBTQ youth and activists. This section explores the theoretical foundations, practical challenges, and exemplary initiatives that embody this vision.

Theoretical Foundations of Scholarships and Grants

Scholarships and grants serve as vital instruments for social equity, particularly in marginalized communities. They provide financial assistance that can alleviate barriers to education and professional development. According to Bourdieu's theory of social capital, access to resources—such as funding for education—can significantly enhance an individual's ability to navigate and succeed in society. This theory underscores the importance of creating opportunities for LGBTQ individuals who may face systemic discrimination in educational and professional settings.

$$SC = \frac{C + E + N}{R} \tag{40}$$

Where:

- SC = Social Capital
- C = Cultural resources (knowledge, skills)
- E = Economic resources (financial support)
- N = Network resources (connections, mentorship)
- R = Risks associated with discrimination or bias

In this context, the equation illustrates how financial support (E) can enhance social capital (SC) for LGBTQ individuals, thereby reducing the risks (R) they face.

Challenges in Establishing Scholarships and Grants

Despite the noble intentions behind scholarships and grants, several challenges persist in their implementation:

- **Funding Sustainability:** Securing ongoing funding for scholarships can be difficult. Many initiatives rely on donations, which can fluctuate. Establishing endowments or partnerships with corporations committed to diversity and inclusion can provide more stability.
- **Eligibility Criteria:** Defining clear yet inclusive eligibility criteria is crucial. Programs must balance the need to target specific populations while ensuring that they do not inadvertently exclude deserving candidates. For instance, scholarships could prioritize LGBTQ individuals from low-income backgrounds or those pursuing studies in social justice.
- **Awareness and Outreach:** Many potential beneficiaries may not be aware of available scholarships. Effective outreach strategies, such as collaborations with LGBTQ organizations, schools, and community centers, can enhance visibility and accessibility.

- **Measurement of Impact:** Evaluating the effectiveness of scholarships and grants poses a challenge. Metrics must be developed to assess not only the academic success of recipients but also their contributions to the LGBTQ community and activism.

Exemplary Initiatives Inspired by Donnya Piggott

Several initiatives have emerged that reflect Donnya Piggott's commitment to supporting LGBTQ youth through scholarships and grants:

- **The Donnya Piggott Scholarship Fund:** This fund could be established to provide financial assistance to LGBTQ students pursuing higher education in fields related to social justice, technology, and advocacy. The scholarship would prioritize applicants who demonstrate a commitment to activism and community service.
- **Mentorship Programs:** In conjunction with scholarships, mentorship programs can be established to connect recipients with established LGBTQ professionals. This approach not only provides financial support but also fosters personal and professional growth through guidance and networking opportunities.
- **Grants for LGBTQ Activism Projects:** Grants could be awarded to individuals or groups developing projects that address pressing issues within the LGBTQ community. For example, funding could support initiatives focused on mental health awareness, educational outreach, or anti-discrimination campaigns.
- **Collaborations with Educational Institutions:** Partnering with universities to create scholarships specifically for LGBTQ students can enhance institutional support for diversity. This collaboration could also include workshops and seminars led by LGBTQ activists, further enriching the academic environment.

Conclusion

Honoring Donnya Piggott's legacy through scholarships and grants is a powerful way to ensure that her vision for an equitable and inclusive world continues to thrive. By providing essential resources to LGBTQ youth and activists, we can cultivate the next generation of leaders who will carry forward the torch of advocacy. As we navigate the complexities of establishing these initiatives, it is imperative that we remain committed to inclusivity, sustainability, and measurable impact. In doing so, we honor not only Donnya's contributions but also the countless individuals who strive for justice and equality in the LGBTQ community.

Creating a roadmap for the continued advancement of LGBTQ rights

The journey towards LGBTQ rights has been marked by both monumental achievements and persistent challenges. As we envision the future, it is crucial to create a structured roadmap that outlines actionable steps for the continued advancement of LGBTQ rights globally. This roadmap must be comprehensive, inclusive, and adaptable, recognizing the diverse needs of LGBTQ individuals across different cultures, societies, and legal frameworks.

1. Establishing Clear Objectives

To create an effective roadmap, we must first establish clear, measurable objectives. These objectives should encompass various aspects of LGBTQ rights, including but not limited to:

- **Legal Protections:** Ensuring that LGBTQ individuals are protected from discrimination in employment, housing, healthcare, and public accommodations.

- **Healthcare Access:** Advocating for equitable access to healthcare services, including mental health support and gender-affirming care.

- **Education:** Promoting inclusive curricula in schools that educate about LGBTQ history, rights, and issues.

- **Social Acceptance:** Fostering environments that celebrate diversity and promote acceptance through community engagement and awareness campaigns.

2. Engaging Stakeholders

The roadmap must involve a wide range of stakeholders, including:

- **Government Entities:** Collaborating with local, national, and international governments to influence policy changes and ensure the implementation of protective legislation.

- **Non-Governmental Organizations (NGOs):** Partnering with NGOs that specialize in human rights, social justice, and LGBTQ advocacy to amplify efforts and share resources.

- **Community Leaders:** Engaging local leaders and influencers who can help mobilize communities and foster grassroots movements.

- **Corporate Sector:** Encouraging businesses to adopt inclusive policies and practices, thereby supporting LGBTQ rights through corporate social responsibility initiatives.

3. Utilizing Technology as a Catalyst

In the digital age, technology serves as a powerful tool for advocacy and mobilization. The roadmap should include strategies for leveraging technology to advance LGBTQ rights:

- **Social Media Campaigns:** Utilizing platforms like Twitter, Instagram, and TikTok to raise awareness and promote LGBTQ issues, creating viral movements that can influence public opinion.

- **Digital Activism:** Encouraging online petitions, virtual events, and webinars that educate and engage supporters from around the world.

- **Data Collection and Analysis:** Using data analytics to understand the needs of LGBTQ communities better and to track the progress of initiatives aimed at improving their rights.

4. Addressing Intersectionality

An effective roadmap must recognize and address the intersectionality of LGBTQ identities. This involves understanding how race, gender, socioeconomic status, and other factors intersect with sexual orientation and gender identity, leading to unique challenges. The roadmap should prioritize:

- **Inclusive Policies:** Crafting policies that consider the diverse experiences of LGBTQ individuals, particularly those from marginalized backgrounds.

- **Culturally Competent Services:** Ensuring that healthcare, legal, and social services are culturally sensitive and accessible to all LGBTQ individuals.

- **Community Representation:** Promoting diverse voices within LGBTQ advocacy to ensure that all identities are represented and heard.

5. Monitoring Progress and Adapting Strategies

A successful roadmap is not static; it requires continuous evaluation and adaptation. Key components include:

- **Regular Assessments:** Conducting periodic assessments to evaluate the effectiveness of initiatives and identify areas for improvement.
- **Feedback Mechanisms:** Establishing channels for community feedback to ensure that the roadmap remains responsive to the needs of LGBTQ individuals.
- **Flexibility:** Adapting strategies based on changing societal dynamics, legal landscapes, and emerging issues within the LGBTQ community.

6. Celebrating Achievements and Building Momentum

Finally, it is essential to celebrate milestones and achievements along the way. Recognizing progress not only fosters a sense of community but also builds momentum for future initiatives. Strategies include:

- **Public Celebrations:** Organizing events that honor the contributions of LGBTQ activists and allies, showcasing the progress made in the fight for equality.
- **Storytelling:** Sharing personal stories of triumph and resilience within the LGBTQ community to inspire others and highlight the importance of continued advocacy.
- **Collaborative Campaigns:** Launching joint campaigns with other social justice movements to emphasize the interconnectedness of various struggles for equality.

Conclusion

Creating a roadmap for the continued advancement of LGBTQ rights requires a multifaceted approach that prioritizes inclusivity, engagement, and adaptability. By establishing clear objectives, engaging stakeholders, leveraging technology, addressing intersectionality, monitoring progress, and celebrating achievements, we can pave the way for a future where LGBTQ rights are universally recognized and upheld. This roadmap not only honors the legacy of activists like Donnya Piggott but also inspires future generations to continue the fight for justice and equality for all.

Index

a, 1–6, 9–13, 15–30, 32–35, 37–57, 61–70, 72–77, 79–84, 86, 88–91, 93, 95, 96, 98, 101, 105, 108–112, 115, 117, 118, 120–122, 125–128, 130, 132–134, 136–141, 144, 147–151, 153–156, 158, 161, 163–166, 168–172, 175, 177–180, 183, 185, 186, 188–193, 195, 197, 198, 200–213, 215–236, 238–241
ability, 20, 27, 29, 30, 33, 43, 70, 126, 132, 146, 153, 172, 191, 192, 203, 223, 235
absence, 76
abuse, 19, 168, 170–172
acceptance, 2, 4, 5, 10, 12, 16–19, 21, 23, 24, 32, 37, 39, 42, 52, 59, 63–68, 70, 72, 74, 76, 86, 88, 89, 93, 110–112, 115–120, 134, 151, 201, 209, 210, 232
access, 27, 30, 32–34, 38–41, 49, 76, 82, 88, 93, 104, 105, 140, 147, 156, 180, 183, 210, 221, 222, 224, 228, 232
accessibility, 26, 97, 151

achievement, 203
acquisition, 158
act, 2, 9, 55, 57, 59, 66, 90, 233
action, 5, 12, 13, 20, 24, 50, 51, 53, 56, 76, 78, 146, 165, 166, 191, 200, 205, 209, 210, 220, 223, 225, 229, 231, 235
activism, 3–6, 9, 12, 15, 17, 19, 26, 27, 30, 53, 76, 84, 89, 90, 130, 139–141, 144–146, 148, 151, 153, 156, 190, 195, 203, 205, 210, 216, 218, 223, 226, 232, 234–236
activist, 69, 210, 216
adaptability, 210, 241
adaptation, 150, 241
addition, 5, 54, 95, 154
address, 29, 33, 40, 42, 43, 47, 52, 58, 82, 127, 134, 138, 139, 148, 151, 153, 156–158, 162, 166, 171, 172, 174, 176, 177, 184, 186, 200, 202, 203, 207, 222–224, 227, 228, 232, 240
adherence, 111
admiration, 206

adoption, 225
advancement, 28, 57, 77, 84, 177, 202, 223, 225, 239, 241
advent, 130, 224
adversity, 10, 19, 44, 50, 207, 208, 210, 213, 218, 220, 232, 236
advice, 224
advocacy, 2–6, 8–11, 13, 15, 17, 19, 20, 24–30, 32–34, 37–39, 42–44, 46, 47, 49–51, 53–56, 59, 61, 66–70, 73, 74, 76–80, 82, 84, 86, 88, 89, 93, 95–98, 103, 105, 108, 120, 122, 125, 127–130, 132–134, 138–141, 143, 144, 146, 148, 151–153, 156, 158, 161, 163, 169, 170, 173, 175, 188–193, 197, 198, 200, 202, 204–207, 209, 211, 213, 216, 219–236, 238, 240
advocate, 3, 5–8, 11, 17, 20, 24, 28, 29, 33, 34, 49–51, 53, 54, 58, 61, 65, 76, 77, 83, 84, 96, 101, 104, 112, 119, 130, 132, 136, 139, 141, 167, 177, 180, 186, 187, 189, 193, 205, 207, 210, 215, 217
age, 3, 4, 6, 10, 16, 27, 28, 35, 39, 111, 139, 141, 146, 148, 163, 170, 172, 226, 240
agency, 84
agenda, 229
algorithm, 149
alienation, 118
alignment, 203
allocation, 82, 138
ally, 30, 128
allyship, 21, 115
analysis, 77, 127
anchor, 23
anomaly, 178
anonymity, 30, 147, 168
anxiety, 5, 23, 58, 62, 96, 221
app, 46
application, 31, 32, 190, 223
approach, 12, 17, 25, 27, 29, 40, 43, 50, 52, 53, 58, 61, 68, 69, 74, 82, 84, 86, 127, 133, 134, 140, 153, 166, 168, 179, 190, 200, 202, 207, 220, 231, 241
area, 170
arena, 3, 6, 120, 178
art, 3, 6, 9–11, 109, 228
artwork, 10
aspect, 19, 21, 37, 43, 56, 70, 170
assistance, 213, 224
asylum, 192
atmosphere, 88, 91
attention, 43, 76, 211, 212, 220
attraction, 16, 111
audience, 10, 29, 39, 43, 132, 149, 191, 235
authenticity, 4, 63, 64, 66, 68, 112
autonomy, 41
availability, 110
avenue, 9
awareness, 3, 5, 9, 19, 21, 29, 30, 43, 74, 76, 77, 79, 83, 88, 89, 97, 98, 103, 139, 141, 146, 150, 164, 166, 191, 216, 222, 228–230, 235

backdrop, 2, 18, 63, 75, 97

background, 29, 33, 175, 226
backlash, 10, 42, 50, 57, 65, 82, 113, 154, 205–207, 209–216, 221, 223, 229, 232
balance, 203
Barbados, 2, 4–6, 9, 10, 12, 18, 19, 23, 24, 26, 28, 29, 40, 42, 46, 51, 54, 63–66, 73–77, 96, 111, 189, 203, 205, 212, 235
barrier, 41, 110, 140, 147
battle, 74, 80
beacon, 2, 4, 17, 21, 35, 44, 50, 98, 191, 193, 234
beginning, 5
behavior, 18, 165
being, 21, 23, 30, 41, 42, 54, 85, 86, 93, 96, 101, 105, 113, 166, 168, 205
Belgium, 189
belief, 12, 233
bell, 10
belonging, 12, 16, 20, 22, 24, 29, 37, 40, 54, 108, 132, 186
benefit, 90, 154, 163
bias, 132, 138, 140
biography, 61
blend, 44, 63, 234
body, 109
breaking, 27, 40, 59, 61, 178, 189, 191
breath, 63
breeding, 168
bridge, 29, 118
Bridgetown, 1–4, 12, 51, 63, 191, 203, 212, 235
bridging, 10, 49, 52, 222
brunt, 166
buffer, 16, 23

buggery, 75
building, 3, 6, 11, 22, 36, 40, 41, 77, 89, 90, 95, 115, 117, 120, 132, 134, 151, 170, 189, 193, 195–197, 205, 209, 212
bullying, 69, 168
burnout, 25, 217
business, 153, 154, 156, 161

call, 122, 205
calling, 28, 53
campaign, 149, 216, 219
capacity, 20, 197, 201, 207
capital, 196, 197
care, 105, 226
career, 211
Caribbean, 1, 3, 6, 43, 75, 235
case, 5, 31, 65, 69, 149, 216, 229
catalyst, 3, 6, 27, 34, 44, 49, 55, 66, 125, 153, 156, 210, 212, 218
cause, 79, 191, 210
celebration, 76
challenge, 6, 9, 12, 13, 18, 20, 24, 30, 34, 40, 50–53, 56, 61, 73, 74, 76, 82, 84, 116, 118, 120, 132, 148, 153, 155, 170, 171, 211, 222, 228
chamber, 142
change, 3, 5, 6, 8, 11, 12, 19, 21, 26–30, 32, 34, 39, 41, 42, 44, 46, 47, 49–51, 53, 55, 57, 58, 66, 77–79, 84, 95, 96, 115, 122, 125, 128, 130, 139, 141, 143–146, 153, 157, 158, 161, 163, 180, 190, 192, 200, 201, 203, 207, 210–213, 215,

218, 223, 224, 228–230, 236
changer, 29
chapter, 59, 61, 125, 189
charge, 90, 155
child, 3, 16
childhood, 3
choice, 3
church, 111
cisgender, 69
clarion, 205
clash, 17, 54
class, 68
clergy, 111
climate, 220, 223
clothing, 3
coalition, 6, 192, 212
coat, 63
coding, 40
coexistence, 120, 121
collaboration, 25, 26, 32, 44, 46, 80, 90, 105, 107, 108, 120, 122, 141, 154, 158, 161, 166, 169, 172, 191–193, 196, 197, 200–202, 204, 231, 234, 235
collection, 29, 77, 139, 225
color, 69
combat, 82, 85, 104, 163, 170, 213, 217, 230
combination, 49, 82
commitment, 2–4, 6, 12, 19, 26, 27, 29, 32, 39, 42–44, 48, 53, 61, 88, 90, 112, 122, 153, 180, 188, 191, 197, 207, 220, 234, 236, 238
communication, 32, 34, 52, 83, 139, 166, 168, 170, 225

community, 1–5, 8–12, 17, 19, 21, 24–29, 33, 34, 36, 37, 39–44, 47, 49–59, 61, 63, 64, 66–70, 72, 75–77, 82–84, 86, 88, 89, 93, 96–98, 104, 105, 108, 111, 112, 120, 126–128, 132, 134, 136, 138, 139, 141, 144, 146–149, 151, 153, 154, 156, 161, 163, 166, 168, 170, 180, 189, 191, 193, 203, 209, 210, 212, 216, 220, 222–225, 227–229, 232, 235, 236, 239, 241
companionship, 16
company, 46
compassion, 52, 118
complexity, 17, 110, 111, 163
compliance, 90
component, 2, 13, 26, 39, 40, 68, 81, 83, 86, 105, 155, 161
compound, 226
concept, 3, 21, 27, 32, 52, 65, 171
concern, 166, 168
conclusion, 2, 4, 8, 10, 13, 17, 24, 29, 39, 55, 56, 61, 70, 76, 79, 86, 90, 96, 97, 101, 108, 112, 128, 132, 139, 141, 155, 170, 172, 191, 205, 212, 215, 218, 220, 225, 231, 234
conduit, 54
confidence, 23, 46, 82
confidentiality, 225
conflict, 15, 18, 51, 96, 110, 118
connection, 2, 11, 13, 52, 109, 130, 170
connectivity, 35, 224, 225

consent, 29, 139
consideration, 226
constructivism, 26
content, 29, 36, 39, 148, 149, 165, 171
context, 17, 24, 26, 27, 57, 62, 65, 75, 126, 144, 220, 225
contrast, 63
controversy, 57, 210–213
conversation, 5
coordination, 225
core, 57, 112, 151
cornerstone, 5, 27, 197
counter, 206, 212
courage, 44, 53, 63, 112, 233
creation, 24, 29, 37, 39, 40, 88, 127, 134, 136, 157, 220, 235
creativity, 2, 4, 9–11, 32, 44, 50, 161, 186, 188
credibility, 154
criminalization, 218
crisis, 121
criticism, 206, 211, 232
culture, 1–4, 39, 72, 93, 168, 175, 186
curiosity, 2–6
curricula, 89, 230
curriculum, 183
cyberbullying, 30, 134, 140, 166, 167, 170, 216, 217, 222
cybersecurity, 45, 225
cycle, 27, 40, 221

data, 5, 8, 28, 29, 32, 46, 58, 77, 127, 133, 134, 138, 139, 158, 172, 224, 225
dataset, 171
David Epston, 2
debate, 211

decision, 42, 227
decriminalization, 218
dedication, 55
demographic, 138
depression, 5, 23, 58, 96, 97, 221
design, 39
designing, 153
desire, 6, 63
determination, 5, 6, 21, 27, 44, 53, 161, 166, 234
development, 9, 16, 25, 29, 39, 41, 46–48, 96, 108, 140, 170, 172, 179, 208, 224, 232
deviation, 75
dialogue, 10, 16, 24, 42, 52, 53, 84, 90, 112–115, 118–120, 142, 143, 164, 217, 220, 232
dichotomy, 1, 63
difference, 63
dignity, 29, 118, 122, 168, 219, 220, 223
disability, 228
disadvantage, 183
discomfort, 17
discourse, 69, 164, 218
discovery, 2, 4, 10, 11, 15, 19, 28, 29, 50, 65
discrediting, 207
discrimination, 4, 5, 18–20, 23, 24, 30, 40, 41, 50, 51, 53, 54, 61, 62, 65, 68, 70, 74–77, 82–84, 86, 89, 91, 96, 97, 99, 103, 121, 134, 148, 155, 156, 166, 168, 170, 172, 186, 189, 195, 203, 212, 213, 218, 219, 221, 222, 226–228, 230, 232, 235

dismantling, 73, 82
disparity, 38, 149, 222
dissemination, 27, 144
dissent, 232
distance, 127
distancing, 210
diversity, 35, 52, 70, 83, 93, 142, 153, 172, 177, 178, 180, 181, 186
divide, 8, 30, 32–34, 38, 41, 134, 136, 138, 140, 147, 148, 183, 185, 235
document, 40, 190
documentary, 12
domain, 110
Donnya, 1–6, 9–12, 15–19, 24–28, 42–46, 50–55, 61, 63, 65–68, 96–98, 239
Donnya Piggott, 2, 4, 9, 11–13, 15, 18, 19, 21, 24, 28, 39, 40, 44, 46–49, 53, 55, 57, 59, 64, 66, 72, 74, 84, 90, 96, 111, 112, 234, 241
Donnya Piggott's, 6, 10, 17, 20, 25–27, 29, 42, 49–51, 53, 56, 61, 63, 97, 236, 238
drafting, 190
duality, 17, 206
dynamic, 17, 90, 146, 171, 180, 220

echo, 142, 143
ecosystem, 158
education, 27, 29, 32, 35–37, 40, 42–44, 52, 53, 82, 84, 86, 88, 90, 92, 93, 108, 120, 164, 166, 168, 176, 177, 180, 183–186, 216–219, 231, 235, 236

effect, 12, 26, 51, 57, 65, 106, 126, 142, 154, 201, 230
effectiveness, 39, 58, 82, 95, 127, 130, 138, 140, 145, 171, 185, 214, 215, 225
effort, 22, 34, 76, 180, 234
element, 67, 229
Eliane, 206, 207, 210–213, 230, 231
Eliane Morissens, 180, 189, 191, 195–197, 201–203, 205, 207, 209, 210, 212, 216, 228, 230, 233
Eliane Morissens', 234
Eliane Morissens's, 193
emergence, 19, 218
emergency, 224
empathy, 5, 8, 10, 11, 23, 52, 54, 55, 112, 119, 120, 122, 128, 164, 228
employee, 188
employment, 40, 219
empowerment, 4, 11, 12, 21, 24, 26, 29, 34, 37, 39, 41, 42, 49, 50, 54–57, 62, 82, 83, 86, 88, 89, 96, 112, 127, 130, 134, 136, 151, 153, 155, 175, 180, 186, 215, 216, 218, 226, 234
endeavor, 27, 32, 39, 90, 136, 150, 153, 158, 207, 234
enforcement, 76, 230
engagement, 3, 5, 6, 8, 24, 26, 37, 39, 49, 50, 88, 126, 127, 139, 141, 144, 146, 148, 149, 163, 168, 173, 175, 190, 207, 212, 227, 228, 234, 241
enrichment, 93
entrepreneurship, 40, 153, 155, 158

environment, 3, 12, 16–18, 25, 35, 41, 52, 54, 73, 75, 83, 86, 88, 89, 93, 105, 108, 109, 112, 118, 126, 142, 147, 153, 154, 166, 168–170, 172, 175, 177, 178, 180, 206, 215, 216, 221, 222
equality, 6, 26, 28, 29, 32, 39, 42–44, 47, 49, 53–55, 66, 77, 79, 90, 120, 122, 125, 128, 134, 136, 146, 148, 153, 155, 156, 158, 163, 175, 177, 180, 183, 185, 193, 197, 200, 203, 205, 207, 210, 212, 219, 223, 225, 228, 230, 231, 233, 234, 236, 239, 241
equation, 7, 8, 20, 28, 33, 40, 49, 53, 74, 77, 88, 91, 96, 104, 106, 110, 119, 126, 127, 137, 156, 163, 171, 178, 183, 196, 203, 208, 229
equity, 39, 93, 149, 178
era, 37, 70, 166
Erik Erikson's, 9
escape, 50
essence, 28, 49, 156
establishment, 25, 67, 87, 108, 196, 235, 236
esteem, 51
ethnicity, 226
evaluation, 241
event, 12, 54, 61, 64, 212
evidence, 58
evolution, 132, 171, 188, 218
example, 3, 5, 10, 12, 21, 23, 27, 29, 34, 41, 52, 57, 63, 69, 76, 83, 111, 127, 164, 171, 180, 190, 192, 209, 216, 219, 227, 229, 232
exception, 153
excitement, 62
exclusion, 22, 40
exercise, 70
exhilaration, 62
experience, 2, 4, 5, 10, 17–19, 22, 23, 49–53, 62, 63, 65–68, 88, 91, 96, 97, 103, 109, 111, 133, 183, 186, 203, 216, 226
expertise, 25, 44, 47
exploration, 3, 9
exposure, 6, 21
expression, 1, 3–6, 9, 10, 16, 19, 28, 35, 40, 50, 51, 121, 156, 168, 173

fabric, 111, 218
face, 10, 17–19, 35, 41, 44, 45, 57, 68, 76, 78, 91, 93, 96, 97, 101, 116, 118, 134, 137, 140, 152, 165, 166, 173, 177, 179, 192, 198, 200, 207, 208, 210, 213, 219, 220, 222, 228, 229, 232, 236
facilitator, 27
faith, 110–112, 115, 117–122
family, 5, 15–19, 21–23, 62, 63, 67, 111
fascination, 28
fatigue, 217
fear, 12, 16, 17, 19, 21, 22, 39, 54, 62, 63, 65–67, 74–76, 86, 89, 111, 113, 119, 154, 168, 221, 231
feedback, 138
feeling, 5, 22, 97

field, 46, 180, 181
fight, 13, 20, 24, 26, 32, 43, 44, 53, 54, 66, 70, 76, 79, 81, 90, 128, 130, 136, 146, 153, 155, 156, 166, 172, 189, 191, 195, 197, 200, 205, 218, 219, 223, 228, 231, 233, 234, 236, 241
fighting, 6
figure, 203, 228
film, 228
finding, 19
firm, 45, 207
flame, 234
fluidity, 5
focus, 39–41, 82, 107, 164, 170, 222, 226
following, 36, 69, 100, 146, 216, 217
force, 27, 32, 42, 46, 125, 128, 134, 218, 223
forefront, 44, 111, 188
form, 4, 133, 168, 207
formation, 9, 11, 15, 23, 146, 148, 192
forum, 52
foster, 3, 8, 13, 17, 19–22, 29, 39, 41, 56, 67, 76, 80, 82, 83, 88, 89, 108–110, 116, 125, 126, 128, 132, 134, 139, 141–143, 148, 153, 164, 169, 178, 202, 218, 228
foundation, 6, 15, 183
fragmentation, 203
framework, 68, 69, 77, 120, 186, 219
framing, 132
freedom, 121
frequency, 33
front, 192, 195, 228
frontier, 172

fuel, 10
function, 8, 126, 183, 229
fund, 197
funding, 25, 27, 158–161, 235
fusion, 203
future, 6, 8, 11, 21, 26, 32, 35, 42, 49, 50, 53, 55, 68, 77, 79, 88, 90, 112, 115, 118, 120, 122, 128, 134, 144, 148, 153, 155, 156, 158, 172, 180, 186, 188, 193, 200, 205, 207, 210, 213, 218, 220, 223, 225, 226, 233–236, 239, 241

game, 29
gap, 10, 29, 30, 32, 33, 147, 178, 180, 219, 222
gay, 68
gender, 3, 5, 18, 22, 35, 40, 43, 51, 52, 65, 68, 75, 79, 91, 105, 109, 110, 115, 154, 175, 178–180, 186, 190, 219, 220, 226, 227, 229, 231, 240
generation, 37, 43, 54, 88, 90, 93, 95, 96, 180, 181, 205, 230, 234, 235, 238
Germany, 165
giant, 46
globalization, 80
globe, 43, 125
goal, 39, 49, 149, 177
good, 30, 47
government, 34, 41
grief, 22
ground, 3, 28, 47, 168
groundbreaking, 44, 132, 235
groundwork, 6, 42, 50, 153

group, 18, 51, 180, 186
growth, 50, 88, 93, 112, 216–218, 232
guidance, 41, 46, 54, 127
guide, 47, 93, 223, 225
guise, 121

hand, 183
harassment, 7, 8, 30, 32, 39, 76, 132, 134, 136, 140, 143, 147, 148, 166–168, 170, 172, 173, 222, 225
harbor, 15
hardship, 210
harm, 212
hate, 30, 76, 140, 147, 163–166, 170, 172, 222
haven, 19
head, 88, 207
healing, 23, 118
health, 5, 19, 20, 23, 29, 33, 41, 42, 51, 58, 69, 75, 85, 86, 96–101, 103–108, 110, 121, 138, 166, 172, 179, 209, 221–224, 228, 232, 235
healthcare, 40, 41, 219, 221, 228, 230
heart, 63, 122, 227
help, 16, 21, 24, 86, 88, 89, 101, 109, 137, 138, 164, 172, 175
heteronormativity, 63
highlight, 21, 46, 58, 120, 164
history, 6, 42, 89
hold, 52, 165
home, 193
homelessness, 19
hometown, 235

homophobia, 4, 51, 76, 80, 81, 203, 232, 235
homosexuality, 54, 75, 121, 222
hope, 2, 4, 17, 21, 35, 44, 50, 55, 63, 98, 112, 191, 193, 234
hopelessness, 97
hostility, 21, 50, 75
household, 111
housing, 41
how, 6, 8, 9, 11, 13, 17, 27–30, 36, 44, 46, 47, 49–51, 53, 56, 68, 120, 125, 128, 139, 162, 164, 186, 189, 197, 205, 208, 210–212, 216, 225, 226, 240
human, 19, 50, 190, 200, 219

ideation, 221
identity, 1–6, 9, 11, 12, 15–19, 22–24, 26, 27, 35, 39, 40, 42–44, 49–52, 59, 61, 63–66, 79, 91, 96, 105, 109–112, 115, 118, 154, 180, 190, 219, 220, 226–228, 231, 240
impact, 4, 11, 12, 15, 20, 21, 23, 24, 29, 44, 47–49, 61, 64–66, 72, 88, 96, 97, 109, 121, 132, 144, 146, 152, 156, 161, 163, 164, 190, 193, 203, 220, 223, 224, 229, 232, 234, 236, 239
imperative, 96, 101, 155, 163, 166, 180, 186, 188, 201, 220, 225, 228, 238
implementation, 41, 90, 205, 225, 237
importance, 2, 4–6, 8, 10–12, 17, 18, 21, 24–27, 29, 41, 42,

51, 52, 54, 70, 71, 78, 86, 88, 98, 103, 110, 115, 178, 180, 186, 191, 195, 209, 212, 214, 215, 230, 232, 236
imprisonment, 222, 229
improvement, 133
in, 1–10, 12, 13, 15–24, 26–34, 36–44, 46, 48–55, 57, 58, 61–77, 79, 81–84, 86–91, 93, 95–99, 103–105, 107–112, 116–122, 125–128, 130, 132, 134, 136, 138, 139, 141, 143–151, 153–156, 158, 159, 161, 163, 164, 166–168, 170–173, 175, 177–180, 183–192, 200, 201, 203–207, 209–213, 215, 216, 218–230, 232–237, 239
incident, 212
inclusion, 41, 42, 93, 111, 115, 136, 178, 186, 190, 229, 236
inclusivity, 3, 5, 43, 48, 83, 84, 88, 132, 134, 153, 155, 172, 186, 188, 239, 241
income, 33
incorporation, 58
increase, 83, 127
indecency, 75
independence, 153
individual, 1, 3, 12, 17, 18, 21, 39, 50, 51, 55, 63, 64, 66, 82, 96, 110, 127, 149, 154
industry, 178–180, 185, 186, 207
inequality, 43, 75, 178, 195
influence, 20, 63, 70, 75, 186, 190, 201, 204, 226, 232, 235

information, 27, 32–37, 139, 144, 149, 172, 173, 224, 225, 232
initiative, 29, 45, 46, 52, 183, 197, 232, 235
injustice, 228
innovation, 28, 41, 42, 47, 49, 141, 150, 153, 154, 158, 177, 178, 180, 186, 188, 225, 236
innovator, 6, 49
insight, 161
inspiration, 2, 44
instability, 76
instance, 3, 10, 12, 16, 17, 25, 29, 40, 43, 50, 54, 58, 63, 68, 75, 111, 126, 134, 138–140, 149, 154, 165, 179, 203, 204, 216, 217, 219, 221, 222, 224–226, 229, 232, 235
integration, 8, 10, 29, 36, 139, 156, 158, 205, 225
intelligence, 220
intentionality, 22
interaction, 149, 183
interconnectedness, 178
intercourse, 75
internet, 8, 30, 38, 41, 127, 134, 140, 146, 147, 168
interplay, 2, 50, 76, 91, 110, 198, 218, 220
interpretation, 111
intersection, 3, 6, 8, 9, 28, 30, 42, 47, 96, 105, 110, 112, 118, 120, 132, 151, 153, 158, 180, 205, 220, 223
intersectionality, 19, 43, 44, 61, 66, 68, 70, 223, 226, 228, 229,

234, 240, 241
intervention, 107
introduction, 205
introspection, 50
investment, 43
involvement, 5, 12, 20, 190, 235
isolation, 16, 19, 22, 23, 75, 91, 96, 103, 109, 118, 173
issue, 32, 40, 41, 76, 147, 164, 183, 221

job, 41
Johnson, 69
journey, 2–6, 9–12, 15, 17–19, 21, 22, 26–29, 42, 43, 46, 49–51, 53–55, 57, 59, 61, 63–67, 79, 88, 96, 98, 112, 115, 118, 122, 128, 158, 161, 180, 186, 191, 203, 205, 210, 213, 218, 231, 233, 234, 236 239
judgment, 12, 17, 19, 21, 54, 67, 89
Judith Butler, 9
justice, 4, 6, 8, 28, 29, 42, 47, 65, 153, 155, 163, 183, 193, 200, 203, 205, 210, 213, 219, 220, 223, 225, 226, 228, 229, 234, 236, 239, 241
juxtaposition, 3

Kimberlé Crenshaw, 68, 186, 226
knowledge, 24, 26–28, 90, 95, 183, 186, 203

lack, 20, 27, 30, 33, 40, 52, 54, 75, 76, 156, 166, 173, 179, 186, 217
landscape, 6, 8, 11, 18, 29, 30, 32, 34, 38, 40, 42, 44, 47, 49, 59, 62, 65, 72, 75, 110, 115, 121, 122, 125, 128, 130, 134, 136, 139, 141, 144, 146, 148, 150, 151, 153, 154, 158, 161, 163, 166, 170, 175, 193, 195, 202, 203, 210, 218, 220, 223, 225–227, 230, 234, 236
language, 109, 171
law, 76, 190, 229, 230
lead, 19, 22, 23, 25, 30, 39, 51, 57, 63, 82, 84, 90, 96, 105, 108, 111, 115, 126, 147, 155, 163, 173, 205, 217
leader, 43, 191, 203–205, 235
leadership, 90, 93, 95, 96, 180, 205
learning, 26–28, 35, 93, 171, 172, 183, 207
leave, 193
legacy, 90, 205, 234, 236, 238, 241
legislation, 77–79, 165, 167, 190, 204, 219, 221, 227
lens, 11, 17, 18, 69, 202
lesbian, 68
leverage, 25, 44, 139, 140, 146, 151, 210
liberation, 64, 67
life, 5, 16, 27, 29, 32, 49, 50, 61, 63, 64, 233
lifeline, 21
light, 101, 191, 236
like, 3, 10, 18, 21, 22, 24, 27, 29, 43, 46, 49, 55, 57, 63–65, 69, 72, 73, 84, 112, 115, 126, 128, 142, 165, 171, 197, 202, 205–207, 241
limit, 142, 178
literacy, 33, 40, 164, 170, 172–175

literature, 5, 89
live, 53, 61, 67, 77, 79, 98, 231
living, 62, 127
lobby, 79, 190
location, 32, 88
loss, 22, 62
love, 10, 16, 19, 21, 23, 24, 52, 63, 66, 112, 118, 120, 122

machine, 171, 172
mainstream, 40, 61, 69–72
maintenance, 87, 136
male, 46, 178
man, 68
management, 39
manner, 63
march, 212
marginalization, 40, 75, 121, 218, 221
mark, 236
marriage, 18, 111
Marsha P. Johnson, 69
material, 27
matter, 44, 88, 155
means, 3, 10, 11, 18, 27, 37, 39, 153, 183, 226
measure, 29, 224
media, 3, 8, 10, 27, 29, 32, 43, 46, 57, 61, 66, 67, 70–72, 74, 84, 126–130, 132, 134, 139, 141, 143, 144, 148–150, 164, 165, 191, 206, 207, 212, 224, 235
medium, 9, 11, 50
member, 9, 17
mentor, 27
mentorship, 5, 29, 43, 46, 54, 55, 68, 88, 90, 93–96, 154, 217, 220, 234, 235

message, 10, 43, 57, 149, 192, 212, 232
messaging, 127, 138
Mia, 23
Michael White, 2
mindfulness, 109
minority, 20, 103
mirror, 12, 70
misalignment, 163
misinformation, 140, 173, 222
mission, 42, 206
misunderstanding, 113
mix, 5, 62
mobile, 46, 158, 224
mobilization, 29, 144, 225, 229, 240
model, 42, 77, 137
mold, 18
moment, 5, 12, 51, 63, 64, 218
momentum, 197, 205, 206, 211, 212, 229, 231, 241
Morissens, 189–193, 203–205, 209, 216, 232
motivation, 26
move, 34, 37, 77, 228
movement, 24, 26, 43, 57, 61, 66, 70, 80, 88, 90, 96, 111, 141, 149, 191, 193, 197, 200, 203, 205, 206, 210, 212, 218, 220, 223, 226, 228, 229, 232, 233, 235, 236
multitude, 208
music, 1
myriad, 18, 66

name, 42, 43, 236
narrative, 2, 4, 12, 51, 52, 57, 61, 98, 120
nation, 18, 42
nature, 10, 65, 166, 171, 186, 215

navigation, 46, 82, 205
necessity, 49, 68, 87, 172, 173, 177, 183, 207, 229
need, 7, 19, 20, 37, 39, 42, 53, 55, 58, 77, 93, 97, 98, 106, 118, 121, 153, 211, 212, 226, 230, 235
negative, 20, 23, 51, 62, 70, 211, 216–218
negativity, 217
negotiation, 83
network, 23, 80, 82, 90, 127, 213, 215
networking, 46, 196
newspaper, 5
non, 99, 171, 220
notion, 6, 21

on, 2–5, 11, 15, 18, 20, 23–25, 28, 34, 40–44, 47, 50, 57, 59, 63, 65, 66, 82, 83, 88, 90, 101, 106, 107, 115, 133, 134, 139, 144, 146, 148, 151, 153, 154, 164, 171, 172, 180, 183, 184, 189–193, 197, 198, 200, 201, 203, 206, 207, 209, 216, 219, 220, 222–224, 226, 229, 230, 232, 234, 236
one, 2, 19, 27, 52, 53, 59, 61, 63, 64, 67, 121, 205, 234
openness, 63
opinion, 127
opportunity, 112, 139, 163, 175, 180, 212
opposition, 76, 205
oppression, 10, 68, 225, 226
ordination, 111

organization, 188
organizing, 5
orientation, 5, 16–18, 22, 35, 40, 51, 52, 65, 68, 79, 91, 105, 109–112, 115, 118, 120, 154, 186, 190, 219, 220, 226, 227, 231, 240
ostracism, 51, 63, 65, 213
ostracization, 111
other, 20, 23, 25, 61, 139, 183, 229, 240
outlet, 50
outrage, 229
outreach, 24–26, 76

painting, 3, 4, 9, 50
pandemic, 76, 209
paradox, 121
part, 205
participation, 10, 21, 32, 66, 138, 140, 147, 168, 177, 178, 221
partnering, 25
partnership, 25, 45, 108, 201
passion, 4, 44, 49, 51, 161
pastor, 52
path, 4, 5, 19, 44, 53, 55, 122
pathway, 66
pay, 180
peer, 86, 109
people, 5, 53, 89
percentage, 7
perception, 70
performance, 4, 9, 228
period, 218
persecution, 192, 219
person, 127, 166
persona, 206, 217
perspective, 27, 219

phase, 220
phenomenon, 51, 126, 130, 142, 149, 206
phrase, 59
Piggott, 28, 29, 40, 41, 57, 58, 235, 236
pillar, 24, 79
pioneer, 226
place, 5
placement, 41
platform, 3, 9, 10, 25, 29, 40, 41, 43, 50, 54, 76, 109, 189, 193, 216
plethora, 170
poetry, 3, 4, 9
point, 63, 111, 211
policy, 46, 55, 58, 118, 144–146, 180, 190, 201, 204, 218, 227–229
population, 18, 21, 77, 103, 168, 179
portion, 18
portrayal, 206
position, 17
positive, 18, 20, 72, 74, 143, 152, 157, 162, 200
positivity, 109
post, 149
potential, 3, 8, 10, 13, 21, 26, 28, 29, 35, 36, 39, 44–47, 62, 78–81, 114, 117, 118, 122, 126, 130, 132, 134, 136, 138, 141–143, 145, 153, 156–159, 161, 162, 172, 173, 175, 186, 200, 212, 213, 217, 221, 223, 225, 230
power, 8–12, 19, 21, 24, 29, 32, 39, 42, 44, 50, 51, 54, 55, 64, 66, 84, 128–130, 134, 136, 141, 143, 146, 155, 172, 189, 191, 193, 197, 200, 205, 213, 225, 231, 234–236
practice, 121, 204, 226
precedent, 46
prejudice, 119
presence, 20, 67
pressure, 51, 57, 216, 217
prevalence, 147
pride, 3, 12, 66
privacy, 29, 45, 134, 138, 225
privilege, 68, 186
problem, 69, 111, 168
process, 22, 26, 39, 55, 61, 62, 64, 83, 84, 110, 153, 179, 217
product, 28, 88
professional, 93
profile, 216
program, 45, 46
progress, 41, 73, 76, 79, 107, 154, 163, 180, 199, 219–221, 229, 241
project, 10, 12, 29, 46, 183
protection, 77
protest, 212
public, 4, 9, 12, 25, 46, 50, 57, 58, 66, 67, 70, 76, 127, 205–207, 212, 216–218, 230
purpose, 44
pursuit, 26, 42, 43, 57, 207, 213, 223, 228
push, 11, 73, 79, 166, 227
pushback, 5, 76, 203

quality, 27
quest, 3, 22, 30, 39, 43, 54, 68, 134, 183

question, 164
questioning, 3, 4, 207
quo, 4, 76, 153

race, 40, 43, 65, 68, 186, 226, 229, 240
raising, 19, 21, 29, 30, 74, 77
rallying, 211
range, 172, 239
re, 119
reach, 10, 20, 29, 126, 149, 161, 191, 192
reaction, 16
reality, 10, 63, 218
realization, 3, 5
realm, 29, 43, 68, 93, 125, 132, 156, 210
recognition, 43, 75, 104, 186, 191, 218, 236
reconciliation, 118
reference, 190
reflection, 28, 183
reform, 55, 121, 201, 211
refuge, 9, 50, 168
region, 138
rejection, 16, 18, 19, 21, 22, 62, 63, 66, 96, 97, 104, 111, 113, 118, 221
relation, 190
relationship, 103
relevance, 232
reliance, 148
relief, 62
religion, 120, 121
reluctance, 51
reminder, 44, 53, 55, 98, 236
report, 33, 62, 76, 97, 164
reporting, 164

representation, 5, 27, 49, 61, 70–72, 74, 109, 132, 134, 147, 149, 178–180, 186, 190, 191, 193, 203
representative, 69, 229
reprisal, 54
research, 5, 58
resilience, 2, 10, 12, 17, 19–21, 24, 42, 44, 49–51, 53, 55, 63, 66, 68, 86, 95, 110, 112, 172, 191, 193, 200, 205, 207–210, 213, 215, 216, 218, 220, 232–234, 236
resistance, 4, 5, 10, 67, 110, 206, 216, 220, 229
resolve, 50
resource, 24, 82, 108, 138, 151, 225
respect, 43, 52, 122, 168, 191, 219
response, 76, 170, 209
responsibility, 55, 90, 168, 234
result, 7, 30, 149
retention, 188
rhetoric, 219
right, 121
rise, 44, 96, 127, 151, 166, 170, 219, 222
risk, 139, 153, 221
roadmap, 239–241
role, 4, 15–17, 19–21, 27, 32, 39, 42, 43, 52, 53, 62, 63, 69, 73, 77, 79, 82, 88, 90, 105, 120, 134, 144, 148, 158, 180, 183, 222–225, 229, 230, 236

s, 2–6, 9–12, 15–17, 19, 20, 23, 25–29, 32, 41–44, 49–51, 53, 56, 59, 61, 63–69, 97, 121, 126, 130, 149, 175,

179, 192, 193, 206, 207, 210, 211, 213, 219, 223, 229, 231, 235, 236, 238, 239
safety, 30, 42, 45, 168–170, 172, 173, 175, 225
sanctuary, 3, 21
Sarah, 111
satisfaction, 188
scale, 190, 191, 197, 198, 200, 201, 203, 224, 229, 230
scarcity, 25
scholar, 68
school, 5, 86, 93
schooling, 27
science, 177
scope, 25, 77
scrutiny, 205–207, 216
search, 2
section, 4, 6, 9, 11, 15, 24, 30, 39, 44, 47, 49, 51, 57, 61, 70, 73, 75, 77, 80, 88, 96, 103, 112, 115, 120, 128, 130, 132, 139, 144, 156, 158, 163, 178, 180, 183, 186, 191, 198, 208, 210, 220, 223, 226, 228, 236
sector, 34
seed, 3
self, 2–4, 9–12, 15, 16, 18, 19, 21, 23, 27, 35, 37, 40, 50, 51, 63, 65, 68, 89, 96, 168, 173, 186, 209
sense, 5, 12, 16, 18, 20, 24, 25, 29, 34, 37, 40, 43, 54, 55, 76, 84, 108, 126, 132, 186, 224, 232, 235, 241
sensitivity, 63, 82, 104
sentiment, 42, 46, 127

series, 52, 61, 218
set, 46, 190
setback, 212
sex, 16, 111, 218, 219, 229
sexuality, 1, 3, 17, 18, 120
shape, 8, 72, 188, 190, 218, 220, 227
share, 2, 3, 11–13, 19, 22, 25, 29, 34, 40, 43, 52, 67, 83, 89, 109, 126, 127, 132, 134, 136, 141, 143, 146, 189, 224, 227
sharing, 2, 10, 12, 13, 20, 34, 52, 54–57, 61, 66, 67, 95, 120, 134, 139, 191, 205, 209, 216, 233
shield, 77
shift, 10, 227
shoestring, 25
significance, 57, 77
silence, 37, 42, 59, 61, 111, 113, 140
skill, 172, 207
skin, 64
slang, 171
society, 2, 13, 15, 16, 18, 19, 21, 24, 33, 34, 37, 39, 42, 51, 53–55, 57, 61, 65–67, 74, 76, 84, 86, 88, 93, 95, 96, 98, 101, 105, 110, 120, 130, 139, 158, 163, 177, 179, 180, 202, 228, 235
socio, 75
software, 179
solace, 21, 50, 111, 217, 235
solidarity, 12, 19–21, 34, 40, 55, 76, 120, 126, 197, 205, 219, 220, 227, 228, 232, 235
solving, 41
source, 15, 16, 112, 226

space, 2, 17, 19, 21, 47, 51, 54, 67, 88, 108, 126, 141
spark, 235
speaking, 4, 12, 50, 57, 58, 67, 205
spectrum, 5, 163, 173
speech, 12, 30, 140, 147, 163–166, 170, 172, 222
sphere, 150
spike, 126
spirit, 19, 20, 41, 50, 93
spread, 225
stability, 41
stage, 42, 44, 57, 189, 191, 192, 195, 232, 235
stance, 57, 232
stand, 53, 82, 84, 193, 207
startup, 41
status, 4, 32, 40, 76, 153, 226, 228, 229, 240
stem, 52
step, 108, 117, 175, 180, 184–186
stigma, 13, 19, 20, 22, 24, 27, 51, 52, 54, 65, 70, 73, 74, 96, 99, 103, 104, 116, 154, 156, 189, 203, 217, 221, 230
Stonewall, 69
story, 4, 23, 29, 44, 52, 66, 67, 73, 98, 111, 191, 205, 209, 216, 236
storytelling, 2, 4, 10–13, 29, 40, 52, 54, 55, 57, 61, 115, 132, 134, 143, 212, 228, 234
strategy, 25, 80, 161, 165, 168, 228
stratification, 68
strength, 17, 19, 23, 24, 55, 70, 82, 84, 112, 134, 207
stress, 20, 62, 96, 103
struggle, 9, 11, 12, 17, 19, 22, 39, 51, 75, 110, 134, 155, 156, 189, 203, 205, 219
study, 5, 69
substance, 19
success, 43, 54, 161, 177, 185, 230
sum, 178
summary, 6, 19, 27, 42, 50, 64
support, 5, 15–25, 27, 29, 32, 34, 37, 43, 46, 51, 54, 58, 63, 67, 75–77, 80, 82, 84, 86, 88–91, 93, 96, 98, 99, 101, 105, 108–110, 113, 121, 126, 127, 134, 136, 138, 141, 143, 150, 153–156, 161, 166, 168, 170, 177, 180, 186, 210, 213–215, 217, 220, 222, 224, 228, 235, 236
surface, 1
surrounding, 5, 6, 27, 51–54, 61, 67, 73, 139, 208, 220, 226
surveillance, 29, 225
sustainability, 43, 88, 239
sword, 46, 77, 210
synergy, 96, 156, 161
system, 21, 93

taking, 153
tapestry, 1, 13, 49, 53, 233
target, 39, 230
task, 43, 76
teaching, 164
tech, 3, 6, 27, 29, 40–49, 161–163, 171, 178–181, 183–188, 207, 235
technology, 3, 4, 6, 8, 10, 26–34, 36–44, 46–49, 84, 90, 125, 126, 128, 130, 132, 134, 136, 140, 146–148, 151, 153, 156–158, 161,

163, 166, 169, 170, 175, 177, 179, 180, 183, 186, 193, 205, 210, 220, 222, 223, 225, 226, 228, 231, 232, 235, 240, 241
teletherapy, 222
tension, 10, 118
term, 186
terrain, 112
territory, 59
testament, 19, 24, 29, 44, 50, 51, 66, 189, 193, 200, 205, 213, 234, 236
the United States, 111, 206, 219, 221
theme, 10
theology, 117
theory, 18, 52, 80, 96, 132, 171, 205, 218, 226
therapy, 2, 52, 108–110
thinking, 42, 48, 164, 184, 226
thirst, 26, 27
thought, 43, 191, 203–205, 235
threat, 163, 219
time, 29, 46, 51, 61, 64, 127
timing, 63
today, 10, 32
tokenism, 163
tool, 4, 11, 13, 28, 34, 37, 40, 43, 49, 50, 89, 125, 127, 128, 130, 144, 148, 226, 240
topic, 96
torch, 231, 234, 238
town, 224
traction, 103, 149, 219
tradition, 3
training, 29, 83, 109, 171, 180, 209, 222, 230
trait, 4, 26

transformation, 55, 120, 186, 203, 217
transgender, 54, 69, 149, 219, 221
transparency, 29, 139, 207
trauma, 217
treatment, 77
triumph, 12, 20, 205
trust, 196
truth, 59, 61, 63, 64, 66
turn, 3, 218
turning, 50, 63, 111, 232

Uganda, 229
underpinning, 156
underrepresentation, 179
understanding, 2, 5, 6, 10–13, 16, 21, 23, 27, 40, 42, 44, 52–54, 57, 67, 68, 75, 77, 83, 86, 88, 89, 96, 101, 109, 112–120, 128, 130, 134, 141–143, 150, 158, 161, 164, 177, 186, 205, 207, 210, 215, 220, 230, 232, 234, 240
uniqueness, 68
university, 25
uprising, 69
urgency, 5
usage, 29, 34, 139
use, 32, 33, 40, 139, 149, 166, 171, 225, 235
user, 149, 164, 172
utilization, 90, 132

value, 52
variety, 198
vehicle, 9, 24, 28
victimhood, 218
victimization, 76

video, 10, 126
view, 18, 121
vigor, 234
violence, 51, 54, 63, 75, 76, 86, 189, 213, 219, 222, 227, 229
visibility, 5, 8, 20, 21, 28, 37–40, 42, 44, 46, 52, 53, 61, 66, 67, 70–72, 76, 88, 126, 132, 134, 148–151, 154, 191, 201, 203, 206, 212, 232, 235
vision, 205, 236, 238
visual, 10
voice, 2, 4, 10, 44, 53, 55, 66, 70, 73, 191
volunteer, 20
vulnerability, 63, 76, 173, 226

wake, 221
warmth, 3
wave, 43, 88, 151, 221
way, 9–11, 35, 39, 44, 49, 53, 55, 61, 67, 72, 74, 79, 84, 88, 90, 112, 118, 120, 128, 130, 153, 155, 180, 188, 210, 218, 224, 231, 238, 241
web, 1, 29, 64
weight, 63

well, 9, 23, 30, 40–42, 85, 86, 93, 96, 101, 105, 149, 166, 168
whole, 180, 188, 218
woman, 23, 43, 111
word, 228
work, 6, 10, 26, 43, 49, 50, 53, 56, 66, 74, 76, 79, 84, 88, 95–97, 112, 115, 118, 122, 172, 180, 184, 191, 193, 206–208, 220, 223, 232, 233, 235
workforce, 177
workplace, 180, 186
workshop, 5
world, 3, 4, 8, 11, 15, 21, 24, 26–29, 32, 35, 39, 42, 49, 57, 61, 72, 74, 112, 115, 118, 134, 146, 156, 163, 168, 180, 184, 186, 189, 191, 197, 210, 219, 220, 226–228, 231, 232, 235, 236, 238
worth, 16
worthlessness, 97
writing, 6

youth, 5, 19, 29, 35–37, 40, 46, 50, 58, 67–69, 86–90, 93–97, 138, 164, 209, 235, 236, 238

Milton Keynes UK
Ingram Content Group UK Ltd.
UKHW020315021124
450424UK00013B/1267